11/03

PENGUIN BOOKS

Judaism

WITHDRAWN

Rabbi Dr Jacob Neusner is Research Professor of Religion and Theology at Bard College, a Member of the Institute of Advanced Study (Princeton) and a Life Member of Clare Hall, Cambridge University.

Jacob Neusner

Judaism
An Introduction

Penguin Books

PENGUIN BOOKS

Published by the Penguin Group

Penguin Books Ltd, 80 Strand, London WC2R ORL, England
Penguin Putnam Inc., 375 Hudson Street, New York, New York 10014, USA
Penguin Books Australia Ltd, 250 Camberwell Road, Camberwell, Victoria 3124, Australia
Penguin Books Canada Ltd, 10 Alcorn Avenue, Toronto, Ontario, Canada M4V 3B2
Penguin Books India (P) Ltd, 11, Community Centre, Panchsheel Park, New Delhi – 110 017, India
Penguin Books (NZ) Ltd, Cnr Rosedale and Airborne Roads, Albany, Auckland, New Zealand
Penguin Books (South Africa) (Pty) Ltd, 24 Sturdee Avenue, Rosebank 2196, South Africa

Penguin Books Ltd, Registered Offices: 80 Strand, London WC2R ORL, England

www.penguin.com

First published 2002
1

Set in 10.5/12.5 pt Monotype Perpetua
Typeset by Rowland Phototypesetting Ltd, Bury St Edmunds, Suffolk
Printed in England by Clays Ltd, St Ives plc

Contents

Prologue

Telling the Story of Judaism

> Religion is experience, image and story before it is anything else and
> after it is everything else . . .
>
> Andrew M. Greeley[1]

To millions of human beings Judaism tells the tale of who they are and
what God wants of them. Here is their story, and mine, too.

In this book I present Judaism by telling the story that Judaism tells,
its master narrative of the human condition. To practise the religion of
Judaism means to take the ancient tale personally. To be a Jew who
practises Judaism is to tell concerning oneself and one's own family the
story that Judaism tells, beginning with the Jewish Scripture (Christianity's 'Old Testament'). Moses delivered God's message to Israel through
narrative. In Scripture's story the prophet tells the tale that conveys who
Israel is, where it comes from, and what it is to do. And how Judaism
has mediated that same story through history shapes the experience and
image and personal narrative for the faithful.

This is no history book. The story Judaism tells brings the past into
the present and imposes upon the present the pattern of the past. It is a
story about eternity in time, made up of narratives conveying timeless
verities. People living anywhere in Creation, at any time in history, in
any realm of language and culture, can tell the story of Judaism about
themselves and find a natural fit. The Judaic way of life acts out, chapter
by chapter, a single narrative of timeless relationships and transactions
with God.

I tell the story by its chapters, as they intersect with the practice of
the faith in everyday life. I do not commence by telling the story told

whole and continuously, for that would require paraphrasing the scriptural narrative without highlighting the telling moments therein, the occasions when the eternal tale intersects with human life and time. Rather I begin with the human here and now and explain through the practice of Judaism at critical moments in the year, and at critical passages of life, how the master narrative works its enchantment. That means identifying when and where and how a chapter of the story takes over and imparts meaning to a concrete transaction or event. First comes the life of home and family, then the social order of corporate community, its law and theology, the whole retelling Scripture's story.

The story is found in the Hebrew Scriptures, as these Scriptures are mediated by the rabbinic sages of ancient times. Writing down an originally oral tradition of Sinai, the great rabbis took Scripture's laws, stories and prophecies and worked them into a systematic account of holy Israel's social order. The documents they produced, from the Mishnah (c. 200 CE) through the Talmud of Babylonia (c. 600 CE), in dialogue with Scripture defined the classical statement of Judaism. The standard prayer books (the *Siddur* and the *Mahzor*) reworked that same story into a theology of worship. To that statement nearly all later formulations of Judaism would refer, down to our own day. The story that I tell, then, defines the touchstone for all that would follow. Once the classical story is told, I turn in Chapters 9 and 11 to its later variations and extensions, particularly the main developments of modern times, all of which refer back to the classical story.

The authoritative sources of Judaism commonly speak of 'Israel', meaning Israelite men and women, both. I have translated 'he' where the original Hebrew or Aramaic requires, while in my own discussions I use gender-neutral formulations. The system of transliteration represents Hebrew as it is pronounced by Israelis today.

In writing this book I consulted Professor Benjamin Brown, Hebrew University, Professor Bruce D. Chilton, Bard College, Professor Andrew M. Greeley, University of Chicago and University of Arizona, Professor William Scott Green, University of Rochester, Professor Ithamar Gruenwald, Tel Aviv University, Professor Allan Nadler, Drew University, Professor Stuart Silverman, University of South Florida, Professor Elliot Wolfson, New York University, and Rabbi Joel Zaiman, Baltimore, Maryland. I appreciate their generosity in giving me their time and critical judgement. I very much enjoyed working with Professor John Hinnells, Editor of this series, and Ms Ellah Allfrey of Penguin Books, London.

Jacob Neusner
Bard College

The Story Judaism Tells
about Israel

1

What Is 'Israel'?

The Community that Tells
about itself the Torah's Story

Imagine a formal dinner at home, served to a family sitting crowded around the table — fathers and mothers, children and grandchildren, uncles and aunts, cousins and friends and guests, including strangers to the family, all in their best clothes and on their best behaviour. The table glows with dishes and silverware, flickering candles and flowers at its centre. All assembled fall silent. Then one of the children exclaims, 'This is not the way we usually have our supper, in the kitchen, in school clothes, how different this night is from all other nights!' And the head of the family responds, 'Yes, but, we were slaves and now we're free, and tonight we remember how come! Now before we eat, we'll tell the story.' And the narrative of the Torah's book of Exodus pours forth.

Such a scene may seem unlikely, but this is exactly what takes place every spring, in the homes and synagogues of every community of Judaism. In a family banquet, held on the festival of Passover, commemorating the liberation of Israel from Egyptian bondage under the leadership of Moses, Jewish families, conventional or as defined for the occasion, retell the tale. Those that practise Judaism thereby answer the question, Who are we? And by that 'we', they mean, What is the community of Israel? — not *was* but *is*, then and now and always. The answer Judaism gives is that *we* are not alone the family and friends we appear to be. Rather, *we* embody the extended family of Abraham and Sarah, of whom the Torah speaks. The family, part of which is assembled at this table, really is an enslaved people, or, if God had not intervened and liberated *us*, that is what *we* should be. But here *we* are, free to live our lives, because God did – through Moses and Aaron and Miriam – keep his promises to Abraham and Sarah and their children.

The people assembled here participate as actors in the narrative of the occasion. It is *our* story, not just *theirs* of long ago. This implausible claim is recited with straight faces around a dining table, and parents teach the lesson through the story they tell their children. It is all set forth in word and symbol, image and experience, and reinforced with a meal of exceptional festival foods. The experienced season of 'our freedom' is not only a story, it is also the smells and tastes and sights and love of a family at supper.

The Passover story provides a working definition of Israel. If religion is story, then 'Israel' is formed by all those who legitimately tell about themselves the tales of the Torah as they carry out the rites thereof.[1] In finding themselves in the Torah, they identify with the Israel of the Exodus and of Sinai and accept God's dominion. And I should claim, most Jews in the world today, when they open Scripture and encounter the story of the Israel portrayed there, take for granted that Scripture speaks of their ancestors and directs its prophecies and promises to them themselves.

Nature Prompts Israel to Tell its Story

Judaism sees Israel's life here on earth as coordinated with the movement of the heavenly bodies, the moon in particular. Harmony characterizes Israel's life on earth and God's abode in heaven. In the words of the *kaddish* prayer of praise, which sanctifies God's name, 'He who makes peace in the heights may make peace for us', meaning that the heavens' regular movements attest to the passage of Israel through the year, eternally. That is why the critical chapters of the story of Israel, observed as festivals, coordinate with the heavenly turning points in the year of nature. These turning points, which take place in spring (the end of the winter rains in the Land of Israel) and autumn (the start of the winter rains) in particular, are indicated by the intersection of solar and lunar movements in the skies. Let me explain the mixed calculation of the Judaic year.

The Jewish Calendar

TISHRI (Sept–Oct)	HESHVAN (Oct–Nov)	KISLEV (Nov–Dec)	TEVET (Dec–Jan)	SHEVAT (Jan–Feb)	ADAR (Feb–Mar)	NISAN (Mar–Apr)	IYAR (Apr–May)	SIVAN (May–June)	TAMMUZ (June–July)	AV (July–Aug)	ELUL (Aug–Sept)
1 New Year	1 New Moon	1 New Moon	1 New Moon Hanukkah	1 New Moon	1 New Moon	1 New Moon	1 New Moon	1 New Moon	1 New Moon	1 New Moon	1 New Moon
2 New Year			2 Hanukkah								
3 Feast of Gedaliah											
10 Day of Atonement			10 Fast		13 Fast		5 Israel Independence Day	6 Shavuot		9 Fast	
15 Sukkot					14 Purim	15 Passover		7* Shavuot	17 Fast		
16* Sukkot					15 Shushan Purim	16* Passover	18 Lag ba-Omer				
17 Intermediate festival days		25 Hanukkah				17 Intermediate festival days					
		26 Hanukkah				20					
21		27 Hanukkah				21 Passover					
22 Shemini Azeret		28 Hanukkah				22* Passover					
23* Simhat Torah		29 Hanukkah									
30 New Moon	29	30 Hanukkah New Moon	29	30	29	30 New Moon	30 Jerusalem Day	30 New Moon	29	30 New Moon	29

☐ festival or feast

*festival day in Diaspora

Judaism celebrates the lunar months, each new moon occasioning a holiday. Israel's months then are signified by the phases of the moon, from the new moon, which signals the first day of the lunar month, to the full moon, the fifteenth day of that same lunar month, and onward to the end of the same lunar month and repetition of the cycle. But, besides the lunar months into which the year is divided, Israel's years are signified by the solar calendar, which governs the seasons here on earth.[2] The solar equinoxes, in spring and autumn, signal critical changes in the ecology of the Land of Israel, marking the end of the winter rains and the advent of the season of dew and the initial barley harvest in March–April, and the final harvest and the beginning of the winter rains to replenish the life-giving water of the Land in September–October. So the two noteworthy occasions in the solar calendar are the spring and autumn equinoxes, on 21 March and 21 September.

And that brings us to the coordination between the lunar and the solar calendars, and how the noteworthy events in Israel's master narrative correspond to the critical turnings in the heavenly hosts. On the first full moon after the spring equinox, the fifteenth day of the lunar month of Nisan, and on the first full moon after the autumn equinox, the fifteenth day of the lunar month of Tishri, Israel tells the stories of its origins in Egyptian slavery followed by its definition at Sinai, then its wandering in the wilderness for forty years. These, specifically, are embodied in two chapters of Israel's tale, told each spring and autumn. First comes the event that defines the beginning of Israel and the definition of Israel, Passover–Shavuot, and then the one that tells the character of Israel and its consequences, Sukkot (the Feast of Tabernacles) the climax of the autumn's penitential season, as we shall see in a moment, which captures the tensions of Israel's ongoing life with God.

The first chapter is formed by the stories told in the span of time from Passover (Pesah) to Shavuot (the Festival of Weeks). These concern the liberation of Israel from Egyptian bondage and its assembly at Mount Sinai to receive the Torah, or Instruction, from God. Passover begins the sequence, on the fifteenth day of the lunar month of Nisan in the spring, the span of time continuing for fifty days (the source of the Greek name for Shavuot, Pentecost), bearing in its wake a sequence of climactic moments in the definition of 'Israel', culminating on the fifty-first day with Shavuot and the complete definition of what is Israel.

The second chapter is told over three weeks in the span of time from the new moon prior to the autumn equinox to the full moon afterwards and a week beyond, twenty-two days in all. The element of the story that concerns us here is realized on Sukkot, beginning on the fifteenth day of the lunar month of Tishri and lasting for seven days thereafter. It concerns Israel's forty years of wandering in the wilderness, until the generation of the Exodus and Sinai died out, when Israel dwelt in *sukkot* or huts,[3] not in permanent houses. So the Israel of Judaism comes to realization in moments of active, participatory narrative, when people both repeat and act out a chapter in the master narrative, to which we now turn.

Passover: 'You shall Tell Your Child, "It is because of what the Lord did for me when I went free from Egypt"'

This brings us back to the Passover banquet or Seder (ceremony) introduced at the outset, which shows how Judaism's Israel is embodied in the common life of an extended family (conventional or otherwise) that forms a holy community through shared song, celebration, storytelling and feasting.

With the advent of spring and renewal after the fructifying winter rains in the Land of Israel comes Passover, signalling the beginning of Israel as a free people called from the slavery of Egypt to bondage to the Torah. Passover carries Israel to Sinai freely to accept God's rule in the Torah. Israel is bidden to form 'the kingdom of priests and the holy people', that is, to accept God's kingdom willingly. In secular language, Passover tells the chapter of the master narrative that accounts for Israel's origin.

The natural year of Judaism begins with Passover for a reason: the celebration of the Exodus from Egypt, matching nature's beginnings in spring, sets the stage for all the other parts of the story. The master narrative of Judaism begins with the story of the origins of Israel: the descent of Israel into Egypt, four centuries of slavery there, then God's sending Moses to the Egyptian Pharaoh to liberate the Israelite slaves and lead them to the Promised Land.

Accordingly, telling the tale of Israel begins annually when the parent tells the child the story of freedom: the liberation of Israel from Egyptian slavery by God's prophet-messenger, Moses. And it is an annual rite that denies the everyday. The family assembled last year, and (God willing) the members expect they will gather next year too. Here, in the Passover liturgy or *haggadah* ('narrative') is a story repeated every year over time beyond reckoning that always surprises; that comes down in tradition but is encountered as fresh and contemporary. The rite shows us how to understand the way in which the past is always present, the present forever part of the past. All depends, then, on the script of the drama in the home. Here is the language that introduces the rite, the exchange between the person representing the child and the voice of the rite, which is the 'we' of both the family and of Israel, the holy people. The child asks four questions as part of the Passover ceremony:

THE YOUNGEST PRESENT: Why has this night been made different from all other nights? On all other nights we eat bread whether leavened or unleavened, on this night only unleavened; on all other nights we eat all kinds of herbs, on this night only bitter ones; on all other nights we do not dip herbs even once; on this night, twice; on all other nights we sit at the table either sitting or reclining, on this night we all recline.

To this we get the following explicit reply:

THE PRESIDING PERSON: We were the slaves of Pharaoh in Egypt; and the Lord our God brought us forth from there with a mighty hand and an outstretched arm. And if the Holy One, blessed be he, had not brought our fathers forth from Egypt, then surely we, and our children, and our children's children, would still be slaves to Pharaoh in Egypt. And so, even if all of us were full of wisdom and understanding, mature and deeply versed in the tradition, we should still be bidden to repeat once more the story of the Exodus from Egypt; and whoever treats the story of the liberation as an important matter is praiseworthy.

The story of Israel then is spelled out, and in the course of the narrative, Israel comes to definition:

Long ago our ancestors were idol-worshippers but now the Holy One has drawn us to his service. So we read in the Torah: 'And Joshua said to all the people, "Thus says the Lord God of Israel: 'From time immemorial your fathers lived beyond the river Euphrates, even to Terah, father of Abraham and of Nahor, and they worshipped idols. And I took your father Abraham from beyond the river and guided his footsteps throughout the land of Canaan. I multiplied his offspring and gave him Isaac. To Isaac I gave Jacob and Esau. And I set apart Mount Seir as the inheritance of Esau, while Jacob and his sons went down to Egypt.' '' '

All of this is deeply relevant to those present, for it says who the assembled family really are, and for whom they really stand. In the here and now this family stands for 'our ancestors', Abraham, Isaac and Jacob.

ALL THOSE PRESENT: Blessed is he who keeps his promise to Israel . . . for the Holy One set a term to our bondage, fulfilling the word which he gave our father Abraham in the covenant made between the divided sacrifice [described in Genesis 15: 7–20]: 'Know beyond a doubt that your offspring will be strangers in a land that is not theirs, four hundred years they shall serve and suffer. But in the end I shall pronounce judgement on the oppressor people and your offspring shall go forth with great wealth.'

Judaism's 'Israel' explicitly defines itself: a family become a people, saved by God from bondage. Through the natural eye, we see ordinary folk, not much different from their neighbours in dress, language or aspirations. The words they speak do not describe reality and are not meant to. When ethnic Jews say of themselves, 'We were the slaves of Pharaoh in Egypt', they transform the exchange. For they know they never felt the lash; but through the eye of faith it is *their* liberation, not merely that of long-dead forebears, that they now celebrate.

That is no exaggeration or conceit. A single formula in words recited in the Passover narrative captures the moment: 'For ever after, in every generation, every Israelite must think of himself or herself as having gone forth from Egypt.' If I think of myself as having gone forth from Egypt, I have to tell about myself personally the story of the Exodus, make the story my own. That means I have to translate my everyday experience into the heightened reality embodied in that story.

And that is what the Passover ceremony accomplishes every year for the vast majority of Jews who practise Judaism, as well as a great many who regard themselves as secular. The power of people to make their own a story of what happened not here and now but there and then comes to expression in the contemporary recapitulation of the Holocaust, with its immediate power to engage and affect. So too it is with Israel at the Red Sea, escaping from the bondage of Egypt to God's rule set forth at Sinai: a vivid event even now, a life-defining narrative for all time. This conviction of the presence, at the Passover table, of episodes in Israel's story, is reinforced in yet another detail. A cup of wine sits by itself on the table, designated the cup of Elijah the prophet. After supper, grace having been recited, the door is opened for Elijah. Everyone rises to greet him and receive his presence, heralding as he does the advent of the Messiah at the end of days. Past and future meet in the Passover ceremony.

What is it that makes it plausible for nearly all Jews all over the world to use the word 'we' in the statement, 'We went forth . . .', and why do people sit down for supper and announce, 'It was not only our forefathers that the Holy One, blessed be He, redeemed; us too, the living, He redeemed together with them'? One theme stands out: we, here and now, are really living then and there ('We were slaves . . .'). The symbols on the table – the unleavened bread (*mazzah*), the bitter herbs, the lamb bone, the hard-boiled egg – explicitly invoke the then and there in the here and now. First comes the unleavened bread:

This is the bread of affliction, which our ancestors ate in the land of Egypt. Let all who are hungry come and eat with us, let all who are needy come and celebrate the Passover with us. This year here, next year in the land of Israel; this year slaves, next year free people.

Now, lest we miss the point that we are there and Moses is here, that this story is about us, the living, not only the long-ago dead, the message is announced in so many words:

This is the promise that has stood by our forefathers and stands by us. For neither once, nor twice, nor three times was our destruction planned; in every generation they rise against us, and in every generation God delivers us from their hands into freedom, out of anguish into joy, out of mourning into festivity, out of darkness into light, out of bondage into redemption.

Passover tells the story of Israel through time, not one time only, but all time, and its message is, 'God delivers us from their hands':

For ever after, in every generation, every Israelite must think of himself [or herself] as having gone forth from Egypt. For we read in the Torah: 'In that day thou shalt teach thy son, saying: "All this is because of what God did for me when I went forth from Egypt." ' It was not only our forefathers that the Holy One, blessed be he, redeemed; us too, the living, he redeemed together with them, as we learn from the verse in the Torah: 'And he brought us out from thence, so that he might bring us home, and give us the land which he pledged to our forefathers.'

There is nothing subtle about Judaic rites. Onlookers are never left in doubt about who, in the series of transformations brought about through the enchantment of the rite, the players are now supposed to be, or where, or when, or why. So we are told what troubles these people. The story the family tells about itself as Israel makes their play-acting at supper plausible as they turn their lives into metaphor, themselves into actors, and the everyday meal into drama. The message penetrates to the heart of people who remember the murder, in the recent past, of approximately six million Jews, and who know that in the Middle East and other anti-semitic settings, Jews are still a minority and at risk.

The power of the Passover ceremony to transform ordinary existence into an account of something beyond lies here. Ordinary existence imposes tensions. By definition Jews are different from gentiles. And now, the difference becomes destiny: it is how Jews transform themselves into the 'Israel' of which Scripture speaks. Scripture's story refers to them. In the transformation at hand, to be a Jew means to be a slave who has been liberated by God. To be Israel means to give eternal thanks for God's deliverance. And that deliverance is not at a single moment in historical time. Transformed into a permanent feature of reality, that story comes true in every generation and is always celebrated. Jews think of themselves as having gone forth from Egypt, and Scripture so instructs them. God did not redeem the dead generation of the Exodus alone, but the living too – especially the living. Thus the family states, recapitulating the entire narrative of Judaism's Israel:

Again and again, in double and redoubled measure, are we beholden to God the All-Present: that he freed us from the Egyptians and wrought his judgement on them; that he sentenced all their idols and slaughtered all their first-born; that he gave their treasure to us and split the Red Sea for us; that he led us through it dry-shod and drowned the tyrants in it; that he helped us through the desert and fed us with manna; that he gave the Sabbath to us and brought us to Mount

Sinai; that he gave the Torah to us and brought us to our homeland, there to build the Temple for us, for atonement of our sins.

Here we find the definition of that 'us' that constitutes Israel, a definition formed of a sequence of events that have designated that group.

What does the Passover rite have to say about Israel's ongoing history? Is it merely a succession of meaningless disasters — worldly happenings without end or purpose, where God intervenes and sets things right? The answer comes in a song sung at the end of the rite:

An only kid, an only kid,
My father bought for two pennies,
An only kid, an only kid.
But along came the cat and ate up the kid,
My father bought for two pennies,
An only kid, an only kid.

And so goes the dreary story. Here is the final verse:

Then the Holy One, blessed be he, came along
And slew the angel of death
Who slew the slaughterer
Who slew the ox
Who drank the water
That put out the fire
That burned the stick
That beat the dog
That bit the cat
That ate the kid
   My father had bought for two pennies,
   An only kid, an only kid.

The history of Israel, the holy people, is the history of the only kid; at the end, the Holy One, blessed be he, comes to slaughter the angel of death, vindicate the long sufferings of many centuries, and bring to a happy and joyful end the times of trouble. That has yet to happen. Here is the whole of Israel's story embodied in the little goat the father bought for next to nothing, his only kid. The fate of Israel, the kid slaughtered not once but many times over, is suffering that has an end and a purpose in the end of days. Death will die, and all who shared in the lamb's suffering will witness the divine denouement of history. To hear such a message of hope and resurrection, deriving from and yet transcending and transforming one's everyday experience, will people not gladly perform the Passover rite each year?

Shavuot: The Season of the Giving of the Torah

In this next chapter of the unfolding narrative of the natural year, Israel emerges as the community of those that accept God's dominion as laid out in the Torah. And in the narrative of Judaism, just as everyone, the living and those destined to live, were saved from Egyptian bondage at Passover, so now at Shavuot every Israelite through all time is regarded as standing at Sinai and receiving the Torah. What is at stake? Israel at Sinai forms not only an ethnic group, an extended family propagated by birth, but also, and especially, a religious community defined by a common commitment to God and his Instruction. Shavuot celebrates God's freely giving, and Israel's willingly receiving, the Torah.

First the slaves are liberated, then they gain the freedom incised on the tablets of the Torah: Israel accepts God's dominion in the covenant of Sinai. Shavuot falls on the fifty-first day from the full moon of Nisan which marked Passover, for 'On the third new moon after the people of Israel had gone forth from the land of Egypt, on that day they came into the wilderness of Sinai' (Exodus 19:1).

In the agricultural year of the Land of Israel, Shavuot marks the end of the barley harvest and the beginning of the wheat harvest. In the sacred calendar of Judaism, the festival of Shavuot embodies the second component of Judaism's definition of Israel: all those present at Sinai who declare, in one voice, 'All the words which the Lord has spoken we will do' (Exodus 24:3). For by 'Israel', Judaism means not only those who have been slaves by circumstance but those who are bonded to God by their choice, freely made, to accept God's sovereignty in the covenant of the Torah of Sinai. These are not only the slaves God has saved from Egyptian bondage but also the community that has entered into the covenant of the Torah defined at Sinai. In the unfolding story, Israel is no longer realized only in home and family, within the paramount metaphor of being children of Abraham and Sarah and the other patriarchs and matriarchs. Judaism's 'Israel' is now redefined as the community of all those who are represented at Sinai, and that means, all those that are bound by birth or by choice to the terms of the covenant of the Torah.

How in the unfolding narrative, does Shavuot encompass all Israel at the giving of the Torah? The key to the story is simple. Just as Israelites celebrating Passover are to think of themselves as having gone forth from Egypt, so when celebrating Shavuot all Israelites are to regard themselves as taking up a presence at Sinai. So just as they themselves are saved from Egyptian bondage, not their ancestors alone, so too, they themselves receive the Torah given by God to Moses. Then they speak in one voice, proclaiming through all time, 'We shall obey and we shall enact' the commandments of the Torah of Sinai, beginning with the Ten Commandments.[4]

So at Shavuot Israel is understood to be those that accepted the Torah at Sinai, and those who do so even now as they take upon themselves God's sovereignty in their lives. And that is not something that comes about by birth, it is the result of a decision to accept God's rule and the Torah and all its commandments as the embodiments of that rule. And any human being may find himself or herself called to Sinai. So Shavuot makes it clear that Israel is the community of those called to the Torah of Sinai, and that encompasses converts, those who join holy Israel by choice. The logic is simple. If 'Israel' encompasses all those that stand at Sinai, not stood *then* but stand here and *now*, then the community of Israel finds room for anyone who shows up and chooses to accept the Torah at Sinai. These are the Israelites by choice, not only by birth. And that is not merely a logical inference drawn from the master narrative sustained by the festival year. It is made explicit in the synagogue liturgy for Shavuot.

This is a festival which is celebrated primarily in public worship in the synagogue, in the declamation of and study of the Torah. The stage is set by the tradition of spending the entire night of the festival, from the sunset that marks its beginning, in community Torah-study organized by the synagogue. That is followed by morning services. So the congregation has re-enacted Israel's action at Sinai in receiving and meditating on the revealed Torah. But at the morning worship the congregation then is given a jarring message, as unanticipated in its way as the surprising message of Passover about the family representing a group of freed slaves.

Specifically, Israel assembled in the synagogue hears, in addition to the obligatory declamation of the Pentateuch and the prophets, the Book of Ruth. That book tells the story of how a woman from Moab, which abused Israel when Israel wandered in the wilderness, and the male heirs of which are excluded from Israel by reason of its churlishness, chose to make herself part of Israel by accepting the yoke of the Torah and the dominion of God.

The singing of the Book of Ruth, interpreted in the manner of the Judaic sages, in celebration of the Festival of the Giving of the Torah, then defines what Shavuot contributes to the definition of Israel. The message of the Book of Ruth is, critically, that 'Israel' is defined by more than worldly ethnicity. A woman of ethnically dubious origin, from outside Israel-by-birth, by accepting the Torah, not only adheres to Israel but becomes the ancestress of the prophesied Messiah.[5] In the patriarchal and genealogical framework of the narrative, which privileges men and favours family ties, one cannot identify an outsider more sharply than as a gentile and a woman. The message of Shavuot conveyed by the climactic inclusion of the Book of Ruth in its Judaic reading is that Israel is Israel by reason of the Torah, and Israel will be saved at the end of time by the Messiah of the house of David, grandson of the outsider on two counts – Moabite and woman – Ruth.

To understand how the story of Ruth when read at Shavuot conveys the Judaic definition of Israel, we have to consider the story not only as Scripture narrates it, but also as the rabbis of the oral Torah interpreted it in *Ruth Rabbah*, a commentary on the Book of Ruth made in the early centuries of the Common Era.[6] The biblical story is simple. It tells the tale of loyalty and love. In a time of famine an Israelite man with his wife Naomi and two sons from Bethlehem left the Land of Israel for Moab. The man died. His sons took Moabite wives, Orpah and Ruth. Then the sons died. Naomi determined to return from Moab to the Land of Israel, advising her daughters-in-law to remain in Moab, 'Go return each to her mother's house', rather than accompanying her to the Land of Israel. The widowed daughters-in-law insisted on remaining with the widowed mother-in-law, even though she had no more sons for them to wed. Eventually, Orpah left. But Ruth said, 'Entreat me not to leave you or to return from following you; for where you go I will go, and where you lodge I will lodge; your people shall be my people, and your God my God' (Ruth 1:16).

Together, Ruth and Naomi returned to Bethlehem in Judah. There Ruth met Boaz, a kinsman of her late husband's, who took her as his wife. Boaz and Ruth married and produced a son, Obed, who fathered Jesse, who fathered David, progenitor of the future Messiah. That is the story of how the Messiah will be born from the house of David, descendant of the gentile woman. It is what is declaimed in the synagogue at Shavuot in celebration of God's self-revelation through the Torah at Sinai: God is the God of all people who accept his dominion in the Torah. And it is the Torah that transforms the gentile into an Israelite. So by 'Israel' the Torah understands everyone who stands at Sinai, just as 'Israel' encompasses everyone who sees himself or herself as liberated from Egypt and rescued at the Red Sea, then and now.

Turning to the way in which the rabbinic sages interpreted that story, meaning what they found noteworthy in it, two points register, one on the surface of their reading, the second in the depths. On the surface, they are struck by the fact that the house of the Messiah begins in Moab with Ruth. At the depths they reflect on how a Moabite becomes an Israelite, so wholly an Israelite as to merit serving as the starting point of the messianic family of David: David's grandmother was not born into Israel but through an act of love and loyalty became an Israelite.

How did that come about? The Judaic answers to that question spelled out in *Ruth Rabbah* simply articulate the inner logic of the scriptural narrative in the light of the occasion at which it is declaimed. At Shavuot, then, to the rabbinic readers of the Book of Ruth, the proposition that Israel is Israel by reason of the Torah, and gentiles are gentiles by reason of their rejection thereof, is self-evident. They find it everywhere, in particular at the critical turning point: 'Your people shall be my people, and your God my God.' Here is the comment of *Ruth Rabbah* on Ruth 1:16:

When Naomi heard her say this, she began laying out for her the laws that govern proselytes.

She said to her, 'My daughter, it is not the way of Israelite women to go to theatres and circuses put on by idolaters.'

[Ruth] said to her, 'Where you go I will go.'

They will say before him, 'Lord of the world, we have thrown up a vast number of bridges, we have conquered a vast number of towns, we have made a vast number of wars, and all of them we did only for Israel, so that they may define as their chief occupation the study of the Torah.'

The Holy One, blessed be he, will say to them, 'Whatever you have done has been for your own convenience. You have thrown up a vast number of bridges to collect tolls, you have conquered a vast number of towns to collect the poll tax, and as to making a vast number of wars, I am the one who makes wars: "The Lord is a man of war" (Exodus 19:17). Are there any among you who have been telling of . . . the Torah?'. . . So they will make their exit, humiliated.

And so it will go with each and every nation.[9]

The lesson is simple. The gentile nations had a chance to accept the Torah but rejected it. That is what brought about the estrangement between God and the gentiles. God is not arbitrary but only responds to how people act. The same rule of justice governs Israel and the gentile nations alike. If Israel inherits the world to come, that is because of its loyalty to the Torah, which also includes suffering in this age in expiation for its sins of rebellion. The other nations commit comparable sins but do not expiate them through suffering in this world, so in the world to come God exacts punishment from them for rejecting his will in the Torah.[10]

So at Shavuot the second element in the Judaic definition of Israel falls into place. Other people rejected the Torah and God's rule set forth therein. Israel accepted the Torah. Those who originate outside Israel but then accept the Torah no longer belong to their original community. They take their place in Israel, the people of the Torah. But what of the house of Israel: where is it located? The answer is, Israel is a pilgrim people, its house is a transient hut as it wanders in the wilderness in quest of the Promised Land.

Sukkot: The Season of Our Rejoicing

Called simply 'The Festival', the festival of Sukkot is about sin, forgiveness and rejoicing. It forms the climax of the autumn holy day season, a counterpart to the spring sequence of Passover and Shavuot. The autumn festival cycle lasts for three weeks, beginning on the first day of the lunar month

(Tishri) in which the autumn equinox takes place. This is Rosh ha-Shanah, the New Year of Judaism. It commemorates the Creation ('today the world was born', the liturgy says), and it is judgement day: the day on which God recalls the deeds of the year past and judges Israel. Ten days later, that is, the tenth of Tishri, comes Yom Kippur, the Day of Atonement, which completes the judgement. The advent of this day in itself atones for Israel's sin and invokes God's mercy and power to forgive sin. Five days later, the fifteenth of Tishri, at the full moon after the autumn equinox, is Sukkot which, like Passover, lasts for seven days. (Actually, in the Diaspora Passover and Sukkot last for eight days, but in the State of Israel, as Scripture requires, seven.) Sukkot forms the third and final component of Judaism's definition of Israel: as a pilgrim people, wandering in the wilderness, expiating the sin of a generation that rebelled against God. It is that aspect of Sukkot that concerns us here: the meaning of the *sukkah*, or hut, itself.

Sukkot places Israel beyond the Red Sea and Sinai, wandering about in the wilderness for forty years. Israel then is reminded that it is a people that has sinned, but that God can and does forgive. After being liberated from slavery in Egypt and receiving the Torah at Mount Sinai, Israel remained in the wilderness until an entire generation had died out, and Israel was ready to enter the Promised Land, that is to say, the land that God had promised to Abraham and Sarah and their descendants when he told them (Genesis 12) to leave their homeland in Babylonia and migrate to the Land that he would show them and give to their descendants, which in Judaism would be known as 'the Land of Israel'. This refers to the location that God had had in mind for his people all along; not merely a geographical area but the location where the life of the faith would be lived out, where God's kingdom would be constructed, the successor to the Garden of Eden.

Passover places Israel's freedom into the context of the affirmation of life beyond sin, whereas Sukkot returns Israel to the fragility of abiding in the wilderness, as Moses explicitly states:

And the Lord said to Moses, 'Say to the people of Israel, On the fifteenth day of this seventh month and for seven days is the feast of huts to the Lord . . . You shall dwell in huts for seven days; all that are native in Israel shall dwell in huts, that your generations may know that I made the people of Israel dwell in huts when I brought them out of the land of Egypt; I am the Lord your God.'[11]

This third stage, following the celebration of freedom and of the giving of the Torah, jars; it is not what we should have expected. The journey across the desert could have been completed in a few weeks, even by a massive caravan. But when the Israelites approached the Promised Land and sent out rangers to report on its condition the people sulked and did not believe they could prevail:

'Yet you would not go up, but rebelled against the command of the Lord your God . . . And the Lord heard your words, and was angered, and he swore, "Not one of these men of this evil generation shall see the good land that I swore to give to your fathers." '[12]

So Israel wandered for forty years in the wilderness, and Sukkot reminds Israel of how, as a result of its rebellion, it lived in temporary hovels for an entire generation.

The principal observance of Sukkot is the construction of a frail hut, for temporary use. This is built from scratch every year; last year's will not do. In it Israel lives once more in the condition of that sinful generation, eating meals and (where the climate permits) sleeping out-of-doors. What defines the hut is the roof, which must cast more shade than light, but not be fully covered over. Roofing of branches, leaves, fruit and flowers allows some light to show through, and at night, the stars. At this time of harvest bounty it is good to be reminded of people's labour and dependence upon heavenly succour. The hut will not provide adequate shelter in the rainy season that is coming. In reverting to the wilderness, Israel is to take shelter in any random, ramshackle hut, covered merely with what nature has provided. The hut in its transience matches Israel's condition in the wilderness, wandering between Egypt and the Promised Land, death and eternal life. The story concerns the generation of the wilderness, that is the generation that must die out before Israel can enter the Promised Land. So entering the hut at Sukkot reminds Israel of the fragility of its condition: still sinful, still awaiting death, so that a new generation will be ready for the Promised Land.

Sukkot focuses on the fragility and culpability of liberated, covenanted Israel. What is underscored in this definition of Israel is the imperfection of the community. In the here and now Israel is still a community of sinners striving to be saints. Israel is en route to the Promised Land that stands for Eden; Israel also, even beyond the penitential season, bears its sin and must, in the short term, die, but in death enjoys the certainty of resurrection, judgement, and eternal life to come.

But this generation of Israel did enter the Land of Israel; a new generation did succeed the old, sinful one. That part of the story is not to be missed. At Sukkot Israel re-experiences not only the wilderness and its message of death but also transcendence over death in its entry into the Promised Land. Sukkot only makes sense in the context of the New Year and the Day of Atonement: as the final act in the penitential season and its intense drama. In the wilderness, en route to the Promised Land, still-sinful Israel depended wholly and completely on God's mercy, goodwill and infinite capacity to forgive in response to repentance and atonement. Israel depended for all things on God, eating food he sends down from heaven, drinking water he divines in rocks, and living in fragile huts constructed of worthless shards and remnants. Even Israel's very household in the mundane sense, its shelter, now is made to depend upon divine grace: the wind can blow it down, rain will render it useless. At Sukkut, each Israelite recapitulates here and now his total dependence upon God's mercy. The hut makes the statement that Israel of the here and now, sinful like the Israel that dwelt in the wilderness, depends wholly upon and looks only to God; lives not only in God's dominion but wholly by God's mercy. Israelites turn their eyes to that God whose recent forgiveness of last year's sins and acts of rebellion and whose acceptance of Israel's immediate act of repentance recapitulates God's ongoing nurture that kept Israel alive in the wilderness.

What Is 'Israel'?

These three festivals have taught us that Israel means those of whom the Torah speaks and their heirs, who are, specifically, those who choose to continue the story through time. Israelites identify with the Israel of Scripture either through family and community heritage (birth and association) or self-selection, the first being most common. The family of Israel is formed through genealogy, reinforced through shared social life. 'Israel' thus refers to the descendants of Scripture's Abraham and Sarah through their grandson Jacob, forming a distinct group that is defined on the analogy of the family. In the law of Judaism a convert abandons his or her entire past and natural genealogy, acquiring a different ancestry and entering into a supernatural family. In simple terms: by the law of Judaism, a Jew, that is, an Israelite in the context of personal status, synagogue and community affairs, is either the child of a Jewish mother[13] or a person who has accepted the kingship of God and the imperatives of the Torah through an act of religious conversion. In contemporary communities of Judaism, converts are supposed to participate. But theology does not tell the entire tale. Converts in Britain, the USA and the State of Israel, alas, tell stories of feeling excluded or taking a second-class position within Jewry. It is not uncommon for converts to attain a higher standard of piety and devotion than the native-born Israelites. These stories of less than full acceptance attest to an imperfect realization of the theology of Israel, God's people, that the Torah sets forth.

The possibility of conversion defines the character of Israel's story. It is not a history of an ethnic group, formed by common ties of blood or a shared culture and language. It is the tale of a community formed by common convictions concerning God's will for Creation and humanity's response thereto. That individuals become Israelites and naturalized to Israel through an act of conversion, entering into that same family of Abraham and Sarah by adopting for themselves Scripture's story as their personal story defines how Judaism conceives of itself. It is, specifically, the conception of Judaism as a religion, not a nationality, race, or ethnicity. Identifying with the story of Israel imposes consequences: obligations to God, responsibilities to the community of Israel. For the Israel defined by the law and theology of Judaism constitutes a community of faith realized in action, a sacred society formed by families and also open to all who undertake the common disciplines. Now it is clear what the community of Israel is, we can look at the individual experience of Judaism.

2
Who Is 'Israel'?

Israelites and Israel: The Moral
Building Blocks of the Social Order

In the tale Judaism tells, all Israel, in one voice and for all time, accepted God's rule in the Torah and made a covenant with God to do his will. Israel speaks in the first person plural: *We* were slaves in Egypt, *we* are free, *we* stand at Sinai, *we* are covenanted to live in God's kingdom. But does the story also speak about the first person singular: who am I, the individual Israelite? The question then is *who* is Israel, meaning, of whom is this corporate community, Israel, comprised? And what role does the master narrative accord to the individuals of that same community?[1]

The answer is ambiguous. On the one hand, the condition of the community of Israel dictates the standing of each individual within it. Judaism's story is clear on that point: the community of Israel are slaves in Egypt; the community of Israel stand at Sinai; and all members are mutually responsible as Israel. And that Israel that is present encompasses every generation. But, the same tale continues, each Israelite bears responsibility not only for all but also for what he or she individually, as a matter of deliberation and intention, chooses to do. So there must also be an occasion to narrate the tale of who the individual Israelite is. Part of a corporate community answerable all together and all at once, the individual also forms a responsible moral actor before God. Judaism values the individual and affirms the singularity of each person, expressing the matter in theological terms:

[Why was man created alone and unique? It is] to portray the grandeur of the

Holy One, blessed be he. For a person mints many coins with a single seal, and they are all alike one another, but the King of kings of kings, the Holy One, blessed be he, minted all human beings with that seal of his with which he made the first person, yet not one of them is like anyone else. Therefore everyone is obligated to maintain, 'On my account the world was created.'[2]

If the Torah's law addresses all Israel, the entire community, just where is the individual recognized within, yet distinct from, all Israel? That dual relationship is captured by the case of Achan, which figures in the Mishnah tractate *Sanhedrin*. In the Scriptural narrative of Joshua's conquest of the Promised Land, Israel suffered a defeat. God explained to Joshua, 'Israel has sinned . . . they have taken some of the devoted things; they have stolen, and lied, and put them among their own stuff . . . Up, sanctify the people . . .' (Joshua 7:10–13). Joshua interrogated each of the tribes, and, in the tribe of Judah, each of the families, and of the families, each of the Zerahites, and of the households, that of Zabdi (Joshua 7:16–18). And the matter came down to Achan, son of Carmi, son of Zabdi, son of Zerah of the tribe of Judah, to whom Joshua said,

'My son, give glory to the Lord God of Israel, and render praise to him; and tell me now what you have done; do not hide it from me.' And Achan answered Joshua, 'Of a truth I have sinned against the Lord God of Israel, and this is what I did . . .'[3]

Achan then confessed to theft. All Israel suffered for the sin of Achan, and Achan bore responsibility for his sin as well. But having paid for his sin, Achan was restored to Israel and with all Israel attained eternal life, according to *Sanhedrin*'s explanation of the implications of the scriptural narrative:

And Achan answered Joshua and said, 'Truly have I sinned against the Lord, the God of Israel; and thus and thus I have done' (Joshua 7:19).

And how do we know that his confession achieved atonement for him?

For it is said, 'And Joshua said, "Why have you troubled us? The Lord will trouble you this day"' (Joshua 7:25), *this* day the Lord will trouble you, but you will not be troubled in the world to come.[4]

Their close reading of the wording, 'this day', leads the rabbinic interpreters to conclude that 'this day' Achan is troubled, but he is not going to be troubled on 'that day' on which the dead are raised for judgement and life eternal. Achan atoned for his sin by being executed, but the rabbinic scholars were clear that, along with nearly all Israel, he would be accorded his individual portion of the world to come, that is, resurrection from the grave at the Last Judgement.

All individuals, Israelite and gentile, are subject to God's rule. The only social group (however classified, whether as people, nation, ethnic tribe, extended family, immediate family) that forms a *moral* entity transcending the individual members thereof is Israel. In this regard Israelites form a species of the genus, humanity. Like the genus of which they are individually part, they are answerable to God for their personal conduct. But, uniquely, Israel is a social entity that is also a moral actor; the holy community of Israel forms a moral whole that exceeds the sum of the parts, as we shall see.

Israel, the community, viewed as a moral actor responsible for its own deeds presupposes Israelites who are also moral actors defined by their deeds. That we see in the story of Sukkot, an entire generation is condemned to dwell in huts and to wander in the wilderness, there to die, because the Israelites, as Moses portrays them, have churlishly rejected the Land God chose for them. And the future generations are to remember. The community of Israel bears responsibility for the actions and attitudes of individual Israelites. British English demonstrates this dual nature: in American English, we say, 'the government is . . . and has decided', but the British also use plural verbs with collective nouns – 'the government are . . . and have decided'. This British reading of the collective noun preserves the elective assent of all individual participants, whereas the American expresses only the corporate assent so that the individual disappears.

If in Judaism's master narrative, individuals were conceived as automatons, always subordinated agencies of the community, the answer to the question, *what* is Israel would automatically define *who* is Israel, the Israelite person, as well. If the community is contemplated as merely the sum total of individual participants, then once we know who the Israelite is, we forthwith can define Israel merely as the sum total of Israelites, therefore never wholly subject to a single judgement, whether of guilt or innocence. But as in the story of Achan, the Torah holds the community responsible for the deeds of Israelites (his theft was the cause of the whole nation's defeat in battle), and further treats individuals as responsible for their own actions. Scripture, continued in the Mishnah, Talmuds and midrash, insists that Israelites are individually responsible for what they do, and further that corporate Israel on its own, not only as the sum of individual actions, forms a moral entity subject to judgement. Achan was individually guilty, but all Israel also was guilty because of the rebellion in its midst.

The festivals of the New Year (Rosh ha-Shanah), fifteen days before the first full moon after the autumn equinox, and the Day of Atonement (Yom Kippur), five days before that same full moon, tell the story that defines who an Israelite is.

The Days of Awe: The New Year, The Day of Remembrance and Judgement, and the Day of Atonement, the Day of Mercy and Forgiveness

The first ten days of the lunar month of Tishri, in the autumn, the New Year, and the Day of Atonement together called 'the Days of Awe', mark days of solemn penitence. The fifteenth day of that same month, the first full moon after the autumn equinox, as we saw in Chapter 1, marks the advent of Sukkot.

The opening ten days then mark the start of the autumn season in connection with the autumnal equinox, marking the end of the dry season and the commencement of the fructifying autumn rains. Israel's collective life in the Land is in the balance; without rain, the summer season of death extends itself, and drought brings famine. With rain, life is renewed. One would expect that the chapter of the narrative told in this season would concern all Israel, and so, at Sukkot, it does. But the individual's conduct enters into the judgement of corporate Israel, and the confrontation with the deeds of the individual over the past year takes priority. Life or death begins with the private person, but always encompasses all Israel.

The story realized in the holy season of the Days of Awe concerns the individual Israelite in the setting of all of humanity. It tells that the New Year commemorates the creation of the world, and at that time, every person comes before God to be judged on their deeds during the past year. Then, ten days later, the decree is sealed on the Day of Atonement, which, on its own, has the power to atone for sin. So the judgement of the New Year is mitigated or even set aside by the atonement of the Day of Atonement, an occasion for forgiveness from sin. Scripture is clear that the advent of the Day on its own brings forgiveness:

It shall be a statute to you for ever that in the seventh month, on the tenth day of the month, you shall afflict yourselves, and shall do no work, either the native or the stranger who sojourns among you; for on this day shall atonement be made for you, to cleanse you; from all your sins you shall be clean before the Lord . . . And this shall be an everlasting statute for you, that atonement may be made for the people of Israel once in the year because of all their sins.[5]

The advent of the Day of Atonement does not mark the sole occasion for forgiveness of sin of individuals and community. Scripture provides for animal sacrifices to atone for unwitting sins. The death of the sinner also atones, as we have already seen in the case of Achan. And then there is repentance, the sinner's statement of regret and remorse for sin, joined with resolve not to repeat the sin.

The liturgical formulation of matters for synagogue worship captures the outcome of the story. The community is judged, so the language is plural ('we . . .') but the individual finds himself or herself in the corporate worship as well. That is because the words of the liturgy create a world of personal introspection and individual judgement. The Days of Awe concern life and death, which take narrative form in affirmations of God's rule and judgement. The New Year celebrates the creation of the world: 'Today the world was born.' At New Year the question is raised: who will live and who will die? At this time, so the words of the service state, humanity is 'inscribed for life or death in the heavenly books for the coming year, and on the Day of Atonement the books are sealed'. The New Year is a day of remembrance on which the deeds of all creatures are reviewed. The principal themes of the words invoke Creation, and God's rule over Creation; revelation, and God's rule in the Torah for the created world; and redemption, God's ultimate plan for the world.

On the birthday of the world God made, God asserts his sovereignty, as in the New Year prayer:

Our God and God of our fathers, rule over the whole world in your honour . . . and appear in your glorious might to all those who dwell in the civilization of your world, so that everything made will know that you made it, and every creature discern that you have created him, so that all in whose nostrils is breath may say, 'The Lord, the God of Israel is king, and his kingdom extends over all.'

God created the world and rules over it, God is made self-manifest in the Torah, and God will at the end of time redeem humanity from the condition of sin and death and accord eternal life to his dominion. God's sovereignty is established by his creation of the world. His judgement follows his revelation of divine law: 'From the beginning you made this, your purpose known . . .'[6] And therefore, since people have been told what God requires of them, they are judged:

On this day sentence is passed upon countries, which to the sword and which to peace, which to famine and which to plenty, and each creature is judged today for life or death. Who is not judged on this day? For the remembrance of every creature comes before you, each man's deeds and destiny, words and way . . .

As this story of judgement unfolds and people grow reflective, the underlying theme of the Days of Awe seizes the imagination: I live and then I die; sooner or later it comes to all. The call for inner contemplation implicit in the liturgy elicits a deep response.

The theme of revelation is further combined with redemption; the ram's horn, or shofar, which is sounded in the synagogue during daily worship for a month before the New Year festival, serves to unite the two:

You did reveal yourself in a cloud of glory . . . Out of heaven you made them [Israel] hear your voice . . . Amid thunder and lightning you revealed yourself to them, and while the shofar sounded you shined forth upon them . . . Our God and God of our fathers, sound the great shofar for our freedom. Lift up the ensign to gather our exiles . . . Lead us happily to Zion your city, Jerusalem the place of your sanctuary.

The most personal, solemn and moving of the Days of Awe is the Day of Atonement, the sabbath of sabbaths. It is marked by fasting and continuous prayer. We should not miss the drama and choreography of the rite of the Day of Atonement. The holy day begins with a public remission of vows, so that the holy community may appear before God unencumbered by vows that, thoughtlessly, they have made to God in the year now coming to a close.

All vows and oaths we take, all promises and obligations we make between this Day of Atonement and the next we hereby publicly retract in the event that we should forget them, and hereby declare our intention to be absolved of them.

At issue are vows taken rashly, not in full deliberation. Not at issue are the solemn commitments, invoking God's name, that people make to each other, for example, contracts and pledges. This prayer, Kol Nidrei ('All Vows'), is sung at sunset on the eve of the Day of Atonement, and moves masses of Jews to come to synagogue who otherwise scarcely find their way there. Hardly poetry, this formulaic passage sung in the synagogue, in front of the open empty ark, with the scrolls of the Torah it usually contains held up before the congregation, marks the single transforming, enchanting moment in the synagogue year. For what the formula, sung dramatically, conveys is the proposition that we sin but may atone, and God judges but will forgive. The power of the Kol Nidrei flows not from its words but from the dramatic staging, formed by the presence of the congregation into a drama of life and death: Who will live, who will die? who by fire? who by water? These are the questions of life and death that are evoked by the melody of Kol Nidrei, with its turning back to the past year and effort to cancel out the vows taken in haste or exasperation in that time.

A day of fasting and prayer, the Day of Atonement is the single most widely observed rite of Judaism. On it the vast majority of Jews in the world, whether otherwise party to Judaism or not, find their way to corporate Israel assembled in synagogue worship, and there they speak of themselves, individuals within the community, Israelites of Israel the holy people. On it, the Israelite individual makes confession:

Our God and God of our fathers, may our prayer come before you. Do not hide yourself from our supplication, for we are not so arrogant or stiff-necked as to say before you . . . 'We are righteous and have not sinned'. But we have sinned.

We are guilt-laden, we have been faithless, we have robbed . . .

We have committed iniquity, caused unrighteousness, have been presumptuous . . .

We have counselled evil, scoffed, revolted, blasphemed . . .

The Hebrew confession is built upon the successive letters of the Hebrew alphabet, from A onward (*ashammu*, 'we are guilt-laden', *bagadnu*, we have been faithless') as if by making certain every letter is represented, God, who knows human secrets, will combine them into appropriate words. The very alphabet bears witness against us before God. Then:

What shall we say before you who dwell on high? What shall we tell you who live in heaven? Do you not know all things, both the hidden and the revealed? You know the secrets of eternity, the most hidden mysteries of life. You search the innermost recesses, testing people's feelings and heart. Nothing is concealed from you or hidden from your eyes. May it therefore be your will to forgive us our sins, to pardon us for our iniquities, to grant remission for our transgressions.

A further list of sins follows, built on alphabetical lines. Prayers to be spoken by the congregation are all in the plural: 'For the sin which we have sinned against you with the utterance of the lips . . . For the sin which we have sinned before you openly and secretly . . .' The community takes upon itself responsibility for what is done in it. All Israel is part of one community, one body, and all are responsible for the acts of each. The sins confessed are mostly against society, against one's fellow human beings; few pertain to ritual laws. At the end the prayer becomes personal:

O my God, before I was formed, I was nothing. Now that I have been formed, it is as though I had not been formed, for I am dust in my life, more so after death. Behold I am before you like a vessel filled with shame and confusion. May it be your will . . . that I may no more sin, and forgive the sins I have already committed in your abundant compassion.

While much of the liturgy speaks of 'we', the individual focus in fact dominates from beginning to end. The Days of Awe speak to the heart of the individual, telling a story of judgement and atonement. So the individual Jew stands before God: possessing no merits, yet hopeful of God's love and compassion.

What story, exactly, does the master narrative of Judaism attach to the Days of Awe? The answer, as with Shavuot, comes to us in the passage of Scripture that is selected for public declamation in the synagogue, and for the New Year that is Genesis 21–2, which tell the story of the birth of Isaac, and then God's commanding Abraham to bring Isaac to Mount Moriah and offer him up as a sacrifice. This Abraham was ready to do and it was only at the last moment, with Abraham's hand raised and his knife poised for the slaughter, that God called Abraham and told him not to offer his son but provided, instead, a ram caught by its horns in a nearby bush.

After these things God tested Abraham, and said to him, 'Abraham!' And he said, 'Here am I.'

He said, 'Take your son, your only son Isaac, whom you love, and go to the land of Moriah [that is, Jerusalem to be], and offer him there as a burnt offering upon one of the mountains of which I shall tell you.'

So Abraham rose early in the morning, saddled his ass, and took two of his young men with him, and his son Isaac; and he cut the wood for the burnt offering, and arose and went to the place of which God had told him.

On the third day Abraham lifted up his eyes and saw the place afar off. Then Abraham said to his young men, 'Stay here with the ass; I and the lad will go yonder and worship, and come again to you.'

And Abraham took the wood of the burnt offering and laid it on Isaac his son; and he took in his hand the fire and the knife. So they went both of them together.

And Isaac said to his father Abraham, 'My father!' And he said, 'Here am I, my son.' He said, 'Behold the fire and the wood; but where is the lamb for a burnt offering?'

Abraham said, 'God will provide himself the lamb for a burnt offering, my son.' So they went both of them together.

When they came to the place of which God had told him, Abraham built an altar there, and laid the wood in order, and bound Isaac his son, and laid him on the altar, upon the wood. Then Abraham put forth his hand, and took the knife to slay his son.

But the angel of the Lord called to him from heaven, and said, 'Abraham, Abraham!' And he said, 'Here am I.'

He said, 'Do not lay your hand on the lad or do anything to him; for now I know that you fear God, seeing you have not withheld your son, your only son, from me.'

And Abraham lifted up his eyes and looked, and behold, behind him was a ram, caught in a thicket by his horns; and Abraham went and took the ram, and offered it up as a burnt offering instead of his son.[7]

This story does not work on its own within the occasion on which it is read, the New Year Day of Judgement. It is woven into the liturgy of worship on that day by the rabbinic sages' interpretation of it, which links the prayers recited at New Year to God's response in Heaven:

When the Holy One, blessed be he, ascends to take his seat on the throne of justice on the New Year, it is for the sake of strict justice that he ascends.

That is in line with the following verse of Scripture: 'God has gone up with the shofar blast' (Psalms 47:5).

But that is not the whole story. For God chooses between two thrones, the throne from which he dispenses strict justice, and the throne from which he dispenses mercy. And when Israel sounds the shofar, his mercy wells up and he shifts to the throne of mercy:

But when Israel take up their shofars and sound them, forthwith: 'The Lord [the name of God that refers to the attribute of mercy] at the sound of the Shofar.'

He rises from the throne of judgement and takes his seat on the throne of mercy. He is filled with mercy for them and for them turns the measure of justice into the measure of mercy.

When?

In the seventh month, on the first day of the month, you shall observe a day of solemn rest, a memorial proclaimed with blast of trumpets (Leviticus 23:24).[8]

The sounding of the shofar sparks God's empathy, which is explained later in the same interpretation, with reference to the narrative of Genesis 22: Abraham's binding Isaac on the altar at Moriah in obedience to God's command, God's remitting the decree and supplying the ram, caught by his horns in the thicket, for the offering in place of Isaac. At that moment Abraham imposed an oath on God. This reading depends on the fact that the letters for the word 'seven' and the letters for the word 'oath' are the same, thus 'the seventh month' of the New Year and the Day of Atonement is recast into 'the month of the oath'. Now we are told what oath is contemplated and how it intersects with God's judgement at the New Year:

'In the seventh (SBY'Y) month' (Leviticus 23:24):

Rabbi Berekhiah would call (that month) the month of the oath (SBW'), namely, the month in which the Holy One, blessed be he, took an oath (NSB')[9] to our father, Abraham, 'By myself have I taken an oath,' says the Lord (Genesis 22:16).

What need was there for this oath?

(Rabbi Bibi bar Abba in the name[10] of Rabbi Yohanan:) Abraham said before the Holy One, blessed be he, 'Lord of the ages! It is perfectly evident before the throne of your glory that, when you said to me, "Take your son, your only son, whom you love, Isaac" (Genesis 22:2), I had in mind what to answer you and to say to you, "Yesterday you said to me, 'For through Isaac shall seed be called forth for you' (Genesis 21:12). And today you say to me, 'Take your son, your only son'."

'But just as I had in mind what to answer you, but [kept my peace and] made no reply to you, so, when the descendants of Isaac will come to the toils of transgression and bad deeds, you must remember in their behalf the binding of Isaac, their father, and therefore effect atonement for them and turn the attribute of justice to the attribute of mercy for them.'

When?

'In the seventh month, on the first day of the month, you shall observe a day of solemn rest, a memorial proclaimed with blast of trumpets' (Leviticus 23:24).[11]

The next chapter makes explicit both the forgiveness of sin and the redemption of holy Israel from bondage to the idolaters:

And Abraham raised his eyes, and he saw, and behold, a ram (Genesis 22:13).

Said Rabbi Yudan, 'That verse teaches that the Holy One, blessed be he, showed Abraham a ram tearing itself out of one thicket and getting caught in another, over and over again. He said to him, "So will your children be trapped by sins and entangled among troubles, but in the end they will be redeemed through the horn of a ram [sounded at the New Year]." Then "the Lord will appear over them, and his arrow go forth like lightning; [the Lord God will sound the trumpet, and march forth in the whirlwinds of the south. The Lord of hosts will protect them]" (Zechariah 9:14–15). That is in line with the following verse of Scripture: "And in that day a great trumpet will be blown" (Isaiah 27:13)].'

Said Rabbi Haninah, 'This verse teaches that the Holy One, blessed be he, showed Abraham a ram tearing itself out of one thicket and getting caught in another, over and over again. He said to him, "So will your children be trapped among the nations and entangled among the kingdoms, and dragged from one kingdom to the next, from Babylonia to Media, from Media to Greece, from Greece to Edom, but in the end they will be redeemed through the horn of a ram [sounded at the New Year]." '[12]

But no account of who is Israel can fail to account for who is *not* Israel? For Judaism divides humanity between Israel, those who know God through the Torah, and everybody else, who deny the Torah and therefore do not know God. Hence humanity consists of Israel and not-Israel. And individual Israelites are represented, always, by 'all Israel', that is, the corporate community, morally responsible for all of its members.[13]

So too here, we know the answer to only part of the question at hand. We turn now to the counterpart to the Israelite. The Israelite and the gentile are both species of a common genus, represented in Scripture by the figure of Adam. So to complete our account of Israel and the Israelite, we have to place the Israelite into the larger setting formed by all humanity.

Israel and Adam

Who is judged at New Year, Israelites alone or all humanity? It commemorates the birth of the world, so the answer can only be, all humanity. Scripture's story of Creation leaves no doubt that all humanity is formed 'in our [God's] image, after our likeness' (Genesis 1:26), and so Judaism provides a place in its narrative for all humanity: on the Day of Judgement, when the Creator judges Creation, everyone comes under judgement. That is only reasonable, since Adam (that is, humanity) was created at New Year, as the following teaching indicates, linking the New Year to the judgement of Adam:

Forever, O Lord, this word is firmly fixed in the heavens (Psalms 119:89).

It was taught on tannaite authority in the name of Rabbi Eliezer, 'On the twenty-fifth day of Elul [the lunar month prior to the lunar month of Tishri, and the New Year], the world was created.'

The following statement of Rav accords with the view of Rabbi Eliezer, for it has been taught in the verses Rav assembled to accompany the sounding of the ram's horn at the New Year, 'This day [marks] the beginning of your works, a memorial to the first day. "For it is a statute for Israel, an ordinance of the God of Jacob (Psalms 81:4)." And concerning all countries, on that day it is declared which is destined for the sword and which for peace, which for famine and which for plenty. On that day all creatures are judged, to be recorded for life or for death.'[14]

Here we find an explicit declaration that on the first of Tishri, all people were created and all people and nations are judged. What has this judgement to do with the creation of the world?

[Since the New Year, the first of Tishri, is the sixth day following the creation of the world, which took place on the twenty-fifth of Elul], you find that on the first of Tishri the first man was created, because he was created on the sixth day of Creation.

In the first hour [the thought of creating him] entered [God's mind], in the second God consulted the ministering angels, in the third he collected dust, in the fourth, he kneaded it, in the fifth he wove together the parts, in the sixth he stood him on his feet as an unformed mass, in the seventh, he blew into him the breath of life, in the eighth, he put him into the Garden of Eden, in the ninth God gave him a commandment, in the tenth Adam violated his commandment, in the eleventh he was judged, in the twelfth God gave him a pardon.

The Holy One, blessed be he, said to him, 'Adam, lo, you serve as omen for your children. Just as you came to judgement before me and I gave you a pardon, so your children will come before me in judgement, and I shall give them a pardon.'

When?

'In the seventh month, on the first day of the month' (Leviticus 23:24).[15]

Here is an explicit statement that God's judgement at the New Year extends to all Creation. And all humanity, just like Israel, is not only to be judged but treated mercifully and pardoned.

How is the Israelite in particular comparable to Adam? To understand the answer to that question, we must try to see the story Scripture tells as the rabbinic sages read it, and assess the the plausibility of that reading. They read the story of Adam and Eve in Eden as a prologue to the story of Israel in the Land of Israel, that long narrative of how Israel took shape in the persons of Abraham and Sarah, created an extended family devoted to the service of God, and were promised a Land of their own, then got the Land but lost it. In the context of that protracted story, the rabbinic sages compare Israel's tenure in the Land of Israel with Adam's tenure in Eden, Israel's exile from the Land of Israel in 586 BCE when the Babylonians captured many Israelites as God's response to Israel's sin, as Adam's loss of Eden was God's response to Adam's sin. The question in their minds is, under what conditions does Adam lose Eden and Israel the Land, and the answer they seek, and set forth, is, how does Israel, returned to the Land that is its Eden, retain the Land, and, by implication, how is Israel to be restored to the Land it has lost, to have and to hold forever. Stated simply, the rabbinic sages want to know how Adam is restored to Eden, Israel to the Land.

Then, as we shall see, Adam and Israel (who can also be seen as individual Israelite and community Israel) work out corresponding stories, both living out the experience of possessing and losing paradise, but with a difference. The Judaic perspective on the comparable stories, Adam's and Israel's, comes to the surface in a simple statement. With Israel's entry into the Land, the story that defines Israel should have come to an end, but it did and does not. The rabbinic sages maintain that had Israel not sinned, the Torah would have contained only the Pentateuch and the book of Joshua:

'If the Israelites had not sinned, to them would have been given only the five books of the Torah and the Book of Joshua alone, which involves the division of the Land of Israel. How come? "For in much wisdom is much vexation" (Ecclesiastes 1:18).'[16]

Adam ought to have stayed in Eden. With the Torah in hand, Israel, the new Adam, ought to have remained in the Land, beyond the reach of time and change, exempt from the events of interesting times. Sin ruined everything, for Adam and Israel, bringing about the history recorded in Scripture. Israel's story therefore encompasses not only entry into the Land but loss of the Land and recovery of the Land.

By reason of disobedience Adam sinned and was justly punished by exile from Eden: that represented an act of mercy – he was not wiped out, as Eve had said he and she would be. Because of disobedience Israel sinned and was justly punished by exile from the Land of Israel, counterpart to Eden. Is Israel then just another Adam, rebellious and permanently punished on that account? There is a distinction: Israel stands at Sinai and accepts God's divinity and sovereignty in the Torah. And that has made all the difference. The Torah, carrying with it the possibility of repentance, changes Israel's condition.

Accordingly, Israel is like Adam, but Israel is also the Last Adam, the opposite of Adam. That theological conviction comes to expression in the telling of the parallel stories of Adam and Israel. We shall now systematically compare Adam and Israel, the first man and the last, and show how the story of Adam matches the story of Israel, but with a difference:

It is written, 'But they are like a man [Adam], they have transgressed the covenant' (Hosea 6:7).

'They are like a man', specifically, like the first man. [We shall now compare the story of the first man in Eden with the story of Israel in its land.]

Now the author identifies an action of God's with regard to Adam with a counterpart action involving Israel, in each case matching verse for verse, beginning with Eden and Adam:

[God speaks] 'In the case of the first man, I brought him into the Garden of Eden, I commanded him, he violated my commandment, I judged him to be sent away and driven out, but I mourned for him, saying, "How . . ." ' [which begins the book of Lamentations, hence stands for a lament].

'I brought him into the Garden of Eden,' as it is written, 'And the Lord God took the man and put him into the Garden of Eden' (Genesis 2:15).

'I commanded him,' as it is written, 'And the Lord God commanded . . .' (Genesis 2:16).

'And he violated my commandment,' as it is written, 'Did you eat from the tree concerning which I commanded you?' (Genesis 3:11).

'I judged him to be sent away,' as it is written, 'And the Lord God sent him from the Garden of Eden' (Genesis 3:23).

'And I judged him to be driven out.' 'And he drove out the man' (Genesis 3:24).

'But I mourned for him, saying, "How . . ." .' 'And he said to him, "Where are you?" ' (Genesis 3:9), and the word for 'where are you?' is written, 'How . . .'

'So too in the case of his descendants, I brought them into the Land of Israel, I commanded them, they violated my commandment, I judged them to be sent out and driven away but I mourned for them, saying, "How . . ." '.

'I brought them into the Land of Israel.' 'And I brought you into a plentiful land' (Jeremiah 2:7).

'I commanded them.' 'And you shall command the people of Israel' (Exodus 27:20); 'Command the people of Israel' (Leviticus 24:2).

'They violated my commandment.' 'All Israel has transgressed thy law' (Daniel 9:11).

'I judged them to be sent out.' 'Send them out of my sight and let them go!'
(Jeremiah 15:1).

'. . . and driven away.' 'I will drive them out of my house' (Hosea 9:15).

'But I mourned for them, saying, "How . . ."' 'How lonely sits the city that
was full of people!' (Lamentations 1:1)[17]

The references are to God's driving Israel out of his house, the Temple
of Jerusalem, and his mourning for Israel in the Book of Lamentations,
which Jeremiah wrote after the destruction of Jerusalem, including the
Temple, in 586 BCE. Here we end where we began, with Israel in exile
from the Land, like Adam in exile from Eden. But the Torah is clear that
there is a difference, which we shall address in its proper place: Israel can
repent.

Scripture, accordingly, tells the story of humanity divided into Israel
with the Torah, and the gentiles with their idols. In a purposeful act of
benevolence, the just God created the world in so orderly a way that the
principle of justice and equity governs throughout. Fair rules apply equally
to all individuals and govern all circumstances. God not only created man
but made himself known to man through the Torah. But man, possessed
of free will, enjoys the choice of accepting and obeying the Torah,
therefore living in the kingdom of heaven, or rejecting the Torah and
God in favour of idolatry and idols.

So much for the story that defines Israel. But there is a simple,
economical definition of who and what Israel is, which we have already
met earlier. That definition focuses upon the individual Israelite and
explicitly speaks of the condition of private individuals: 'All Israelites
have a share in the world to come', meaning, every individual Israelite
(with a paltry handful of exceptions, not all of them Israelite at all) will
be resurrected, stand and be judged, and then live for ever. We may
reverse the subject and predicate: all who have a share in the world to
come are Israelites. And all who do not cannot fall into the category,
'Israelites', as framed in that same sentence.

At the most profound level, therefore, to be 'an Israelite' means to be
one of those destined to rise from the dead and enjoy the world to come.
Specifically, Israel is defined as those who maintain that the resurrection
of the dead is a teaching of the Torah, and that the Torah comes from
heaven. So to be an Israelite is to rise from the dead to the world to

come. Gentiles, by contrast, are not going to be resurrected when the dead are raised, but those among them who are innocent will not be eternally damned. If at the end of time Israel is comprised of those who will rise from the dead, in the interim it finds its definition in those who live the holy life and so imitate God; those who are, so far as they can be, like God. For Israel to be holy means that Israel is to be separate, and if Israel sanctifies itself, it sanctifies God:

'And the Lord said to Moses, "Say to all the congregation of the people of Israel, You shall be holy, [for I the Lord your God am holy.]"' (Leviticus 19:1–4):

  'You shall be holy.'

  'You shall be separate.'

  'You shall be holy, for I the Lord your God am holy.'

  That is to say, 'If you sanctify yourselves, I shall credit it to you as though you had sanctified me, and if you do not sanctify yourselves, I shall hold that it is as if you have not sanctified me.'

  Or perhaps the sense is this: 'If you sanctify me, then lo, I shall be sanctified, and if not, I shall not be sanctified'?

  Scripture says, 'For I . . . am holy', meaning, 'I remain in my state of sanctification, whether or not you sanctify me.'[18]

This final, bold assertion completes Judaism's story of what and who Israel is and raises the question, What is the task of the Israelite and of all Israel? And once more, by now predictably, a chapter of the tale that Judaism tells contains the answer. And, in line with our encounter with other chapters in that simple story, an occasion in the sacred calendar precipitates the telling. This one is the seventh day of Creation, *shabbat*, the sabbath, a word that cannot be translated into any language, being unique to Judaism.

Restoring Eden: The Sabbath

How is Israel to regain the Land, which is its Eden? Israel on the sabbath restores the conditions that prevailed when God and Adam were last together, that perfect sabbath when God, having perfected Creation, blessed and sanctified the sabbath day in celebration of the perfection of

Creation, and then rested. (According to some of the rabbinic sages, Adam sinned on the sixth day and did not enter the bliss of the sabbath of Eden. In that framework, Israel's task is to attain what Adam denied humanity – the sabbath spent with God in Eden.) In so many words, we are told that Israel's perfect sanctification of a single sabbath day represents that repair and perfection of the world that marks the recovery of the Land that is Israel's Eden:

The Israelites said to Isaiah, 'O Isaiah, our rabbi, what will come for us out of this night?'

He said to them, 'Wait for me, until I can present the question [to God].'

Once he had asked the question, he came back to them.

They said to him, 'Watchman, what of the night? What did the Guardian of the Ages say?' [A play on 'of the night' and 'say']

He said to them, 'The watchman says: "Morning comes, and also the night. [If you will inquire, inquire; come back again]"' (Isaiah 21:12).

They said to him, 'Also the night?'

He said to them, 'It is not what you are thinking. But there will be morning for the righteous, and night for the wicked, morning for Israel, and night for idolaters.'

Now comes the main point in the exchange: when will this happen? It will happen when Israel wants. And what is standing in the way is Israel's arrogance, to be atoned for by Israel's remorseful repentance:

They said to him, 'When?'

He said to them, 'Whenever you want, he too wants [it to be], if you want it, he wants it.'

They said to him, 'What is standing in the way?'

He said to them, 'Repentance: "come back again"' (Isaiah 21:12).

This is stated in the clearest possible way: one day will do it.

Rabbi Aha in the name of Rabbi Tanhum ben Rabbi Hiyya, 'If Israel repents for one day, forthwith the son of David [the prophesied Messiah] will come.

'What is the scriptural basis? "O that today you would hearken to his voice!"' (Psalms 95:7).

Now comes the introduction of the sabbath as a test case:

Said Rabbi Levi, 'If Israel should keep a single sabbath in the proper way, forthwith the son of David will come.

'What is the scriptural basis for this view? "Moses said, 'Eat it today, for today is a sabbath to the Lord; [today you will not find it in the field]' " (Exodus 16:25).

'And it says, "[For thus said the Lord God, the Holy One of Israel,] 'In returning and rest you shall be saved; [in quietness and in trust shall be your strength.' And you would not]" (Isaiah 30:15). By means of returning and [sabbath] rest you will be redeemed.'[19]

The main point is the linkage of repentance to the coming restoration of Israel to the Land, the dead to life, by the Messiah. But the advent of the Messiah depends wholly upon Israel's will. If Israel will subordinate its will to God's, all else will follow. And the sabbath stands at the very centre of the Judaic master narrative.

No wonder then, that in the liturgy of home and synagogue, to the sabbath-observing Israelite the Sabbath is the chief sign of God's grace. The sanctification of the sabbath wine states, 'For thou hast chosen us and sanctified us above all nations, in love and favour has given us thy holy sabbath as an inheritance.' Likewise in the sabbath morning liturgy:

You did not give it [sabbath] to the nations of the earth, nor did you make it the heritage of idolaters, nor in its rest will unrighteous men find a place.

But to Israel your people you have given it in love, to the seed of Jacob whom you have chosen, to that people who sanctify the sabbath day. All of them find fulfilment and joy from your bounty.

For the seventh day did you choose and sanctify as the most pleasant of days and you called it a memorial to the works of Creation.

Here again we find a profusion of themes, this time centred upon the sabbath. The sabbath is a sign of the covenant. It is a gift of grace, which neither idolaters nor evil people may enjoy. And it is the most pleasant of days. Keeping the sabbath is living in God's kingdom: 'Those who keep the sabbath and call it a delight will rejoice in your kingdom.' Keeping the sabbath brings the Israelite into the kingdom of God. So states the additional sabbath prayer (keeping the sabbath now is a foretaste of the redemption): 'This day is for Israel light and rejoicing.' The rest of the sabbath is, as the afternoon prayer affirms, 'a rest granted in generous love, a true and faithful rest'.

Let us briefly turn aside to the actuality of living Judaism, realized on the sabbath day. How, ideally, do people keep the sabbath? All week long through the six days of activity and creation, the Israelite will look forward to the sabbath and this anticipation enhances the ordinary days. By late Friday afternoon those who keep the sabbath will usually have bathed, put on their sabbath garments, and set aside the affairs of the week. At home, the family will have cleaned, cooked, and arranged the finest table. It is common to invite guests for the sabbath meal. The sabbath comes at sunset and leaves when three stars have appeared on Saturday night. After a brief sabbath eve service the family comes together to enjoy its best meal of the week, a meal at which particular sabbath foods are served. In the morning comes the sabbath service, including a public reading from the Five Books of Moses (the original Torah), and prophetic writings, and an additional service in memory of the Temple sacrifices on sabbaths of old. Then home for lunch and very commonly a sabbath nap, the sweetest part of the day. As the day wanes, the synagogue calls for a late afternoon service, followed by Torah-study and a third meal. Then comes a ceremony, *havdalah* (separation), involving spices, wine and candlelight, between the holy time of the sabbath and the ordinary time of the rest of the week.

What has the sabbath to do with the restoration of Israel to the Land, humanity to Eden? The connection between the sabbath, on the one side, and Eden and its counterpart, the Land, is made explicit in Scripture's law. There, in Leviticus 25: 1–4, the Torah accords to not only the people, but also the Land of Israel a sabbath, observed every seven years, when all labour on the Land ceases, and the Land enjoys the repose that the sabbath brought to God in Creation and brings to Israel every seventh day:

The Lord said . . .

'When you come into the land which I give you, the land shall keep a sabbath to the Lord. Six years you shall sow your field . . . but in the seventh year there shall be a sabbath of solemn rest for the land, a sabbath to the Lord; you shall not sow your field . . .'

The Torah leaves no doubt that the sabbatical year finds its place in the context of how God undertook the creation of the world: first perfecting the world order, next sanctifying Creation, and then celebrating the sabbath in response to that sanctification. In his exposition of the laws of the sabbatical year, Alan J. Avery-Peck states:

In modeling their lives on the perfected character of the universe that once existed, Israelites make explicit their understanding that this order will exist again, that God's plan for the Israelite people still is in effect . . . Israelites themselves, through their actions, participate in the creation of that perfected world. They do this through their intentions and perceptions in defining proper observance of the sabbatical year.[20]

The sabbatical year recovers that perfect time of Eden when the world was at rest, all things in place. Before the rebellion, man did not have to labour on the land; he picked and ate his meals freely. And, in the nature of things, everything belonged to everybody; private ownership in response to individual labour did not exist, because man did not have to work anyhow. Reverting to that perfect time, the Torah maintains that the land will provide adequate food for everyone, including the flocks and herds, even if people do not work the land. But that is on condition that all claim of ownership lapses; the food is left in the fields, to be picked by anyone who wishes, but it may not be hoarded by the landowner in particular; what has been hoarded has now to be removed from the household and moved to public domain, where anyone may come and take it. Avery-Peck states this matter as follows:

Scripture thus understands the sabbatical year to represent a return to a perfected order of reality, in which all share equally in the bounty of a holy land that yields its food without human labor. The sabbatical year provides a model through which, once every seven years, Israelites living in the here-and-now may enjoy the perfected order in which God always intended the world to exist and toward which, in the Israelite world-view, history indeed is moving . . . The release of debts accomplishes for Israelites' economic relationships just what the agricultural sabbatical accomplishes for the relationship between the people and the land. Eradicating debt allows the Israelite economy to return to the state of equilibrium that existed at the time of Creation, when all shared equally in the bounty of the land.[21]

Scripture expresses that same concept when it arranges for the return, at the jubilee year, of inherited property to the original family ownership:

You shall count seven weeks of years, seven times seven years, so that the time of the seven weeks of years shall be to you forty-nine years . . . And you shall hallow the fiftieth year, and proclaim liberty throughout the land to all its inhabitants; it shall be a jubilee for you, when each of you shall return to his property and each of you shall return to his family.[22]

The jubilee year follows a sabbatical year, meaning that for two successive years the land is not to be worked. The halakhah we shall examine in due course will establish that when land is sold, it is for the span of time remaining to the next jubilee year. That then marks the reordering of land-holding to its original pattern, when Israel inherited the land to begin with and commenced to enjoy its produce. In the State of Israel today, the laws continue to be taken into account in a variety of ways; they are not ignored by any means.

We now see how, through the law of the Torah, Judaism embodies in rules for the Israelite social order that same narrative of Creation perfected on the sabbath that the rabbinic sages find in Scripture and express in the liturgy. But, just as Passover comes to its full realization around the domestic table, so the Israelite household embodies the perfection of Creation on the sabbath. Judaism tells its story through the family first of all. The Israelite household at rest recapitulates the celebration of God at the moment of the conclusion and perfection of Creation. Then the Israelite household, like Creation at sunset marking the end of the sixth day of Creation, is sanctified: meaning, separated from the profane world and distinguished as God's domain. With all things in place and in order, at the sunset that marks the advent of the seventh day, the rest that marks the perfection of Creation descends. The sanctification takes place through that very act of perfect repose that recapitulates the one celebrated at the climax of Creation. Like God at the celebration of Creation, man now achieves perfect, appropriate rest. That takes place when time, circumstance, and space too, come together. The advent of the Sabbath marks the time; the conduct of home and family life, the circumstance; and the household, the space.

As the advent of the sabbath, holy time, originally required preparation in the Temple, so there is a set of rules for sanctifying the household. The Torah has set the stage. The sabbath marks the celebration of Creation's perfection (Genesis 2:1−3). Food for the day is to be prepared in advance (Exodus 16:22–6, 29–30). Fire is not to be kindled on that day, thus no cooking (Exodus 35:3). Hard work is not to be done on that day by the householder and his dependents, including his slaves and material possessions (Exodus 20:8–11, Exodus 23:12, 31:12–17, 34:21). The where matters as much as the when and the how: people are supposed to stay in their place: 'Let each person remain in place, let no one leave his place on the seventh day' (Exodus 16:29–30), 'place' meaning here the private domain of the household. Here then we encounter that individual Israelite, in the context of the household, whom we distinguished to begin with from the entirety of the community of Israel.

The theology of the sabbath put forth in the law of Judaism derives from a systematization of definitions implicit in the story of Eden that envelopes the sabbath. The rabbinic sages devote their interpretation of the law concerning the sabbath above all to two matters: the systematic definition of private domain, where ordinary activity is permitted, and the rather particular definition of what constitutes a prohibited act of labour. Their consideration of these two points precipitate deep thought and animate the handful of principles brought to concrete realization in the two bodies of law they engender.

Taking the second point first, the commandment not to labour on the sabbath (Exodus 20: 8–11) refers in a generic sense to all manner of work; but in the law of Judaism, 'labour' has very particular meanings and is defined in a quite specific, and somewhat odd, manner. We can make sense of the law only by looking at the story of Creation. The sabbath precipitates the imitation of God on a very particular occasion and for a very distinctive purpose. The meeting of time and space on the seventh day of Creation, God having formed space and marked time, finds its counterpart in the ordering of Israelite space at the advent of the birthday of time, space being ordered through the action and inaction of the Israelites themselves.

On the sabbath, the distinction between public and private domain is set aside. Rather, on that day, the commingling of ownership of private property into a shared domain for the purpose of sabbath observance and the commingling of meals to signify shared ownership, accomplishes for Israel's sabbath what the sabbatical year achieves for the Land's. On the sabbath inaugurated by the sabbatical year the Land, so far as it is otherwise private property, no longer is possessed exclusively by the householder.

So too, the produce of the Land consequently belongs to everybody. Commingling domains and sharing private property in observance of the sabbath realize for the ordinary sabbath of Israel the very same principles that are embodied in the law of Judaism for the seventh year.

So on the sabbath established arrangements as to ownership and possession are set aside, and a different conception of private property takes over. What on ordinary days is deemed to belong to the householder and to be subject to his exclusive will on the sabbath falls into a more complex web of possession. The householder continues to use his property but not as a proprietor does. He gives up exclusive access thereto, and gains in exchange rights of access to other people's property. Private property is commingled; everybody shares in everybody's. The result is, private property takes on a new meaning, different from the secular one. In contemporary Judaism, an *eruv* or symbolic fence joining private properties over a considerable area allows people to carry things outside their own homes. Such fictive boundaries are common in areas where Orthodox Jews live.

So far as work is concerned, on the sabbath it is prohibited deliberately to carry out in a normal way a completed act of constructive labour, one that produces enduring results, and carries out one's entire intention. But there is no prohibition on performing an act of labour in an other-than-normal way. In theory, a man may go out into the fields and plough, if he does so in some odd manner. He may build an entire house, so long as it collapses promptly.

The issue of activity on the sabbath therefore is removed from the obvious context of work, conventionally defined. A person is not forbidden to carry out an act of destruction, or an act of labour that produces no lasting consequences. He may start an act of labour if he does not complete it. He may accomplish an act of labour in some extraordinary manner. None of these acts of labour are forbidden, even though, done properly and with consequence, they represent massive violations of the halakhah. Nor is part of an act of labour that is not brought to conclusion prohibited. Nor is it forbidden to perform part of an act of labour in partnership with another person who carries out the other requisite part. Nor does one incur culpability for performing an act of labour in several distinct parts, for example, over a protracted, differentiated period of time. One may tie a knot, but not one that stands. One may carry a package, but not in the usual manner. And one may do pretty much anything without penalty, *if* one did not intend matters as they actually happened.

Clearly, this particular definition of the act of labour that is prohibited on the sabbath has taken over and recast the commonsense meaning of the commandment not to labour on the sabbath. The metaphor of God in Eden gave the rabbinic sages the governing principles that define forbidden labour. What God did in the six days of Creation provides the model: the work of Creation involved a single actor, accomplishing his goals in a single completed action.

Let us review the main principles item by item. They involve the three preconditions. The act must fully carry out the intention of the actor, as Creation carried out God's intention. The act of labour must be carried out by a single actor, as God acted alone in creating the world. An act of labour is the like of one that is required in the building and maintenance of God's residence in this world, the tabernacle[23] – such as transporting objects from one place to another or building a structure. The act of labour prohibited on the Sabbath involves two further considerations. The act must be done in the ordinary way, just as Scripture's account leaves no doubt that God accomplished Creation in the manner in which he accomplished all his goals from Creation onward, by a simple act of speech. And, weightier still, the forbidden act is one that produces enduring consequences. God did not create only to destroy, he created the enduring world. The act was important, involving what was not negligible but what man and God alike deemed to make a difference.

If this is what is forbidden, what then takes place inside the walls of the Israelite household when time takes over space and revises the conduct of ordinary affairs? Israel goes home to Eden. Israel imitates God by keeping the sabbath. To restore its Eden, Israel must sustain its life, nourish itself, where it belongs. That is the story Judaism tells about the Israelite through the tale of the sabbath day. Now that we know what Israel is and who Israel is, we ask the final question: how do they relate?

Israel and the Israelite

Which comes first, the individual Israelite or the corporate community of Israel? According to the story that Judaism tells about Adam and Eve and the creation of the world, first comes the individual, the Israelite, then comes the corporate moral entity, Israel, a whole that exceeds the sum of its parts.

In the beginning, representing undifferentiated humanity, are Adam and Eve, bearing individual responsibility. Each forms in his or her person a moral entity, a responsible actor, subject to divine judgement. There was no Israel then. Only with the advent of Abraham, twenty generations later, would the moral entity, Israel, emerge, and in the divine calculus, there was never any other such corporate community that registered. Only Israel is called into being at Sinai and made responsible for its collective character as 'a kingdom of priests and a holy people'. The language of Sinai, 'We shall do and we shall obey', speaks of the entire community, not only of individuals. There is no counterpart moment in which any other nation or people accepts collective responsibility for the actions of individuals. None other is like Israel, responsible as whole and indivisible, not merely as the sum of the individual parts.

Stated in more abstract terms, Judaism holds that the entirety of humanity by nature, from creation on, is comprised of individuals, each unique in some aspect from all others. That is the point of the statement, 'On my account the world was created.' But, we now realize, humanity is divided into two parts: the part made up of mere, differentiated individuals, on the one side, and the part that out of individuals constitutes a corporate moral entity, on the other. The individuals who cohere in Israel form a whole that transcends the sum of the parts. While individuals, all children of Noah, are responsible for what they do, corporate Israel, alone among all collectivities of humanity, constitutes a moral entity as well. Then, it follows, by way of definition, gentiles are individuals that add up to no more than themselves, while Israelites are individuals that surrender personal autonomy to form themselves into Israel. Being Israel imposes upon individuals rights and responsibilities vastly in excess of the basic obligations incumbent upon all individuals, the children of Noah. To them, several duties pertain: to establish courts of justice, refrain from murder and adultery, treat animals humanely. To Israel hundreds of imperatives (613 it is alleged) pertain: 'You only have I known of all the families of the earth; therefore I will punish you for all your iniquities' says God (Amos 3:2).

Israel is subject to divine imperatives in such a way that belonging to that society has consequences that make each individual responsible for all others and vice versa. Then, in a profound sense, according to that teaching, humanity at large is unsocialized. That is to say, gentiles are deemed not formed by either nature or nurture (genealogy or conversion) into larger entities (families, societies, peoples, nations and the like). Groups of gentiles constitute individuals on their own, nothing more. The collectivities, however classified, that they manifestly do form represent a mere happenstance, having no standing in the divine scheme of things. The miracle of society requires God's intervention. Israel comes about by reason of God's activity: his call to Abraham, his self-manifestation in the liberation of Israel from Egypt, his revelation at Sinai. Israel as a whole, not only severally but jointly, for that reason is judged by God by the criterion of the Torah, which captures in narrative terms precisely how individuals form the corporate community through divine activity: engagement, intervention, revelation.

The festivals, the Days of Awe, the sabbaths, each tells its part of the story of God in search of humanity, his discovery of Abraham and Sarah, and election of Israel, the body of their heirs in the flesh and after the spirit, both. The story unfolds by the rhythm of the year, as the heavenly bodies, the sun and the moon, mark time into its consequential components. The seasons and the months, recapitulating in the heavens the liberation from Egypt, the self-manifestation of God at Sinai, the wandering in the wilderness; the creation, Eden, loss, and restoration tell a simple story, subject to infinite articulation but little variation.

3
The Historical View
of the Formation of Judaism

From Story to History

The participant in a religious tradition tells its master story, seeing the whole, from the interior, as a complete and coherent narrative and taking it all personally. The observer of that same system, standing outside, studies the history of the story, seeing the parts in exterior context. The story synthesizes, history analyses. The story sees matters in the eye of eternity, history in the setting of time. In this chapter we shift our perspective from that of the participant in the tradition to that of the observer of the tradition. Going over the same ground, the journey takes its own route, guided by a different reading of the maps held in common.

Accordingly, it is in narrative form that the Judaic world-view sets forth the transcendent rules of engagement with God. Judaism's theology moves from the account of what happened to generalize and so define what *is*. That is because the theology of Judaism sets forth the rules revealed in the narrative that govern the actions of the One Who Acts and what he wants of us. The Judaic way of life recapitulates moments of the same enduring pattern, now realized in law, specifying acts of omission or of commission. Food, clothing, shelter, vocation, work and rest, above all, patterns of human relationship and interaction, all are shaped within a single pattern, which re-enacts in gesture and symbol the implicit message of that master narrative.

The Torah's story is told in the past tense, but the story is acutely contemporary at all points in time. For most of the events and transactions of the narrative are not such as to yield material evidence for archaeological verification. History records the results of our investigation of the past, tentative and subject to revision always. Story is narrative that the past is transmitting to us. Most of the important statements that the Torah makes about God and his transactions with humanity cannot be proved or disproved by objects buried in the ground. But, more to the point, Judaism's story concerns history in not only the past tense, but the perpetual present tense.

This does not mean that Judaism rejects history.[1] On the contrary, the rabbinic sages through all time understood that the Jewish people literally were slaves in Egypt, literally were freed by God, literally stood at Mount Sinai, and in the wilderness literally received the text of the Pentateuch with its accompanying oral tradition. Any understanding of Judaism that denies these historical claims takes its leave of the Judaism of Moses our Rabbi. That also is not to say this historical understanding is literalist. The meaning of Scripture as set forth by the oral tradition takes its leave of the meaning gained from a naïve, literal reading (as in the case of Genesis 1, the story of creation). Scripture requires decoding, which is what the rabbinic sages accomplish. But, unlike archaeology, with its narrow scope of material culture, Judaism is not engaged only or primarily by history. Findings of fact about the past occupy only a modest place among the priorities of the sages. Above all else, the Judaic tradition prizes eternal truths, which transcend history.

The Pentateuch in Historical Context

The greater part of the faithful to this day (and all the faithful of Judaism until the nineteenth century) perceive the Torah as a single text, revealed by God to Moses at Mount Sinai. The entire narrative is taken literally and at face value, though it sustains profound and dense layers of interpretation. There is no gap between story and history. But that is not the view of most historians of ancient Israel, though their accounts of matters are hardly uniform. The following description, analysis and interpretation of Judaism represents the broad academic consensus.

Speaking of Creation, the beginnings of Israel, Egyptian bondage, wandering in the wilderness, the laws of the Torah of Sinai, and the approach to the Promised Land, the Pentateuch refers to events of a long-ago past. Much, though not all, scholarship concurs, that the Pentateuch took shape in the aftermath of the destruction of the Temple of Jerusalem in 586 BCE (about 700 years after the revelation at Sinai), when the community of Israel was exiled to Babylonia, returning to the Land of Israel after 539, and was completed c. 450 BCE. In the Pentateuch therefore we deal with a composite of materials, some from before 586 BCE, some from afterwards, each with its own viewpoint and traits of mind.

So only in the aftermath of the destruction of that first Temple and the later restoration of the exiles to the Land was Judaism's story first told whole and complete. In the light of Israel's ultimate destiny, which the authorship of the Pentateuch took to be the loss and restoration of the Land, the origins of the people in its Land took on cogent meaning: Israel began with its acquisition of the Land, through Abraham, and attained its identity as God's people through the promise of the Land, in the covenant of Sinai, and the entry into the Land, under Joshua. The issue became, what are the conditions of Israel's tenure of the Land of Israel? Israel's history, from its entry into the Promised Land (told in the Book of Joshua) to the fall of Jerusalem in 586 BCE (2 Kings), as interpreted by the prophets, then formed the story of how, because of its conduct in the Land, Israel lost its Land, first in the north, then in the south, despite the prophets' persistent warnings. From the exile in Babylonia, the authorship of the Torah recast Israel's history into the story of the conditional existence of the people. Everything depended on carrying out a covenant that was articulated, for example, in Leviticus 26 and Deuteronomy 32–4: do this, get that; do not do this, do not get that. Nothing formed a given, beyond all conditions. The task of that authorship demanded the interpretation of the condition of the present, and their message in response to the uncertainty of Israel's life beyond exile and restoration underlined the uncertainty of that life.

To the priests of Jerusalem, the Temple built by Solomon in c. 900 BCE, destroyed by the Babylonians in 586 BCE, rebuilt under Persian auspices between 530 and 450 BCE, and destroyed by the Romans in 70 CE, formed the place where God took up residence within humanity. Mount Zion, on which the Temple was built, was held to be the highest of all mountains. The Pentateuch devotes much of its law to the building of the tabernacle in the wilderness, model for the Temple later on, and the conduct of the sacrifices offered there. These served various purposes, some votive, some obligatory. The principal sacrifice, the daily whole offering, made at dawn and dusk, atoned for the sins of all Israel as a corporate community. When the Temple was destroyed by the Romans, the importance of the Temple to that time was captured in this story, involving Yohanan ben Zakkai, leader of the rabbinical group before and after 70, and his disciple, Joshua ben Hananiah:

One time [after the destruction of the Temple] Rabban Yohanan ben Zakkai was going forth from Jerusalem, with Rabbi Joshua following after him. He saw the house of the sanctuary lying in ruins.

Rabbi Joshua said, 'I grieve for this place which lies in ruins, the place in which the sins of Israel used to come to atonement.'

He [Rabban Yohanan] said to him, 'My son, do not be distressed. We have another mode of atonement, which is like [atonement through sacrifice], and what is that? It is deeds of loving kindness.

'For so it is said, "For I desire mercy and not sacrifice, [and the knowledge of God rather than burnt offerings]" ' (Hosea 6:6).[2]

The Temple altar defined the meeting point between God and Israel, and its blood-rite of atonement secured atonement for Israel's sins, both collective and individual. No wonder, then, that every turning point in the calendar called for offerings to commemorate and celebrate the events of nature, just as the obligatory daily offerings celebrated events in Israel's life with God. It was with the catastrophe of the loss of the Temple and its means of atonement that the priests, drawing on ancient traditions, recast the entire history of Israel as the story of Israel's covenant with God realized in the Temple rites, a covenant violated by the sins of the generations past, re-established by God in his mercy in response to Israel's repentance for those sins, and embodied in the restored Temple. Then Adam's loss of Eden afforded perspective on Israel's loss of the Land, and the rest followed. So the question asked in 586 BCE — has God forsaken us? — found its answer in the restoration from 530 to 450 — God forgives us when we atone and repent for sin and do what the covenant set forth by the Torah requires.

The Pentateuch as fully formulated comes from that small number of Israelite families, many of them Temple priests, who remembered the exile, survived in Babylonia, and then, fifty or 150 years later, returned to the Land of Israel. They knew things that Israel before 586 could never have imagined: the experiences of exile and return. To the priests who rebuilt the Temple and gave the Pentateuch its final form, what mattered in 586 was the destruction of the Temple, and what made a difference three generations later was the restoration of the Land of Israel and the rebuilding of the Temple. To them religion was the key, the Temple the nexus between heaven and earth. The Pentateuch set forth their conception of a shared consciousness, a collective story of a people subject to condition and stipulation, forever threatened with desolation, always requiring renewal. The original Torah, or Pentateuch, declaimed in the synagogue from week to week, taught that one lesson of the human condition of Israel. To Israel the Torah imparted the picture of society subject to judgement, and the story of exile and return and the conditional possession of the Land embodied that picture. And it was the priests' judgement in particular that prevailed. All Judaisms to come would in some way or other find in the priests' paradigm the model to which either to conform or object. The priests' Torah, the Pentateuch in its final statement, constituted the first and enduring Judaism, with its paradigm of exile and return for all to follow.

The Three Focal Points of the Second Temple Judaism, 450 BCE to 70 CE

Once the Pentateuch took shape, along with other components of the ancient Israelite heritage of history, prophecy and poetry, the work of interpretation got under way. That produced a variety of Judaic religious systems of social order (or Judaisms), each with its way of life, world-view and definition of 'Israel'; each responding with a self-evidently valid answer to an urgent question. Among them we may discern three ideal types.

The Judaisms that emerged from Scripture centred upon three points of emphasis: first, the one that stressed doctrine, law and way of life, which emerged from the priestly viewpoint, with its interest in sanctification; second, the one that took a special interest in the wise conduct of everyday affairs, which emerged from the wisdom-writings, with their emphasis on the here-and-now of ordinary life; and third, the one that emphasized the meaning and purpose of history, which emerged from the prophetic viewpoint, with its focus on salvation. The principal strands of ancient Israelite life come to realization in the three distinct types of holy men we identify as priests, scribes, and messiahs, and their definitive spheres of activity – Temple, yeshivot (Talmudic academies) and government offices, and (ordinarily, since 'messiah' originally meant 'anointed leader in battle') battlefield. Ancient Israel's heritage yielded the religious system with its priests, the Torah with its scribes and teachers, and the prophetic and apocalyptic hope for meaning in history and a vision of the end of the world embodied in messiahs.

Viewed as ideal types, the Judaic systems in Second Temple Times yielded two ways of life. The priest described society as organized through lines of structure emanating from the Temple. His caste stood at the top of a social scale in which all things were properly organized, each with its correct name and proper place. The inherent sanctity of Israel, the people, came down through genealogy to its richest embodiment in him, the priest. Food set aside for his rations at God's command possessed that same sanctity; so too did the table at which he ate his food. To the priest the sacred society of Israel produced history as an account of what happened in, and (alas) on occasion to, the Temple. To the scribe or sage, the life of society demanded wise regulation. Relationships among people required guidance by the laws embodied in the Torah, which were best interpreted by the sage. Accordingly, the task of Israel was to construct a way of life in accordance with the revealed rules of the Torah. The sage, master of the rules, stood at the head of this society. As for prophecy's insistence that the fate of the nation depended upon the faith and moral condition of society, history testified to the external context and inner condition of Israel, viewed as a whole. Both sage and priest saw Israel from the aspect of eternity. But the nation lived out its life in the history of this world, among other peoples coveting the very same Land, within the politics of empires. The Messiah's kingship would resolve the issues of Israel's subordinated relationship to other nations and empires, establishing once and for all time the correct context for priest and sage alike.

Among a number of Judaic groups that distinguished themselves between 450 BCE and 70 CE, I shall focus on two: first, the Judaic system (by some deemed similar to that of the Essenes) described in the documents found at Qumran (the Dead Sea Scrolls), and second, the Pharisees, because there is sufficient evidence to describe these sects in their broader social context, not merely as statements of belief. Each in its way realized in sharp and extreme form the ideals of the normative system of the priests' Torah of Moses. Both groups lay stress on religious cleanness and uncleanness, and the preservation of food and of meals in conditions required, in the priestly code laid down in the Books of Leviticus and Numbers, only for the Temple and its priests when eating their share of the Temple sacrifices. By such imitation, both groups entered into that state of holiness achieved by the priests in the Temple.

The Judaic System Portrayed by the Library at Qumran

The Judaic religious system portrayed by the library found at the Dead Sea site called Qumran flourished in the last two centuries BCE up to 68 CE. The main component of the world-view of the library's Judaism was the conviction that the community formed the final remnant of Israel, and that God would shortly annihilate the wicked. These converts to the true faith would be saved, because their founder, the 'teacher of righteousness', established a new contract or covenant between the community and God. So this 'Israel' would endure. The task of the community was to remain faithful to the contract or covenant, endure their exile in the wilderness, and prepare for the restoration of the Temple in its correct form. So this community recapitulated the history of Israel, seeing itself as the surviving remnant of some disaster that had destroyed the faith, preparing for that restoration that they anticipated would soon come, just as it had before.

In all, therefore, we find in the Qumran system a replication of the Judaic system of the priesthood, with one important qualification. While the Judaic system represented by the Pentateuch laid great stress on the holy way of life, the Qumran system as represented by its library added a powerful element of eschatological expectation and so combined the holy way of life with a doctrine of salvation at the end of time. The principal components of the scriptural composite – Torah laws, prophetic historical interpretation, sagacious rules on the conduct of everyday life

– found counterparts in the library of the Qumran community. The Qumran Judaism reworked these various strands into a distinctive and characteristic statement of its own.

The Qumran library sets forth the Judaic system of a holy community in the here and now, awaiting an eschatological climax. The elements of the original paradigm are three: first, the notion of a saving remnant, a chosen few, which surely originated in the pattern of Israel that endured beyond 586; second, the conception of a community with a beginning, middle and end, rather than a community that exists more or less permanently; third, the notion that that Israel is holy in the way in which the Temple is holy. All commentators on the library of Qumran have found striking the community's sense of itself as different, separate from the rest of Israel, the clean few among the unclean many, the saved few, the children of light. The fundamental notion that the small group constituted in microcosm the Israel that mattered rests on the premise that the 'Israel' out there, the nation as a whole, lives only on condition that various demands made by God are met.

The Qumran community saw the Temple and its priestly leadership as having become corrupt and false. The 'Israel' out there had failed; it is now (in the mind of the Israel at hand) the children of darkness. Such a distinction between an old Israel and a new Israel requires the conviction that the life of Israel is not a given, a fact of ordinary reality, but a status to be achieved, a standing to be attained through appropriate regeneration and sanctification. And that basic notion in detail expresses the general pattern of the Pentateuchal structure: Israel is called, formed as something out of nothing, a very particular entity, subject to very special conditions: the children of light, as opposed to the rest, the children of darkness. So the conviction of the Qumran community is nothing more than a restatement, in fresh terms, of the conclusions of the experience of death and resurrection that, as an entity, the nation of Israel (in its priests' vision of the nation) had endured. The prerequisite for an acutely self-conscious understanding of one's community as the children of light, of the rest as the children of darkness is the original and paradigmatic experience of national death and resurrection.

The Pharisees before 70 CE

Rabbinic Judaism, the standard form of the religion from antiquity to our own day – represented by Scripture as mediated by the Mishnah, Talmuds and midrash – drew upon the heritage of two distinct groups in Second Temple times: Pharisees, a religious community, and scribes, a profession. The message of the one joined with the method of the other formed the Judaic religious system represented by the rabbinic writings of the period after the destruction of Jerusalem in 70 CE, the concentric stories, theology and law of which are explored in this book.

The Pharisees laid stress on the keeping of the laws concerning the correct preparation of food, including the proper separation, for the support of the priesthood and other scheduled castes, of a portion of the crops. Scripture had specified a variety of rules on the matter, in general holding that God owned a share of the crops, and God's share was to go to the holy castes (the priests and the tribe of the Levites, who were restricted to religious duties and held no land). When the Pharisees made sure that everything that was supposed to be tithed to the holy castes was, they therefore obeyed those rules concerning the preparation of food that linked meals to the altar and its service. The Book of Leviticus had furthermore laid down rules governing uncleanness: its sources and effects. Such sources, specified in Leviticus 11–15, are the discharge of bodily fluids and certain deceased creatures, for example. The result of contact with such sources of uncleanness was not hygienic but, mainly, religious: one affected by uncleanness could not enter the Temple (Leviticus 12, 13–14). Another result of uncleanness deriving from certain sources was to prohibit sexual relations (Leviticus 15), but one made unclean in that way also could not go to the Temple. For the authors of the Priestly Code, the concern for the cleanness or uncleanness of utensils and people, therefore, derived from the protection of religion and the Temple from those dangers seen to lurk in the sources of uncleanness, which were death or things comparable to death (menstrual blood, for example).

But the rules affecting uncleanness laid out in the Mishnah, many of them going back to the earliest stratum of the mishnaic system, before 70 CE (hence, many assume, to Pharisaic origins), deal with domestic matters. The fundamental assumption throughout is that one eats in a state of ritual cleanness not only food deriving from the altar, but meals eaten at home. The further and more important assumption is that ordinary people, not only priests, keep those rules. Put together, the two premises point to a group that is made up of lay people pretending to be priests, much on the order of the Qumran Judaism, and treating their homes as temples, their tables as altars.

The Pharisaic stress on the sanctification of the home as if it were the Temple points to a more extreme position within the priestly paradigm of the Pentateuch than that of the priests themselves. What the priests wanted for the Temple, the Pharisees wanted for the community at large. Admittedly, we know little of the positions taken in the first century by the Pharisaic system on other matters, besides those represented by the Christian Gospels and the later rabbis of the Mishnah. No one can imagine that the group took positions only on these subjects, which deal with partial aspects of a complete system. The Qumran Judaism presented a substantial account of the meaning and end of history, a doctrine of salvation; they spelled out in so many words their doctrine of Israel, or themselves as the final remnant of Israel. In these and other ways they point to areas of the Pharisaic system – their world-view, perhaps also aspects of their way of life – of which we presently know nothing. But what we do know allows us to characterize the Pharisaic system as at least a Judaism of sanctification.

No wonder Pharisees, by all accounts, affirmed the eternity of the soul (as the first-century Jewish historian Josephus says) and the resurrection of the dead (as Luke's picture of the Pharisee Paul in Acts maintains). For the way of sanctification led past the uncleanness of the grave to the renewed purity of the living person, purification out of the most unclean of all sources of uncleanness, the realm of death itself. The pattern of sanctification of the everyday brought immediacy to the cosmic pattern of death and resurrection. For the nation earlier and always, and for the individual even now, in the priests' system of the Torah of Moses, as much as in the Pharisees' system, that enduring paradigm of life flowed from the altar, nexus of heaven and earth.

The First Phase of Rabbinic Judaism,
70–200 CE: The Judaism of the Mishnah

Emerging after the second destruction of the Temple in 70 CE (this time by the Romans), but calling upon resources from Scripture onward, rabbinic Judaism responded to this second destruction of the Temple by maintaining that the holiness of the life of Israel the people, a holiness that had formerly centred on the Temple, still endured. Israel's sanctification thus transcended the physical destruction of the building and the cessation of sacrifices. Israel the people was holy, was the medium and the instrument of God's sanctification. The religious system developed by the rabbinic sages then instructed Israel to act as if there was a new Temple formed of Israel, the Jewish people. Joined to the Pharisaic mode of looking at life, now centred in the doctrine of the holiness of Israel the people, was the substance of the scribal ideal, the stress on learning the Torah and carrying out its teachings. The emerging system would claim, like the scribes of old, that it was possible to serve God not only through sacrifice, but also through study of the Torah. So the question is the question of the priests and Pharisees: how to serve God? But the answer is the answer of the scribes: through Torah-learning.

The method, the way of life, of that system of Judaism as it would reach its final definition was the Pharisaic method, with its stress on the everyday sanctification of all Israel. The world-view, the substance of that Judaism, was the scribal message, with its stress on the Torah. Pharisaism laid stress upon universal keeping of the law, obligating every Jew to do what only the elite, the priests, were normally expected to accomplish. The professional ideal of the scribes stressed the study of Torah and the centrality of the learned person in the religious system. But there was something more: it was the doctrine of Israel that made all the difference. If the world-view came from the scribes and the way of life from the Pharisees, the doctrine of who is Israel, and the social reality beyond that doctrine, was fresh and unpredictable. It was surviving Israel, the Jewish people beyond the pause marked by the second destruction of the Temple. The crisis of the destruction centred attention on what had endured, persisting beyond the end: the people; the community of Israel itself. The conviction that Israel was special, and that what happened to Israel signified God's will was already established. Israel, because of its (in its mind) amazing experience of loss and restoration, death and resurrection, had attained remarkable self-consciousness. In the life of a nation that had already ceased to be a nation on its own Land (when the first Temple was destroyed and the Israelites taken into exile in Babylonia in 586 BCE) and then had regained that condition, the present calamity represented once more the paradigm of death and resurrection. Consequently, the truly fresh and definitive component of the new system after 70 CE, the collection of oral laws compiled c. 200 and known as the Mishnah, in fact restated in contemporary terms the fixed and established doctrine with which the first Judaism, the Judaism of the Torah of Moses after 450 BCE, had commenced.

The stress of the initial statement of rabbinic Judaism lies on sanctification, understood as the correct arrangement of all things, each in its proper category, each called by its rightful name, just as at the Creation: everything having been given its proper name, God called the natural world very good and sanctified it. The Mishnah makes a statement of philosophy concerning the order of the natural world in its correspondence with the supernatural world. The system of philosophy expressed through the concrete and detailed law presented by the Mishnah, consists of a coherent logic, a cogent world-view and a comprehensive way of life. It is a world-view which speaks of transcendent things, a way of life in response to the supernatural meaning of what is done, a heightened and deepened perception of the sanctification of Israel in deed and in deliberation. Sanctification thus means two things: first, distinguishing Israel in all its dimensions from the world in all its ways; second, establishing the stability, order, regularity, predictability and reliability of Israel in the world of nature and supernature in particular at moments and in contexts of danger. Danger means instability, disorder, irregularity, uncertainty and betrayal. Each topic of the system as a whole explores a critical and indispensable moment or context of social being. Through what is said in regard to each of the Mishnah's principal topics, what the halakhic system as a whole wishes to declare is fully expressed. Yet if the parts severally and jointly give the message of the whole, the whole cannot exist without all of the parts, so well joined and carefully crafted are they all.

The world addressed by the Mishnah is hardly congruent with the world-view presented within the Mishnah. In the aftermath of the second war against Rome in 132–5, the Temple was declared permanently prohibited to Jews, and Jerusalem was closed off to them as well. So there were no sacrificial offerings, no Temple, no holy city to which, at this time, the description of the Mishnaic laws applied. We observe at the very outset, therefore, that a sizable proportion of the Mishnah deals with matters to which the sages had no material access or practical knowledge at the time of their work. The Mishnah contains a division (the fifth) on the conduct of religious rites, as well as one (the sixth) on the conduct of matters so as to preserve the ritual purity of the sacrificial system along the lines laid out in the Book of Leviticus. In fact, a fair part of the second division, on appointed times, deals with the conduct of religious rites on special days, for example, the sacrifices offered on the Day of Atonement, Passover, and the like. Indeed, what the Mishnah wants to know about appointed seasons concerns the religious rites of the Temple (the place where sacrifices were made to God) far more than it does the synagogues (places of group prayer and scriptural study). The fourth division, on civil law, presents an elaborate account of a political structure and system of Israelite self-government. This system speaks of king, priest, Temple, and court. But it was not the Jews, through their kings, priests and judges, but the Romans who conducted the government of Israel in the Land of Israel in the time in which the second-century authorities did their work. So it would appear that well over half of the Mishnah speaks of religious rites for the Temple, government, and Temple priesthood. The Mishnah takes up a profoundly priestly and Levitical conception of sanctification. When we consider that, in the very time in which it was written, the Temple lay in ruins, the city of Jerusalem was prohibited to all Israelites, and the Jewish government and administration which had centred on the Temple and based its authority on the holy life lived there were in ruins, the fantastic character of the Mishnah's address to its own catastrophic day becomes clear. Much of the Mishnah speaks of matters not in being in the time in which the Mishnah was created, because the Mishnah wishes to make its statement on what really matters.

In the age after the catastrophe, the challenge is to reorder a world off-course and adrift, to gain reorientation now the sun has come out after the night and the fog. The Mishnah is a document of imagination and fantasy, describing how things 'are' out of the shards and remnants of reality, but, in larger measure, building social being out of beams of hope. The Mishnah tells us something about how things were, but everything about how a small group of rabbinic sages wanted things to be. The document is orderly, repetitious and careful in both language and message. It is small-minded, petty, obvious, dull, routine: everything its age was not. The Mishnah stands in contrast to the world to which it speaks. Its message is one of small achievements and modest hope. It means to defy a world of large disorders and immodest demands. The heirs of heroes build an unheroic community in the new and ordinary age. The Mishnah's message is that what a person wants matters in important ways. It states that message to an Israelite world which can shape affairs in no important ways and speaks to people who by no means desire the way things now are. The Mishnah therefore lays down a practical judgement upon, and in favour of, the imagination and will to reshape reality, regain a system, and re-establish that order upon which trustworthy existence is to be built.

The Mishnah's principal message is that man is at the centre of Creation, the head of all creatures upon earth, corresponding to God in heaven, in whose image man is made. The way in which the Mishnah makes this simple and fundamental statement is to impute power to man to inaugurate and initiate those corresponding processes, sanctification and uncleanness, which play so critical a role in the Mishnah's account of reality. The will of man, expressed through the deed of man, is the active power in the world. Will and deed constitute those actors of Creation which work upon neutral realms, subject to either sanctification or uncleanness: the Temple and table, the field and family, the altar and hearth, women, time, space, transactions in the material world and in the world above as well. An object, a substance, a transaction, even a phrase or a sentence is inert but may be made holy, when the interplay of the will and deed of man arouses or generates its potential to be sanctified. Each may be treated as ordinary or (where relevant) made unclean by the neglect of the will and the inattentive act of man. Man is counterpart and partner in Creation in that, like God, he has power over the status and condition of Creation, putting everything in its proper place, calling everything by its rightful name.

So, stated briefly, the question taken up and answered by the Mishnah is, what can a man do? And the answer laid down by the Mishnah is that man, through will and deed, is master of this world, and the measure of all things. Since when the Mishnah thinks of man, it means the Israelite, who is the subject and actor of its system, the statement is clear. This man is Israel, who can do what he wills. In the aftermath of the two wars against the Romans, the message of the Mishnah could not have been more pertinent, or poignant and tragic. The first of the two stages of the formation of rabbinic Judaism therefore answered a single encompassing question: what, in the aftermath of the destruction of the Temple and the Temple rites, remained of the sanctity of the holy caste, the priesthood, the holy Land and, above all, the holy people and their holy way of life? The answer, that sanctity persists, indelibly, in Israel the people – in their way of life, in their Land, in their priesthood, in their food, in their mode of sustaining life, in their manner of procreating and so sustaining the nation – would endure. But that answer found itself absorbed, in time to come, within a successor system, with its own points of stress and emphasis.

The Second Phase of Rabbinic Judaism, 200–600 CE: The Judaism of the Talmud

Rabbinic Judaism as put forth by the Mishnah, c. 200, ignored Christianity and its emphases. But with the world-shaking events of a century later, that was no longer possible. The fourth century witnessed a drastic change in the situation faced by the Jews of the Land of Israel and the Roman Empire. Five events of fundamental importance for the history of Judaism took place in the fourth and fifth centuries (all of them except for the last were well known in their day):

1. The Roman Emperor Constantine declared Christianity a permitted religion in 312; by the end of his life he had converted and made Christianity the state religion. Christianity had triumphed, and three centuries of sustained persecution came to an end.

2. Twenty-four years later, Emperor Julian reverted to paganism. As part of his effort to embarrass Christianity, he gave the Jews permission to rebuild the

Temple of Jerusalem in 360. But nothing came of it since he died soon after, succeeded by another Christian emperor.

3. After the death of Julian, Rome was securely Christian. This led in time to the beginning of the de-paganization of the Roman Empire, a programme of attacks on pagan temples and, along the way, synagogues.

4. In the third and fourth centuries, the majority of the population of Palestine, Israelites in origin or otherwise, became Christian.

5. At the end of the fourth century and during the fifth century, the important documents of rabbinic Judaism – the Talmud of the Land of Israel, a commentary on the Mishnah, and works of scriptural exegeses (*Genesis Rabbah* and *Leviticus Rabbah* in particular) – were completed.

What happened with the legalization of Christianity followed by its establishment as the official religion of the Roman Empire was a world-historical change, one that could not be absorbed into Israel's available system of theories on outsiders, in general, and the meaning of the history of the great empires, in particular. The Christian Empire was fundamentally different from its pagan predecessor in two ways. First, it shared with Israel reverence for exactly the same Holy Scriptures on which Jewry based its existence. So it was no longer a wholly other, entirely alien Empire that ruled from over the horizon. It was now a monotheist, formerly persecuted, biblical Empire, not awfully different from Israel in its basic convictions about all important matters of time and eternity. And it was near at hand (in the new capital of the Eastern Empire, Constantinople) and interested. Second, established policies of more than a half a millennium, from the time of the Maccabees' alliance with Rome to the start of the fourth century, now gave way. The Romans' original agreement to tolerate Judaism in exchange for the Jews' alliance with Rome and acceptance of its imperial role was overthrown when the Jews revolted in 70 and 132. Instead, there was intolerance of Judaism and persecution of Jews through attacks on their persons and property.

The rabbinic sages worked out in the pages of the Talmud of the Land of Israel and in the exegetical compilations of the age a Judaism intersecting with the Mishnah's but essentially asymmetrical with it, providing answers to the urgent questions posed by historical change. Christian theologians held that the Christian triumph confirmed the Christhood of Jesus; that the old Judaism and Israel's hope for salvation at the end of time had been superseded by the new messiah and his new religion. Now the rabbis, augmenting the Mishnah's corpus, put forth a system for salvation focused on the salvific power of the sanctification of the holy people, the descendants of Abraham, Isaac and Jacob. The age had brought enormous political change, which had weighty, and negative, implications for the meaning and end of history as Israel would experience it. In response, the rabbis laid fresh emphasis on salvation and on the figure of the true Messiah of Israel, who was now portrayed as the goal and the end of Israel's history. Indeed, the system as a whole was made into a messianic statement: the Messiah will come to Israel; he will be a rabbi; and he will bring about the resurrection of the dead and the end of history.

The rabbinic sages provided responses to those very specific points at which the Christian challenge met old Israel's world-view head on. What did Israel's sages have to present as the Torah's answer to the Cross? The Torah itself. This took three forms. First, they insisted on the high status of the Torah as oral and memorized revelation, including the Mishnah and other rabbinical writings. Second, it was presented as the encompassing symbol of Israel's salvation. Third, at the end of the world the Torah would be embodied in the person of the Messiah who, of course, would be a rabbi. The Torah in all three aspects confronted the Cross, with its doctrine of the triumphant Christ, Messiah and king, ruler now of earth as of heaven. The outcome was the stunning success of that society for which the sages and, in their view, God, cared so deeply: eternal Israel in the here and now. For the Judaism formulated by the rabbis did endure in the Christian West, imparting to Jews the secure conviction of constituting that Israel in the here and now to which the Torah continued to speak. We know the sages' Judaism won because when, in turn, Islam conquered the region, Christianity throughout the Middle East and North Africa gave way, leaving only pockets of the faithful to live out the long story of Islamic dominance. But the rabbinic sages' Judaism in those same vast territories retained the loyalty and conviction of the people of the Torah. The Cross would rule only where the Crescent and its sword did not. But the Torah of Sinai everywhere and always sanctified Israel in time and promised secure salvation for eternity.

The entire history of Judaism is contained within these simple propositions. The symbolic system of Christianity, with Christ triumphant on the Cross as its reigning symbol, and with the canon of Christianity now defined and recognized as authoritative, called forth from the sages of the Land of Israel a symbolic system strikingly responsive to the crisis. This took the form of the symbolic power of the newly expanded Torah, with its explicit claim that the rabbinic sages' authority here and now represented the will of God in heaven. The fifth-century Torah included as much of the written and oral Torah as everyone acknowledged as authoritative as well as the entirety of the sages' teachings. This canonical shift assigned to the rabbis' own writings a position in the revelation by God to Moses of the entire Torah, oral and written. The important doctrinal change was the inclusion into the Mishnaic system of the belief, omitted in the original Mishnah, in the coming of the Messiah and a new emphasis on salvation at the end of the world.

Rabbinic Judaism consisted of more than a symbolic structure and a narrative system embodied in the figures of the Torah and the rabbi and the themes of sanctification in the here and now and salvation at the end of time. Rabbinic Judaism also set forth a systematic theology, contained within its canonical writings, those of the written and oral Torah alike. That is the theology we examine in Chapter 6, the law we consider in Chapter 7, the theology that animates the stories in Chapters 1, 2, 4 and 5.

Israel's Story
   in Everyday Life

4

Chapters of the Story of Judaism in the Life Cycle of the Israelite

When Israel's Master Narrative Shapes the Life Cycle, and When It Does Not

Individuals are not only Israelites, species of the genus Israel. They have their own story to tell, the story of their own lives, not only of Israel. For they also bear names, come from particular mothers and fathers, have private lives and personal preferences and traits. They each live out their individual existence, they are born one by one and die one by one. Each is possessed of an utterly personal biography. And that unique story figures particularly at certain passages of life.

When we survey the life cycle as defined by Judaism – entry into Israel (through birth or conversion), puberty, marriage and death – we find stories of two types. First come occasions in the private life at which the individual invokes in his or her personal framework a chapter in Israel's story. Second are moments that are utterly private in formulation, yet profoundly Judaic in meaning. In them we see how, at particular turning points in life, the individual tells his or her own story, intersecting with, but not embodying, Israel's at all. These stories are rarely original, but always unique to the person who tells them. Then, at the end, when we have reviewed the Judaic shaping of the life cycle, I will explain why this, not that: when and why Israel's master narrative imposes itself on events in the individual's course through life, and where the public master narrative stands back, falls silent, and does not come into play at all, leaving the individual to stand alone on the stage of human existence.

Birth into the Covenant of Abraham Our Father

The beginning of an Israelite life, whether at birth or by the choice and rite of conversion, marks a moment of eternity because the Israelite now bears within himself or herself the promise of eternal life. Stated simply, when a baby is born or an adult converts to Judaism, a unique and eternal life commences within Israel. Because the advent of an Israelite concerns all Israel, we should expect to invoke a chapter of the master narrative. The only question is, which chapter? Our first answer to that question comes with the rite of circumcision, which marks the entry of the newborn son into the covenant of Abraham.

What is the effect of the story upon the event? In the case of circumcision it transforms a surgical operation into a moment of sanctification. The rite of passage of circumcision in Judaism takes a most personal moment, the birth of a child as a result of the private sexual relation of the mother and the father and the personal labour of the mother. That most individual occasion, the beginning of a boy's life, links in a concrete way to specific moments and personalities in the public and supernatural life of Israel. These envelop a surgical operation in the name of the faith, which requires cutting off the foreskin of the penis on the eighth day after birth, a rite called *berit milah*, 'the covenant of (or "effected through") circumcision'. *Berit milah* seals with the blood of the infant son the contract between Israel beginning with its birth in Abraham and Sarah, and God, a covenant made generation by generation, father to son to grandson through remembered time.

Before we turn to the stories, let us consider the rite itself. Circumcision must take place on the eighth day after birth, normally in the presence of a quorum of ten adult males. Very commonly, it is done in the home, not in the hospital, and crowded into a few rooms will be relatives and friends. There is nothing private nor merely surgical about the operation. The contemporary practice of having a surgical operation in no way carries out the rite of circumcision. For what changes the matter is not only circumstance. It is the story contained in the ritual formula that transforms the birth of a child to an individual couple into an event heavy with meaning: a metaphor for something more, a simile of something that transcends. The tale tells how God sees the family beyond time, joined by blood of not pedigree but circumcision, genealogy framed by 150 generations of loyalty to the covenant in blood and birth from the union of the womb of a Jewish woman with the circumcised penis of her husband: this is the fruit of the womb.

There are four aspects in which the operation is turned into an act of sanctification. When the rite begins, the assembly and the mohel (ritual circumciser) together recite the following passage from the Book of Numbers (25: 10–12):

The Lord said to Moses, 'Phineas, son of Eleazar, son of Aaron the priest, has turned my wrath from the people of Israel by displaying among them his passion for me, so that I did not wipe out the people of Israel in my passion. Therefore say, "Behold, I give to him my covenant of peace."'

The passage is from the incident in the wilderness when the Israelites were sexually involved with Moabite women and made offerings to Baal of Peor, the god of Moab. Phineas, son of Aaron, who was the brother of Moses and the chief priest, took action against these sexual acts of idolatry. Commenting on this passage, the American rabbi Lifsa Schachter states,

Phineas is identified with zealously opposing the . . . sins of sexual licentiousness and idolatry. He is best known for an event which occurred when the Israelites, whoring with Moabite women in the desert, were drawn to the worship of Baal-Peor . . . Phineas leaped into the fray and through an act of double murder . . . quieted God's terrible wrath.[1]

In the room where the rite of circumcision takes place a chair is set out for Elijah, as at the Passover Seder. The presence of Elijah attests to Israel's persistence in its unique covenant with God. For Elijah had called into doubt Israel's loyalty, explicitly complaining to God that Israel neglected the covenant (I Kings 19:10–14). So here and now he is required to come to bear witness that Israel observes the covenant of circumcision. Elijah's presence marks those occasions when Israel assembles in the hope of the Messiah (Malachi 4:5). The newborn son is set on Elijah's chair, and the congregation says, 'This is the chair of Elijah, of blessed memory.' The story embodied in the chair of Elijah is as follows:

Elijah was living in a cave when suddenly the word of the Lord came to him asking, 'Why are you here, Elijah?'

'Because of my great zeal for the Lord, the God of hosts,' he said. 'The people of Israel have forsaken your covenant, torn down your altars, and put your prophets to death with the sword. I alone am left, and they seek to take my life.'

And the answer came: 'Go and stand on the mount before the Lord.'

For the Lord was passing by: a great and strong wind came rending mountains and shattering rocks before him, but the Lord was not in the wind; and after the wind there was an earthquake, but the Lord was not in the earthquake; and after the earthquake fire; but the Lord was not in the fire; and after the fire a still small voice.

When Elijah heard it, he muffled his face in his cloak and went out and stood at the entrance of the cave. Then there came a voice: 'Why are you here, Elijah?'

'Because of my great zeal for the Lord, the God of hosts,' he said. 'The people of Israel have forsaken your covenant, torn down your altars, and put your prophets to death with the sword. I alone am left, and they seek to take my life.'[2]

When Elijah says, 'The people of Israel have forsaken your covenant', he means that they no longer practise circumcision. This passage stands behind the story told in a medieval document, *Pirke deRabbi Eliezer*, that Elijah attends the rite of circumcision of every Jewish baby boy:

The Israelites were wont to circumcise until they were divided into two kingdoms. The [northern] kingdom of Ephraim [Israel] cast off from themselves the covenant of circumcision. Elijah, may he be remembered for good, arose and was zealous with a mighty passion, and he adjured the heavens to send down neither dew nor rain upon the earth. [Queen] Jezebel heard about it and sought to slay him.

Elijah arose and prayed before the Holy One, blessed be he. The Holy One, blessed be he, said to him, 'Are you better than your fathers (1 Kings 19:4)? Esau sought to slay Jacob, but he fled before him, as it is said: And Jacob fled into the field of Aram (Hosea 12:12).

'Pharaoh sought to slay Moses, who fled before him and he was saved, as it is said: Now when Pharaoh heard this thing, he sought to slay Moses. And Moses fled from the face of Pharaoh (Exodus 2:15).

'Saul sought to slay David, who fled before him and was saved, as it is said: If you save not your life tonight, tomorrow you will be killed (1 Samuel 19:11).

'Another text says, And David fled and escaped (1 Samuel 19:18). Learn that everyone who flees is sad.'

Elijah, may he be remembered for good, arose and fled from the Land of Israel, and he betook himself to Mount Horeb, as it is said, and he arose and ate and drank (1 Kings 19:8). Then the Holy One, blessed be he, was revealed to him and said to him, 'What are you doing here, Elijah?'

He answered him saying, 'I have been very zealous.'

The Holy One, blessed be he, said to him, 'You are always zealous. You were zealous in Shittim on account of the immorality. For it is said, Phineas the son of Eleazar, the son of Aaron the priest, turned my wrath away from the children of Israel, in that he was zealous with my zeal among them (Numbers 25:11).

'Here you are also zealous, by your life! They shall not observe the covenant of circumcision until you see it done with your own eyes.'

Hence the sages have instituted the custom that people should have a seat of honour for the messenger of the covenant, for Elijah, may he be remembered for good, is called the messenger of the covenant, as it is said, And the messenger of the covenant, whom you delight in, behold he comes (Malachi 3:1).[3]

Elijah then serves as the guardian for the newborn, just as he raised the child of the widow from the dead (1 Kings 17:17–24). The gesture of setting out the empty chair sets the stage for an event in the life of the family not of the child alone but of all Israel. The chair of Elijah, filled by the one who holds the child, sets the newborn baby into Elijah's lap. There the rite is performed.

The blessing said before the rite itself, as the mohel takes the knife to cut the foreskin of the penis, transforms the act into one of sanctification: 'Praised are you . . . who sanctified us with your commandments and commanded us to bring the son into the covenant of Abraham our father.' This introduces the narrative of the first act of circumcision that of Abraham, as a sign of the covenant between God and Israel.

When Abram was ninety-nine years old the Lord appeared to Abram, and said to him, 'I am God Almighty; walk before me, and be blameless. And I will make my covenant between me and you, and will multiply you exceedingly.' Then Abram fell on his face; and God said to him, 'Behold, my covenant is with you, and you shall be the father of a multitude of nations. No longer shall your name be Abram, but your name shall be Abraham . . .'

And God said to Abraham, 'As for you, you shall keep my covenant, you and your descendants after you throughout their generations. This is my covenant, which you shall keep, between me and you and your descendants after you: Every male among you shall be circumcised.'[4]

The explicit invocation of Abraham's covenant in the blessing turns the concrete action in the here and now into a simile of the archetype: the Israelite circumcises his son just as Abraham circumcised Isaac at eight days. The rite by itself is a surgical operation. Done in the presence of Phineas, Elijah and Abraham, invoking their stories, it turns into an embodiment of Israel's loyalty to its covenant with God.

Lest people miss the point of the stories that are called to mind, the rite makes matters explicit. This is in an act of sanctification. Once the operation has been performed, wine is blessed:

Praised are you, Lord our God, who sanctified the beloved from the womb and set a statute into his very flesh, and his parts sealed with the sign of the holy covenant. On this account, Living God, our portion and rock, save the beloved of our flesh from destruction, for the sake of his covenant placed in our flesh. Blessed are you . . . who makes the covenant.

The covenant is not a generality; it is specific, concrete. By virtue of the rite, the child enters the covenant, meaning that he joins that unseen 'Israel' that through blood enters an agreement with God. Then the blessing of the covenant is owing to the child. For covenants or contracts cut both ways.

After the father has recited the blessing, '. . . who sanctified us with your commandments and commanded us to bring the son into the covenant of Abraham our father' the community responds, 'Just as he has entered the covenant, so may he be introduced to the Torah, the huppah [marriage canopy] and good deeds'. Lifsa Schachter interprets those who are present as follows:

In the presence of Elijah . . . Torah, as against idolatry; in the presence of Phineas . . . huppah, as against sexual licentiousness; in the presence of Abraham . . . good deeds: 'For I have singled him out that he may instruct his children and his posterity to keep the way of the Lord by doing what is just and right' (Genesis 18:18).[5]

Scripture's stories, chapter by chapter, once again define the scene: Elijah complaining to God, Abraham obediently circumcising his sons, Phineas, calming God's wrath by an act of violence, with whom a covenant of peace then is made. These are the right chapters of Scripture's story, recast into a coherent narrative and message for the boy and his family. They take this very personal and private occasion and transform it into an event for the community of Israel before God.

The advent of daughters is celebrated by contemporary Judaic families as well. They are received in covenanted Israel through rites in Orthodox, Reform, Conservative and Reconstructionist synagogues. The *simhat habat* or 'rejoicing over the advent of a daughter' takes a variety of liturgical forms. In Conservative and Reform congregations, where women along with men are called to the Torah, the parents bring the daughter to the Torah and recite the blessings before and after the Torah is declaimed, after which they recite a blessing of thanks for having reached this joyous occasion and the daughter is blessed.

Conversion: Abraham and Sarah's New Child

The counterpart to the covenant of circumcision, the rite of conversion, which we met in connection with Ruth at the Festival of Shavuot, marks the other way in which a human being becomes an Israelite. The story goes over the same ground, namely, the beginning of immortality in another Israelite soul. The convert, one who accepts the unity and sovereignty of God embodied in the Torah of Sinai, acquires a genealogy, a story to explain his or her share in the God of Israel. The genealogy is via Abraham and Sarah, who even before reaching the Promised Land had made converts in the kingdom of Haran. This is how the rabbinic sages explain matters, shaping the story to the occasion:

'And Abram took Sarai his wife, and Lot his brother's son, and all their possessions which they had gathered, and the soul that they had made . . .' (Genesis 12:5):

Rabbi Eleazar in the name of Rabbi Yose ben Zimra: 'If all of the nations of the world should come together to try to create a single mosquito, they could not put a soul into it, and yet you say, "And the soul that they had made"? [They could not have created souls.] But this refers to proselytes.'

Then why should not the text say, 'The proselytes whom they had converted.' Why stress, 'whom they had made'?

This serves to teach you that whoever brings a gentile close [to the worship of the true God] is as if he had created him anew.

And why not say, 'That he had made'? Why, 'That *they* had made'?

Said Rabbi Huniah, 'Abraham converted the men and Sarah the women.'[6]

The point needs no elaboration. Abraham and Sarah are mother and father of not only their biological descendants, born into Israel, but also their descendants by choice, those who adopt Abraham and Sarah as their ancestry and enter into the covenant of Abraham with God.

What this means in practical terms is simple. The convert is equivalent to the native-born Israelite, and, as I have stressed from the outset, the 'Israel' of which Judaism speaks encompasses all those who accept God's dominion and select for themselves a place in the family of Israel. The convert adopts a new, Israelite name, and is called to the Torah as 'So-and-so, son [or daughter] of Abraham our father and Sarah our mother', thus securing a new, Israelite, genealogy and standing in holy Israel. The convert to Judaism is now deemed to have no prior genealogy. Their natural mother and father, brothers and sisters are no longer regarded as relatives; by the law of Judaism they do not stand in line to inherit the estate of the convert; nor do any children already in existence – only those born after conversion.

Accordingly, like a newborn son, the male convert is circumcised into the covenant of Abraham. Both the male and the female convert are also immersed in water that has collected naturally, for example, a lake, river, ocean or special immersion pool (*mikveh*). In his account of the rite, Rabbi Jules Harlow states, 'Conversion is more than a change in religion; it is a new birth, involving many changes and adjustments.'[7]

But to enter into the eternal life of Israel does not come easily. For many centuries Judaism has discouraged proselytism for two reasons. First, to ensure that the prospective convert is sincere. Second, to make sure the convert knows what the costs are: accepting both God's rule and gentiles' enmity. Only if he or she persists will the rabbi who is approached convene a rabbinical court of those rabbis to act on the petition. The convert is not encouraged to adopt the Torah and enter holy Israel. Instead, the rabbi repeats a rite meant to discourage conversion, and to filter out all but the most determined, so as to make conversion to Judaism a sincere and strong commitment.

Our rabbis have taught on Tannaite authority:
A person who comes to convert at this time [after the destruction of the Second Temple in 70 CE], they say to him, 'How come you have come to convert? Don't you know that at this time the Israelites are forsaken and harassed, despised, baited, and afflictions come upon them?'

If he says, 'I know full well, and I am not worthy [of sharing their suffering],' they accept him forthwith. And they inform him about some of the lesser religious duties and some of the weightier religious duties.

He is informed about the sin of neglecting the religious duties involving gleanings, the forgotten sheaf, the corner of the field, and the poor man's tithe. They further inform him about the penalty for not keeping the commandments.

This shows that the convert is not encouraged but fully informed of the disadvantages of the contemplated change in life. At issue is not only adopting the status of a group subject to hatred, but also taking on the obligations of an Israelite and the penalties for violating them.

They say to him, 'You should know that before you came to this change of status [to being part of Israel], if you ate forbidden fat, you would not be penalized by extirpation [execution]. If you violated the sabbath, you would not be put to death through stoning. But now if you eat forbidden fat, you are punished with extirpation. If you violate the sabbath, you are punished by stoning.'

These represent details of the Torah that, in theory, the convert accepts. The gentile is not obliged to keep the sabbath, the Israelite is. And the rest follows. But so too, the stakes are very high. To be Israel is to inherit the world to come, in so many words:

And just as they inform him about the penalties for violating religious duties, so they inform him about the rewards for doing them. They say to him, 'You should know that the world to come is prepared only for the righteous, and Israel at this time is unable to bear either too much prosperity or too much penalty.'

They do not press him too hard, and they do not impose too many details on him.

Once the male candidate for entry into Israel accepts the obligations of the Torah and affirms his desire to enter into the covenant of Abraham, the rite of circumcision is performed forthwith, and he is immersed later. The female candidate is immersed on the spot.

If he accepted all this, they circumcise him immediately. If any shreds that render the circumcision invalid remain, they do it a second time.

Once he has healed, they immerse him right away.

And two disciples of sages supervise the process and inform him about some [more] of the lesser religious duties and some of the weightier religious duties.

He immerses and comes up, and lo, he is an Israelite for all purposes.

In the case of a woman, women sit her in the water up to her neck, and two disciples of sages stand there for her situated outside, and they inform her about some [more] of the lesser religious duties and some of the weightier religious duties.[8]

Two details are striking in this Talmudic account of the process of conversion, which is still the dominant view of matters today. First, what is at stake in accepting God's rule in the Torah is eternal life, that is, becoming part of Israel both in this world and in the world to come. That is stated in so many words. Second, the rewards for becoming part of holy Israel come in the world to come; in this world one is asking for trouble. Conversion for personal gain, for the sake of marrying a particular Israelite, for example, is not countenanced.

After the immersion of the convert, some rabbis recite:

With pure water will I cleanse you and you shall be clean; from all your impurities will I cleanse you. A new heart will I give you and a new spirit will I put within you. I will cause you to follow my teachings and you shall keep my statutes. You shall be my people, and I will be your God.[9]

Besides circumcision and immersion, there is, in addition, a synagogue rite. A court of three rabbis questions the convert, who makes a declaration of faith. Some rabbinical authorities ask the convert to recite the following:

I hereby declare my desire to accept the principles of the Jewish religion, to follow its practices and ceremonies, and to become a member of the Jewish people . . . I pray that I may always remain conscious of the duties that are mine as a member of the House of Israel. I declare my determination to maintain a Jewish home. Should I be blessed with male children, I pledge to bring them into the Covenant of Abraham. I further pledge to rear all children with whom God may bless me in loyalty to the Jewish faith and its practices.

'Hear O Israel, the Lord our God, the Lord is one . . .'[10]

Ruth 1:16–17, 'Entreat me not to leave you . . .', which we met earlier, is sometimes recited. A blessing is asked for the convert: 'May he who blessed our ancestors, Abraham, Isaac and Jacob, Sarah, Rebecca, Rachel and Leah, bless . . . a true proselyte among the people of the God of Abraham . . .'

Here is another occasion on which a story turns what is personal and private into an event in the life of holy, corporate Israel. What is important in the rite of passage into Judaism locates itself on the surface of matters: the persistent invocation of the figures of Abraham and Sarah, and entry into Israel as their child. It is the story that is told that transforms the acts of circumcision and immersion into moments of sanctification and transcendence. But not all events in the Judaic life cycle come under the master narrative of Israel, and here we come to the first important chapter in an individual's autobiography that does not take shape in dialogue with that narrative. Scripture scarcely figures.

Entering the Age of Responsibility

The advent of puberty is marked by the bar mitzvah rite for a young man, and a bat mitzvah rite for a young woman, at which a young person becomes obligated to keep the commandments. '*Bar*' means son and '*bat*' means daughter, with the additional sense of 'one who is subject to'; and '*mitzvah*' means a divine commandment. In Reform, Conservative, Reconstructionist and other non-Orthodox Judaic settings, women as well as men are called to the Torah. Hence outside Orthodoxy, girls as much as boys undertake the public rites of responsibility. The rite is unadorned: the young person is called to pronounce the blessing over and then to read one or two passages from the Torah in the synagogue. In olden times it was not so important an occasion as it has become in modern America. Only when an Israelite achieves intelligence and self-consciousness, normally at puberty, is he or she expected to accept the full privilege and responsibility of *mitzvah* (commandment) and to regard himself or herself as commanded by God. Judaism perceives the commandments as expressions of God's love, his engagement with the Israelite's doings.

The Israelite accepts the yoke of the kingdom of heaven and submits to God's will. That acceptance cannot be coerced, but requires thoughtful and complete affirmation. The bar or bat mitzvah thus represents the moment that the young Israelite first assumes full responsibility before God to keep the commandments. Calling the young person to the Torah and conferring upon him or her the rights of a full member of the community ratify what has taken place. But this marks a stage in personal development, not a significant change in status (as there was at circumcision), nor any real alteration in the condition of the community.

And that observation carries us to the question, when does a life-cycle event *not* situate itself within a chapter in Israel's story? For puberty represents one such omitted turning point, not framed within a chapter of the master narrative. No tale is told to link the personal to the public, the unique individual to the status of Israelite. No story serves to impart larger significance to the event. When an 'I' reaches the age of responsibility for carrying out religious duties, the 'I' personally becomes responsible. The 'I' is changed, Israel is not. That is because the child was an Israelite from birth, remains an Israelite through death and will rise from the grave to judgement, resurrection and eternal life.

Reform Judaism has invented a rite to mark bar and bat mitzvahs. The generations of the family, as far back as great-grandparents in some cases, down to the bar or bat mitzvah child, line up before the ark where the Torah is kept. The rabbi takes a Torah and hands it to the oldest generation, who hand the Torah on to their children and so on to the bar/bat mitzvah child. The ceremony expresses the desire, 'Just as we have received and guarded this precious faith and handed it on to you, so you receive and guard the Torah, and keep it, for another generation.' The story then is personal and familial, but by reason of this rite it also involves the community of Israel, past, present, and future, as much as the first act of giving the Torah at Sinai did and does. The rite celebrates the fact that the parents, grandparents and great-grandparents (often present these days) are not the end of the line.

Marriage: Adam and Eve in Eden

If puberty provokes no public storytelling, the marriage rite makes up for it, invoking the great themes of the restoration of Israel to the Land and of Adam and Eve to Eden, the matching moment that forms a principal part of the master narrative of Judaism. That invocation of critical chapters in Israel's story is, as usual, articulate and explicit. The rite maintains that Adam and Eve in Eden are present under the marriage canopy, along with the memory and hope of the Israelites beyond the destruction of Jerusalem in 586 BCE, destined once more to rejoice. The words and deeds of the wedding rite transform the space, time, action and community of the 'I' of the groom and the 'I' of the bride into the 'we' of Israelites, and of Adam and Eve. The space is contained by the huppah, translated as marriage canopy, which should properly be constructed under the open sky: a contained space of heaven representing heaven. Stripped down to essentials, the stories that are invoked transform the union of woman and man into the beginning of a new Creation, so that the woman becomes Eve, the man, Adam. In this way the prophecy of the snake in Eden is realized, as the great Bible interpreter, Rashi (Rabbi Solomon ben Isaac, 1040–1105), explains. When the snake says, 'For God knows that when you eat of it your eyes will be opened, and you will be like God . . .' (Genesis 3:5), the meaning, Rashi maintains, is that 'you will become creators of worlds'.[11] At the marriage rite a new world begins: a family in the house of Israel, the beginning of a new creation of life.

The rite unfolds in stages, beginning before the couple reaches the marriage canopy. First, the *ketubah*, or marriage contract, is validated by the signatures of the witnesses. This guarantees support for the wife in the event of divorce or the death of the husband. Judaism lives in stories, but it also provides for the ordinary world. The bride is not only Eve, she is also a woman who has obligations to her husband, and the groom, Adam, is reciprocally responsible. So the marriage rite represents not only an occasion in Israel's story but a legal transaction by which the rights and obligations of each party have to be expressed and guaranteed by a contract. The *ketubah* is appropriately signed and delivered from the groom to the bride's possession.

This *ketubah* witnesses before God and man that on the——day of the week, the——of the month——, in the year——, the holy covenant of marriage was entered between bridegroom and his bride, at——. Duly conscious of the solemn obligation of marriage the bridegroom made the following declaration to his bride: 'Be consecrated to me as my wife according to the laws and traditions of Moses and Israel. I will love, honour and cherish you; I will protect and support you; and I will faithfully care for your needs, as prescribed by Jewish law and tradition.' And the bride made the following declaration to the groom: 'In accepting the wedding ring I pledge you all my love and devotion and I take upon myself the fulfilment of all the duties incumbent upon a Jewish wife.'[12]

The contract is in Aramaic, as all valid contracts in Judaism must be. The language of the *ketubah* specifies the legal standing of the husband's obligation to the wife. In order to pay what is owing to her, should he divorce her, or in order to provide for her if he dies before she does, the husband pledges even the shirt off his back.

Next comes the touching moment at which the groom places the veil over the bride's face, before they take their places under the marriage canopy, and makes the following statement to her:

May you, our sister, be fruitful and prosper. May God make you as Sarah, Rebecca, Rachel and Leah. May the Lord bless you and keep you. May the Lord show you favor and be gracious to you. May the Lord show you kindness and grant you peace.[13]

To understand the next stage, the betrothal, we have to call to mind the law of Judaism. That law recognizes a two-stage process, roughly equivalent to betrothal then marriage. In the first stage, *erusin*, the woman is sanctified, or designated as holy, to a particular man, and in the second, *nissuin*, the actual union is consecrated through the Seven Blessings. In ancient times there was an interval of as much as a full year between these stages, but in our own day the wedding rite encompasses both. The first of the two is carried out under the marriage canopy by the drinking of a cup of wine with this blessing:

Blessed are you, our God, king of the world, who creates the fruit of the vine.

Blessed are you, Lord our God, king of the world, who has sanctified us by his commandments and commanded us concerning proper sexual relations, forbidding to us betrothed women but permitting to us married women through the rites of the huppah and sanctification. Blessed are you, Lord, who sanctifies his people Israel through the marriage canopy and the rite of sanctification.

Then there is a gift of a ring to the bride, with this formula: 'Behold you are sanctified to me by this ring in accord with the tradition of Moses and Israel.' This concludes the betrothal.

Then come the Seven Blessings that mark the stage of *nissuin*, the fully realized union. The blessings are recited over a cup of wine, and they complete the rite under the huppah. They embody the chapters of the Israelite narrative that animate the occasion. The first blessing introduces the wine itself: 'Praised are you, O Lord our God, king of the universe, creator of the fruit of the vine.' Then comes the first act, the chapter of Eden, Adam and Eve:

Praised are you, O Lord our God, king of the universe, who created all things for your glory.

Praised are you, O Lord our God, king of the universe, creator of Adam.

Praised are You, O Lord our God, king of the universe, who created man and woman in his image, fashioning woman from man as his mate, that together they might perpetuate life. Praised are you, O Lord, creator of man.

The sequence of three is perfectly realized: first, creation of all things, then creation of man, then creation of man and woman in his image. The theme of ancient paradise is introduced by the simple choice of the word Adam, so heavy with meaning. The story of man's creation is rehearsed: man and woman are in God's image, together complete and whole, creators of life, 'like God'. Woman was fashioned from man in order together with him to perpetuate life. And again, 'blessed is the creator of Adam'.

Then comes the second act, introducing that other actor in Creation, counterpart to Adam and Eve in Eden, which is Israel in Zion. But what about Zion, with the Temple in ruins? That is to say, until the coming of the Messiah and the end of days, the loss of the Land of Israel by holy Israel, comparable to the loss of Eden by Adam and Eve, casts shadows over all rejoicing. So by 'Zion' here is meant the Temple now in ruins but one day to be restored with the advent of the Messiah. Zion's children today rejoice under the huppah, in time to come they will rejoice in the restoration of Zion itself: 'May Zion rejoice as her children are restored to her in joy. Praised are you, O Lord, who causes Zion to rejoice at her children's return.' What a jarring intrusion! We move from Eden to Zion, Adam and Eve to Israel. In truth, Zion comes uninvited. No one mentioned her. But in Judaism and its narrative, Jerusalem forms a perpetual presence.

So it is a natural sequence. For this Adam and this Eve are also Israel, children of Zion the mother, as expressed in this fifth blessing. Zion lies in ruins, her children scattered. Adam and Eve cannot celebrate together without thinking of the condition of the mother, Jerusalem. The children will one day come home for the resurrection of the dead and the reunion of all Israel over all eternity in the world to come of Eden. But that is then, this is now. The mood is hopeful yet sad, as it was meant to be, for Israel mourns as it rejoices and rejoices as it mourns.

Quickly then, back to the happy occasion, for we do not let mourning lead to melancholy: 'Grant perfect joy to the loving companions', for they are creators of a new line in mankind, the new Adam and the new Eve, and may their home be the Garden of Eden. And if joy is there, then 'praised are you for the joy of bride and groom'. What is the upshot? The joy of the moment gives a foretaste of the rejoicing of restoration, redemption, return. Now the two roles become one in that same joy, first Adam and Eve, now groom and bride; Eden then, the marriage canopy now: 'Grant perfect joy to these loving companions, as you did to the first man and woman in the Garden of Eden. Praised are you, O Lord, who grants the joy of bride and groom.'

That same joy comes in the metaphors of Zion the bride and Israel the groom. But this is made very specific, for the words of the final blessing allude to the vision of Jeremiah, when all seemed lost, that Jerusalem, which was about to fall and lose its people, will one day ring with the shouts of not the slaughtered and the enslaved but the returned and redeemed. That is why the concluding blessing returns to the theme of Jerusalem. This time it evokes the tragic hour of Jerusalem's first destruction. When everyone had given up hope, supposing that with the end of Jerusalem had come the end of time, only Jeremiah counselled renewed hope. With the enemy at the gate, he sang of coming gladness:

Thus says the Lord: In this place of which you say, 'It is a waste, without man or beast,' in the cities of Judah and the streets of Jerusalem that are desolate, without man or inhabitant or beast, there shall be heard again the voice of mirth and the voice of gladness, the voice of the bridegroom and the voice of the bride, the voices of those who sing as they bring thank offerings to the house of the Lord . . .

For I will restore the fortunes of the land as at first, says the Lord.[14]

The joy is not in two but in three concentric moments – then, now, tomorrow – Eden then, marriage party now, and Zion in the coming age:

Praised are you, O Lord our God, king of the universe, who created joy and gladness, bride and groom, mirth, song, delight and rejoicing, love and harmony, peace and companionship. O Lord our God, may there ever be heard in the cities of Judah and in the streets of Jerusalem voices of joy and gladness, voices of bride and groom, the jubilant voices of those joined in marriage under the bridal canopy, the voices of young people feasting and singing.

Praised are you, O Lord, who causes the groom to rejoice with his bride.[15]

This closing blessing is not merely a literary artifice or a learned allusion to the ancient prophet. It defines the exultant, jubilant climax of this acted-out story: just as here and now there stand before us Adam and Eve, so here and now in this wedding, the ancient sorrow having been rehearsed, we listen to the voice of gladness that is coming. The joy of this new Creation prefigures the joy of the Messiah's coming, hope for which is very present in this hour. And when he comes, the joy then will echo the joy of bride and groom before us. Zion the bride, Israel the groom, united now as they will be reunited by the compassionate God, these stand under the marriage canopy.

What follows is a moment of privacy for husband and wife. In the received tradition immediately upon leaving the canopy, they head for bed, then for celebration. In the innocent world in which sexual relations commence after the marriage, a rite known as *yihud*, where the bride and groom are all by themselves for the first time, in order to consummate their union completes the seven blessings.

These seven blessings serve, then, to call to mind a sequence of stories, free-standing chapters arranged in a particular way to convey a distinctive statement. They say nothing of private people and of their falling in love. Nor do they speak of the community of Israel, as one might expect on a public occasion. Rather, they transform the singular individuals into actors in the story of humanity and Israel. Lover and beloved are transformed from natural to archetypal figures. The natural events of human life, here the marriage of ordinary people, are by narrative heightened into a re-enactment of Israel's life as a community. What gives the love of bride and groom its true meaning is their acting out the story of Creation, revelation and redemption, here and now embodied in that love. The marriage rite shows how, seeing Judaism as story, image and experience, we may say that an Israelite is any person who tells concerning himself or herself in particular the story of Israel in general.

Death and Resurrection

No Moses, no Elijah, no David join the flights of angels that will carry me to my rest. Unlike birth and marriage, death, marking the penultimate stage in the Israelite life cycle (to be followed by resurrection), embodies no chapter in Israel's narrative. The birth of an Israelite does define a major event for Israel, the advent of an eternal Israelite: for Israel never dies, nor, ultimately, does the Israelite. At death the Israelite does not perish but only sleeps in the dust, awaiting resurrection: death is only a chapter en route to eternal life. That is why death does not mark an event in the story of Israel or correspond to an occasion in that story. No metaphor, no incident from the corporate experience of Israel fetched from beyond the here and now intervenes to turn death into something other than it is, the stark fact of the end of the life of an individual.

A review of the rites of death shows us that all things focus upon the individual, always 'I', never 'we, Israel'. At the onset of death, the dying Jew says a confession:

My God and God of my fathers, accept my prayer . . .

Forgive me for all the sins which I have committed in my lifetime . . .

Accept my pain and suffering as atonement and forgive my wrongdoing for against you alone have I sinned . . .

I acknowledge that my life and recovery depend on you.

May it be your will to heal me.

Yet if you have decreed that I shall die of this affliction, may my death atone for all sins and transgressions which I have committed before you.

Shelter me in the shadow of your wings.

Grant me a share in the world to come.

Father of orphans and Guardian of widows, protect my beloved family . . .

Into your hand I commit my soul. You redeem me, O Lord God of truth.

Then comes the declaration of the faith:

Hear O Israel, the Lord is our God, the Lord alone.

The Lord, he is God.

The Lord, he is God.

What is important in the confession in comparison to other critical rites of passage is its silence, for what the dying person does not invoke tells us more than what is said. To state matters very simply, except for the final 'Hear O Israel', there is not a word here that could not be said by any monotheist who believes in God, sin, atonement, judgement and reconciliation, and life eternal, which is to say, by any Christian or Muslim. The concluding sentences identify the dying person with the holy community and its faith. But they too do not call to witness, to name familiar spirits, the slaves in Egypt, Israel at Sinai, let alone Adam and Eve, Elijah, or even the divine Judge seated before an open book and inscribing the fate of each person.

Nor does the law of Judaism require a gesture to suggest otherwise. Everything that is done concerns the corpse, little invokes that transforming metaphor that makes of a meal a celebration of freedom, of having an outdoor picnic in a hut a commemoration of Israel's wandering in the wilderness, a surgical operation a mark of eternal loyalty to God engraved in the flesh. The corpse is carefully washed and always protected. The body is covered in a white shroud, then laid in a coffin and buried. Normally burial takes place on the day of death or on the following day.

The burial rite at the graveside is laconic. The prayers that are said are exceedingly brief. One prayer that is commonly recited is as follows:

The dust returns to the earth, as it was, but the spirit returns to God, who gave it. May the soul of the deceased be bound up in the bond of life eternal. Send comfort, O Lord, to those who mourn. Grant strength to those whose burden is sorrow.

It is common to intone the prayer, *El Male Rahamim*, 'O God full of compassion':

O God, full of compassion and exalted in the heights, grant perfect peace in your sheltering presence, among the holy and pure, to the soul of the deceased, who has gone to his eternal home. Master of mercy, we beseech you, remember all the worthy and righteous deeds that he performed in the land of the living. May his soul be bound up in the bond of life. The Lord is his portion. May he rest in peace. And let us say, Amen.

The body is placed in the grave. Three pieces of broken pottery are laid on the eyes and mouth as signs of their vanity. A handful of earth from the Land of Israel is laid under the head.

The family recites the *kaddish*, in Aramaic (the vernacular language when it was composed) the prayer that sanctifies God's name and, appropriately on the occasion of death, looks forward to the messianic age and the resurrection of the dead. The prayer expresses the hope that the Messiah will soon come, 'speedily, in our days', and that 'he who brings harmony to the heavens will make peace on earth'. It concludes

THE FAMILY:

May the great name [of God] be magnified and sanctified in the world which [God] created in accord with his will. And may his kingdom come in your life and days, and in the life of all the house of Israel, speedily, promptly. And say, Amen.

THE CONGREGATION:

May the great name be blessed for ever and all eternity.

THE FAMILY:

May the holy name of the blessed one be blessed, praised, adorned, exulted, raised up, adorned, raised high, praised; yet beyond all of those blessings, songs, praises, words of consolation, which we say in this world. And say, Amen.

THE CONGREGATION: Amen.

THE FAMILY:

May great peace [descend] from heaven, [and] life for us and for all Israel. And say Amen.

THE CONGREGATION: Amen.

Now the final part is repeated in Hebrew:

THE FAMILY:
He who makes peace in the heights will make peace for us and for all Israel. And say Amen.

The family of the deceased as well as the assembled mourners now shovel earth on to the body, until the grave is filled. Then two lines are formed, leading away from the grave, and the mourners are given the following blessing: 'May the Omnipresent comfort you among the other mourners of Zion and Jerusalem.' The appeal to Zion and Jerusalem, of course, refers to the Temple of old, which people mourn until the coming restoration; it is thus the only messianic and eschatological reference. The family mourners remain at home for a mourning period of seven days and continue to recite the *kaddish* for eleven months. There is in all of this no appeal to a presence other than God's, no metamorphosis of death into something more.

But death does not mark the end of life. In God's time, the dead will live again. The resurrection of the dead stands for the thoroughgoing metamorphosis of a this-worldly experience: death stands for the opposite, life eternal. In the law of Judaism, the response to the anticipated transformation takes the form of a particular and strict rule against autopsy or any disfiguring of the corpse. The dead will live, therefore the body must be preserved as in life, so far as one can, for the coming resurrection. Israel, the holy community, transcends death. No chapter in the master narrative tells that story: the entire narrative embodies it. That is the fundamental conviction of Judaism, repeated in public worship three times daily in the second of the Eighteen Benedictions we shall meet in the next chapter:

Your might, Lord, is eternal; your saving power brings the dead to life again.

You sustain the living with loving kindness, with great mercy you bring the dead to life again.

You support the fallen, heal the sick, free the captives, and keep faith with those who sleep in the dust.

Who can compare with your might, O Lord and King?

You are master over life and death and deliverance.

Faith are you in bringing the dead to life again.

Praised are you, lord, master over life and death.[16]

The occasion of death, then, is transformed both in deed and in doctrine by the belief in the resurrection, and that belief is tied to the final judgement at which Israel attains its ultimate salvation at the end of time. But on the occasion of death, the story has not yet run its course; it is not time to take up the narrative.

Israel and the Israelite at Life's Turning Points

Where, then, do the chapters of Israel's story pervade the everyday life of the Judaism's Israelite, and where does the master narrative fall silent, leaving the Israelite to tell his or her unique and personal tale? What decides is this criterion: does the event in the individual Israelite's life affect the condition of the holy community of Israel? Then the pertinent chapter of Israel's story imposes itself on the shaping and meaning of the event. But when what happens to the Israelite has no bearing on Israel's public, social order, then the public narrative of Judaism gives way to the Israelite's private story; the 'we' encompassing the 'I' falls silent, leaving the still small voice of the unique person.

To grasp the difference, we have to call to mind the Judaic doctrine concerning the individual. Once born into Israel (by nature or by choice), the unique individual, in God's image, lives for ever in its individuality. The belief in the resurrection of the dead at the end of days illuminates all else. The Israelite (with few exceptions) rises from the grave, is judged, and enters into Eden or the world to come. The corporate community is affected by Israel's own creation: a birth, a marriage or a conversion all represent public events of eternal consequence. Israel is augmented, for a soul has come into life, never again to perish for all eternity. Who would not take note? Surely Abraham and Sarah celebrate, and Elijah once more is confounded. Birth, conversion, and marriage, these constitute events for Israel, marking the advent of new life, in birth or conversion, and a new Eden, in marriage.

But two noteworthy stages in the passage through life and beyond, reaching the age of responsibility, passing to the grave for the interval from death to resurrection, do not change the condition of all Israel.

Israelites live for ever, and one by one and all together they constitute the Israel that endures for all eternity; time and change, either maturity or death, make no difference once life eternal has begun.

5
God in the Here and Now

Israel meets God at the Red Sea, at Mount Sinai, in the wilderness, and intersecting with historical time, in losing the Land and at the end of days being restored to the Land. But what of ordinary life: what story imposes sense and meaning in the workaday world? How does the transformation by the master narrative take place in the everyday and the here and now?

There are three critical transactions of the ordinary weekday at which the Israelite meets God: eating a meal while acknowledging who affords nourishment and what a meal calls to mind; reciting the obligatory prayers three times a day; and devoting some portion of each day to studying the Torah, understood as God's word. These occasions stand out even among the constant round of acts of sanctification and experience of the sacred in which a pious person engages. At a meal the entire Israelite story is invoked, past, present and future. Praying three times a day forms an act of direct address to God, as 'you', on the part of the Israelites, 'we'. Time spent studying the Torah is the climax, when God speaks to Israel through a passage of the Torah.

Eating

Sustaining life, which is a gift from God, involves two matters: first, what Israelites are to eat or refrain from eating; and second, how they are to eat. Scripture, for example Leviticus 11–15, as interpreted by the rabbinic sages in the oral part of the Torah, specifies a variety of foods that may or may not be eaten. All fruits and vegetables are permitted, so too fish that have fins and scales, but not scavengers or bottom-feeders. For meat, only animals that have cloven hoofs and chew the cud may be consumed by Israelites ('kosher' or suitable meat). Animals must be slaughtered with a perfectly sharp knife, swiftly to prevent suffering, with the recitation of a blessing; the blood is drained, and the meat inspected for blemishes and indications of disease. 'You shall not boil a kid in its mother's milk' (Exodus 23:19) is understood by the sages to mean also not consuming dairy products for a span of time after eating meat (from two to six hours, depending on the custom), and two sets of dishes, one for meat, the other for dairy products, are required.

In general, the food regulations form an exercise in sanctification, a perpetual discipline of divine service; obedience to God's will in the humblest transactions of everyday life. Among contemporary practitioners of Judaism practice varies, with Reform Judaism not requiring the observance of dietary rules and Orthodox Judaism strictly keeping those rules. It is not uncommon for Conservative Jews to keep the dietary laws at home but to ignore them when eating outside the home. Most public institutions of the Jewish community of the Diaspora and Israeli government facilities follow the dietary rules. So much for the 'what' of eating.

The 'how' is more readily grasped. The meal presents itself as an occasion of thanksgiving, which encompasses the entirety of the story Judaism tells. To put matters simply: every time the faithful Israelite eats a meal, he or she rehearses the whole Judaic narrative – Land, exile, redemption – every chapter. Blessings before eating food and an elaborate grace after each meal transform the act of nourishment to a direct encounter with God, deemed to provide the food that is eaten, and a reprise of Israel's condition in time and eternity. The secular facts of hunger and satisfaction now are made, in an exact sense, to *embody* exile and return, sin and remission of sin, this world and the world to come. The blessing before eating food and the grace afterwards work out the meaning of a metaphor, and three meals a day transform the here and now into something other. The routine experience of hunger and satisfaction changes into a metaphor for Israel's life of anguished reality but ultimate redemption. So a meal turns into a moment of communion with the meaning of life as part of Israel, God's people.

One psalm prefaces the grace on routine weekdays; another is sung on sabbaths and festivals. The two, quite naturally, form a match and a complement. Let us consider them in sequence, first for the everyday:

By the rivers of Babylon, there we sat down and wept, when we remembered Zion . . . If I forget you, O Jerusalem, let my right hand wither away! Let my tongue cleave to the roof of my mouth if I do not remember you, if I do not set Jerusalem above my highest joy![1]

Now for the sabbath or festival days:

When the Lord restored the fortunes of Zion, we were like those who dream. Our mouth was filled with laughter, and our tongue with shouts of joy . . . Restore our fortunes, O Lord, like the streams in the dry land. May those who sow in tears reap with shouts of joy![2]

On weekdays Israel at table is located in the here and now of exile; on the sabbath or festival we refer to the then and there of Zion as the world of redemption and salvation. If we did not know a thing about the sabbath, from the liturgy and its contrasts we should be able to reconstruct the difference between the holy sabbath and the secular days of the week and know that the sabbath represents Israel's salvation in the here and now.

But more strikingly: the eating of a meal involves more than an individual's eating food. Predictably, it involves 'us', Israel today, at this table, with history and destiny. The humble act of eating invokes the specific moments, time past on weekdays, time future on holy days, that make the group distinctive, with a destiny all its own. So the setting of the meal tells Israelites that they represent more than who, when they sat down because they were hungry, they thought they were. It identifies the experience of hunger with one historical moment, the satisfaction of hunger with another: 'We hungered but were fed and will have enough.' From the 'I' and the here and now, the occasion of the meal has moved people to the 'we' of time and eternity.

Now to the action. The grace after meals is comprised of four principal paragraphs, moving from the here and the now to the time to come, from the meal just eaten to the messianic banquet. We start with the ordinary and say what is required, which is thanks for a real meal in today's world:

Blessed are you, Lord our God, king of the universe, who nourishes all the world by his goodness, in grace, in mercy, and in compassion: he gives bread to all flesh, for his mercy is everlasting. And because of his great goodness we have never lacked, and so may we never lack, sustenance, for the sake of his great name. For he nourishes and feeds everyone, is good to all, and provides food for each one of the creatures he created. *Blessed are you, O Lord, who feeds everyone.*

This first paragraph leaves those present where they were: at the table at which they ate their meal. It effects no transformation, and simply expresses the unexceptional thought that God has given food, which any religious person may affirm. Now comes the first unanticipated statement:

We thank you, Lord our God, for having given our fathers as a heritage a pleasant, good and spacious Land; for having taken us out of the land of Egypt, for having redeemed us from the house of bondage; for your covenant, which you have set as a seal in our flesh, for your Torah which you have taught us, for your statutes which you have made known to us, for the life of grace and mercy you have graciously bestowed upon us, and for the nourishment with which you do nourish us and feed us always, every day, in every season, and every hour.

For all these things, Lord our God, we thank and praise you; may your praises continually be in the mouth of every living thing, as it is written, 'And you shall eat and be satisfied, and bless the Lord your God for the good Land which he hath given you.' *Blessed are you, O Lord, for the Land and its food.*

The diners have now moved from what they have eaten to *where* they have eaten. But that introduces a dissonant note. The thanks go for more than the food. Now the grace refers to a 'good and spacious Land' meaning only what Judaism knows as the Land of Israel; to 'us', not me; to 'our fathers'; to having been taken 'out of the land of Egypt', to having been redeemed from slavery; to a covenant 'in my flesh', to Torah and statutes; and on and on, down to land and food.

The master narrative once more has imposed itself whole and complete. A considerable realm of being has taken over everyday reality. Now on the occasion of a cheese sandwich the entire sacred history of Israel comes into play, from the exodus from Egypt to the circumcision of my penis. All are invoked for a single occasion, a meal, which marks a human experience that has changed one's condition from hunger to satisfaction. The occasion points towards the end as well:

O Lord our God, have pity on your people Israel, on your city Jerusalem, on Zion the place of your glory, on the royal house of David your Messiah, and on the great and holy house which is called by your name. Our God, our Father, feed us and speed us, nourish us and make us flourish, unstintingly, O Lord our God, speedily free us from all distress.

And let us not, O Lord our God, find ourselves in need of gifts from flesh and blood, or of a loan from anyone save from your full, generous, abundant, wide-open hand; so we may never be humiliated, or put to shame.

O rebuild Jerusalem, the holy city, speedily in our day. *Blessed are you, Lord, who in mercy will rebuild Jerusalem. Amen.*

The climax refers to Jerusalem, Zion, David, the Messiah, the Temple, where God was sustained in times past; then dependence on God alone, not on mortals; and the rebuilding of Jerusalem. All of these closely related symbols invoke the single consideration of time at its end: the coming of the Messiah and the conclusion of history as we now know it. The opening psalms have prepared us for this appeal to the end-time: exile on weekdays, return to Zion on sabbaths and holy days.

Blessed are you, Lord our God, king of the universe, thou God, who art our Father, our powerful king, our creator and redeemer, who made us, our holy one, the holy one of Jacob, our shepherd, shepherd of Israel, the good king, who visits his goodness upon all; for every single day he has brought good, he does bring good, he will bring good upon us; he has rewarded us, does reward, and will always reward us, with grace, mercy and compassion, amplitude, deliverance and prosperity, blessing and salvation, comfort and a living, sustenance, pity and peace, and all good; let us not want any manner of good whatever.

This concluding paragraph returns us to the point at which we began: thanks for lunch. Of the four paragraphs, the first and the fourth, the one at hand, which multiplies prayers for future grace alongside thanks for goodness now received, begin and end in the here and now. The two in the middle invoke a different being altogether.

The transformation of the ordinary into the unusual effected by the reminder of holy land and sacred history moves present time and perceived space from now to then – then-past and then-future. In seeing matters in this way, Judaism perceives things as other than what they are, all through the power of the story. What has happened at the meal? The diner was hungry and ate, a commonplace, entirely secular action. But the experience of hunger and of eating is turned through the story that is told into an encounter with another world of meaning altogether. The rite, an act of thought and imagination, transforms time and space, moving the diners from nowhere in particular to a very particular place, changing those present into actors in eternity.

Praying

The master narrative is always in the background of Jewish prayers, referred to, while its implications are translated into rules of engagement that govern God's response to Israel's prayer. That God hears and answers prayer is a leitmotif of the master narrative. And principal elements of same grand story, for instance, the story of God's creating the world, forming Israel at Sinai through the Torah, and ultimate redemption of Israel at the end of time as at the crossing of the Red Sea, figure prominently. To put the matter differently, without knowing the story that Judaism tells, the prayers that Israelites recite lack context and coherence.

Prayer in Judaism is obligatory and may be voluntary as well. The community and its members pray upon rising, at dusk and after dark. Public prayers encompass three important matters: to whom is the prayer addressed, the petition that is presented, and the identification of the community by whom the petition is set forth. These take shape in the recitation of 'the Shema' ('Hear . . .', from the first word, 'Hear O Israel . . .') or creed twice daily, morning and night; the petition, called The Prayer (also known as the Amidah or Eighteen Benedictions) at the three specified times, for the needs and welfare of the community and the individual and the prayer identifying the community in its larger setting, called 'Aleinu' ('It is our duty . . .'); this is also said morning, dusk and night.

As we examine the texts that everywhere define obligatory prayer, we find a systematic and comprehensive handbook of the faith, its conception of the One before whom Israel stands in prayer, its programme of belief in divine providence and mercy, and its definition of itself. Thus we learn to whom Israel accounts itself as responsible and obligated; what it seeks in response; and how it understands itself within the realm of humanity at large. But these represent only the systematization and abstract formulation of the master narrative. God is creator of the world, made self-manifest in the Torah, aiming at redemption through the restoration of Israel to the Land, Adam to Eden. Israel, for its part, in formal prayer, petitions God for blessings, at the same time acknowledging the blessings of the sacred narrative: shield of the patriarchs and matriarchs, keeping faith with those that sleep in the ground, sacred and holy God. And as Israel turns from addressing God to the workaday world, the embodied community reminds itself of who it is and why God cares. None of these statements of direct address is comprehensible outside of the framework of the narrative: the story and its images impart sense to the experience in the here and now for those that recapitulate it.

The Shema

Evening and morning, Israel individually and communally proclaims the unity and uniqueness of God. The proclamation is preceded and followed by blessings. The whole constitutes the creed of the Jewish faith. The three elements of the Shema cover Creation, revelation and redemption, that is to say, God as creator of the world, God as revealer of the Torah and God as redeemer of Israel. The recital of the Shema is introduced by a celebration of God as creator of the world. In the morning (ideally at sunrise), the individual, in community or not, recites these preliminary benedictions:

Praised are you, O Lord our God, king of the universe.
You fix the cycles of light and darkness;
You ordain the order of all Creation
You cause light to shine over the earth;
Your radiant mercy is upon its inhabitants.
In your goodness the work of Creation
Is continually renewed day by day . . .
O cause a new light to shine on Zion;
May we all soon be worthy to behold its radiance.
Praised are you, O Lord, creator of the heavenly bodies.

The corresponding prayer in the evening refers to the setting of the sun:

Praised are you . . .

Your command brings on the dusk of evening.

Your wisdom opens the gates of heaven to a new day.

With understanding you order the cycles of time;

Your will determines the succession of seasons;

You order the stars in their heavenly courses.

You create day, and you create night,

Rolling away light before darkness . . .

Praised are you, O Lord, for the evening dusk.[3]

So Creation embodies God's will and plan, and Israel takes note. Morning and evening, Israel responds to the natural order of the world with thanks and praise of God who created the world and who actively guides the daily events of nature. Whatever happens in nature gives testimony to the sovereignty of the Creator. And that testimony takes shape in the ordinary events: sunrise and sunset. These, especially, evoke the religious response to set the stage for what follows.

For Israel God is not merely Creator, but purposeful Creator. His purpose is set forth in the Torah. For Israel God is made known in the Torah, the mark not merely of divine sovereignty, but of divine grace and love, source of life here and now and in eternity. So goes the second blessing:

Deep is your love for us, O Lord our God;

Bounteous is your compassion and tenderness.

You taught our fathers the laws of life,

And they trusted in you, Father and king,

For their sake be gracious to us, and teach us,

That we may learn your laws and trust in you.

Father, merciful Father, have compassion upon us:

Endow us with discernment and understanding.

Grant us the will to study your Torah,

To heed its words and to teach its precepts . . .

Enlighten our eyes in your Torah,

Open our hearts to your commandments . . .

Unite our thoughts with singleness of purpose

To hold you in reverence and in love . . .

You have drawn us close to you;

We praise you and thank you in truth.

With love do we thankfully proclaim your unity.

And praise you who chose your people Israel in love.

In these blessings before the declaration of the faith, then, the important point is that we refer in abstract language to the concrete narratives of creation and Sinai. The narrative gives concreteness to the abstractions of theology, and the theology translates the implications of the narrative into generalizations, complete with evidence and argument. Then the liturgy turns the whole into the language of dialogue between Israel and God: 'You' and 'we'.

In the Shema, the Torah leads Israel to enunciate the chief of its revelations: 'Hear, O Israel, the Lord our God, the Lord is One.' This proclamation is followed by three scriptural passages. The first is Deuteronomy 6:5–9: 'You shall love the Lord your God with all your heart, and with all your soul, and with all your might.' And further, one must diligently teach one's children these words and talk of them everywhere and always, and place them on one's forehead, doorposts and gates. The second set of verses is Deuteronomy 11:13–21, which emphasizes that if Jews keep the commandments, they will enjoy worldly blessings; but that if they do not, they will be punished and disappear from the good Land God gives them. The third is Numbers 15:37–41, the commandment to wear fringes on the corners of one's garments.[4]

The final component of the recitation of the Shema completes the trilogy by reciting the story of God's redemption of Israel at the Red Sea, model for God's redemption of Israel at the end of days. So God the Creator and Revealer of the Torah now gives way to God as Redeemer:

You are our king and our fathers' king,

Our redeemer and our fathers' redeemer.

You are our creator . . .

You have ever been our redeemer and deliverer

There can be no God but you . . .

You, O Lord our God, rescued us from Egypt;

You redeemed us from the house of bondage . . .

You split apart the waters of the Red Sea,

The faithful you rescued, the wicked drowned . . .

Then your beloved sang hymns of thanksgiving . . .

They acclaimed the king, God on high,
Great and awesome source of all blessings,
The ever-living God, exalted in his majesty.
He humbles the proud and raises the lowly;
He helps the needy and answers his people's call . . .
Then Moses and all the children of Israel
Sang with great joy this song to the Lord:
Who is like you O Lord among the mighty?
Who is like you, so glorious in holiness?
So wondrous your deeds, so worthy of praise!
The redeemed sang a new song to you;
They sang in chorus at the shore of the sea,
Acclaiming your sovereignty with thanksgiving:
The Lord shall reign for ever and ever.
Rock of Israel, arise to Israel's defence!
Fulfil your promise to deliver Judah and Israel.
Our redeemer is the Holy One of Israel,
The Lord of hosts in his name.
Praised are you, O Lord, redeemer of Israel.

The congregation repeats the exultant song of Moses and the people at the Red Sea not as scholars making a learned allusion, but as participants in the salvation of old. We recall in this connection the admonition at the Passover ceremony for Israelites to see themselves as redeemed from Egyptian bondage. Here is how the act of liberation is recalled and renewed. Then at prayer the people turn to the future and ask that Israel once more be redeemed. But what exactly is meant by redemption, and is it a matter of past and future alone, but not of the present? This prayer says that when the needy are helped, when the proud are humbled and the lowly are raised – in such commonplace daily events – redemption is already present. And that explicit statement alerts us to what is happening in the act of prayer.

Prayer turns the story into an account of the acutely present situation of Israel. Creation, revelation and redemption represent the here and now of Israel's everyday experience, and the act of reciting these prayers serves to transform the commonplace events of nature and the social order – sunrise, provision for the poor – into echoes of Israel's embodied life with God. In simple language: just as Creation is not only in the beginning but happens every day, morning and night, so redemption is not only at the Red Sea, but every day, in humble events. Just as revelation was not at Sinai alone, but takes place whenever people study the Torah or whenever God opens their hearts to the commandments. When at the outset I said, to practise Judaism is to take the Torah personally, this is what I meant: to turn the implications of the Torah and its narrative into direct speech to God.

The great cosmic events of Creation in the beginning, redemption at the Red Sea, and revelation at Sinai, are everywhere, every day, near at hand. Israel views secular reality from the perspective of eternal, ever-recurrent events. What happens to Israel and to the world, whether good or evil, always falls into the pattern revealed of old and made manifest each day. Historical events produce a framework in which future events will find a place and by which they will be understood. Nothing that happens cannot fit the paradigm. The principal chapters in the master narrative – Creation, the Exodus from Egypt, and the revelation of the Torah at Sinai – are commemorated and celebrated, not merely to tell the story of what once was and is no more, but to recreate out of the raw materials of everyday life the 'true being': life as it was, always is, and will be for ever. At prayer Israel repeatedly refers to the crucial elements of its corporate being, thus uncovering the sacred both in nature and in history. What happens in the proclamation of the Shema is that the particular events of Creation – sunset and sunrise – evoke in response the celebration of the power and the love of God, of his justice and mercy, and of revelation and redemption.

The Prayer

The immense statement of the creed in the Shema gives way to the second of the three required components of obligatory public worship, *The Prayer* par excellence, comprised on weekdays of prayers of petition. What the community asks for, always in the plural, concerns public welfare and covers matters we should today assign to the category of public policy as much as personal need. In the morning, noon and evening these weekday prayers of petition are called 'the Eighteen Benedictions' (Hebrew: *shemoneh-esreh*), although they are actually requests concluding with a blessing. Some of these, in particular those at the beginning and the end, recur in sabbath and festival prayers.

The Prayer is also called the 'Amidah', meaning the prayer said standing; it is said silently. Each individual prays by and for himself or herself, but in community, together with other silent, praying individuals. The prayer is then repeated aloud by the prayer leader, for encounter with God through prayer is both private and public, individual and collective. To contemplate the power of these prayers imagine a room full of people, all standing by themselves yet in close proximity, some swaying this way and that, all addressing themselves directly and intimately to God, some silently and some in a whisper. They do not move their feet, for they are now standing before the King of Kings, and it is not appropriate to shift and shuffle. If spoken to, they will not answer. Their attention is fixed upon the words of supplication, praise and gratitude. When they begin, they genuflect, and again towards the end, and at the conclusion they step back and withdraw from the Presence.

These, on ordinary days, are the words they say. The introductory three paragraphs define the One to whom petition is addressed, the God of the founders, who is omnipotent and holy.

Praised are you, Lord our God and God of our fathers, God of Abraham, God of Isaac and God of Jacob, great, mighty, revered God, exalted, who bestows loving kindness and is master of all things, who remembers the acts of loyalty of the founders and who in love will bring a redeemer to their descendants for his great name's sake. King, helper, savior and shield, praised are you, Lord, shield of Abraham.

You are powerful for ever, Lord, giving life to the dead. You are great in acts of salvation. You sustain the living in loyalty and bring the dead to life in great mercy, holding up the falling, healing the sick, freeing the prisoners, and keeping faith with those who sleep in the dust. Who is like you, Almighty, and who is compared to you, King who kills and gives life and brings salvation to spring up. And you are trusted to give life to the dead. Praised are you, Lord, who gives life to the dead.

We shall sanctify your name in the world just as they sanctify it in the heights of heaven . . . Holy, holy, holy is the Lord of hosts, the whole earth is full of his glory . . .

On weekdays petitionary prayers follow, each concluding by blessing God ('Praised are you . . .').

Wisdom—Repentance

You graciously endow man with intelligence;
You teach him knowledge and understanding.
Grant us knowledge, discernment, and wisdom.
Praised are you, O Lord, for the gift of knowledge.

Our Father, bring us back to your Torah.
Our King, draw us near to your service;
Lead us back to you truly repentant.
Praised are you, O Lord who welcomes repentance.

Forgiveness—Redemption

Our Father, forgive us, for we have sinned;
Our King, pardon us, for we have transgressed;
You forgive sin and pardon transgression.
Praised are you, gracious and forgiving Lord.

Behold our affliction and deliver us.
Redeem us soon for the sake of your name,
For you are the mighty Redeemer.
Praised are you, O Lord, Redeemer of Israel.

Heal Us—Bless Our Years

Heal us, O Lord, and we shall be healed;
Help us and save us, for you are our glory.
Grant perfect healing for all our afflictions,
O faithful and merciful God of healing.
Praised are you, O Lord, Healer of his people.

O Lord our God! Make this a blessed year;
May its varied produce bring us happiness.
Bring blessing upon the whole earth.
Bless the year with your abounding goodness.
Praised are you, O Lord, who blesses our years.

Gather Our Exiles—Reign Over Us

Sound the great shofar to herald [our] freedom;

Raise high the banner to gather all exiles;
Gather the dispersed from the corners of the earth.
Praised are you, O Lord, who gathers our exiles.

   Restore our judges as in days of old;
Restore our counselors as in former times;
Remove from us sorrow and anguish.
Reign over us alone with loving kindness;
With justice and mercy sustain our cause.
Praised are you, O Lord, King who loves justice.

Humble the Arrogant—Sustain the Righteous
   Frustrate the hopes of those who malign us;
Let all evil very soon disappear;
Let all your enemies be speedily destroyed.
May you quickly uproot and crush the arrogant;
May you subdue and humble them in our time.
Praised are you, O Lord, who humbles the arrogant.

   Let your tender mercies, O Lord God, be stirred
For the righteous, the pious, the leaders of Israel,
Toward devoted scholars and faithful proselytes.
Be merciful to us of the house of Israel;
Reward all who trust in you;
Cast our lot with those who are faithful to you.
May we never come to despair, for our trust is in you.
Praised are you, O Lord, who sustains the righteous.

Favor Your City and Your People
Have mercy, O Lord, and return to Jerusalem, your city;
May your presence dwell there as you promised.
Rebuild it now, in our days and for all time;
Re-establish there the majesty of David, your servant.
Praised are you, O Lord, who rebuilds Jerusalem.

   Bring to flower the shoot of your servant David.
Hasten the advent of the messianic redemption;
Each and every day we hope for your deliverance.
Praised are you, O Lord, who assures our deliverance.

   O Lord, our God, hear our cry!

Have compassion upon us and pity us;
Accept our prayer with loving favor.
You, O God, listen to entreaty and prayer.
O King, do not turn us away unanswered,
For you mercifully heed your people's supplication.
Praised are you, O Lord, who is attentive to prayer.
    O Lord, Our God, favor your people Israel
    Accept with love Israel's offering of prayer;
May our worship be ever acceptable to you.
May our eyes witness your return in mercy to Zion.
Praised are you, O Lord, whose presence returns to Zion.

Our Thankfulness

We thank you, O Lord our God and God of our fathers,
Defender of our lives, shield of our safety;
Through all generations we thank you and praise you.
Our lives are in your hands, our souls in your charge.
We thank you for the miracles which daily attend us,
For your wonders and favor morning, noon, and night.
You are beneficent with boundless mercy and love.
From of old we have always placed our hope in you.
For all these blessings, O our King,
We shall ever praise and exalt you.
Every living creature thanks you, and praises you in truth.
O God, you are our deliverance and our help.
Praised are you, O Lord, for your Goodness and your glory.

Peace and Well-being

Grant peace and well-being to the whole house of Israel;
Give us of your grace, your love, and your mercy.
Bless us all, O our Father, with the light of your presence.
It is your light that revealed to us your life-giving Torah,
And taught us love and tenderness, justice, mercy, and peace.
May it please you to bless your people in every season,
To bless them at all times with your fight of peace.
Praised are you, O Lord, who blesses Israel with peace.[5]

The first two petitions pertain to intelligence. Israel thanks God for mind: knowledge, wisdom, discernment. But knowledge is for a purpose, and the purpose is knowledge of the Torah. Such knowledge leads to the service of God and produces a spirit of repentance. We cannot pray without setting ourselves right with God, and that means repenting for what has separated us from God. Torah is the way to repentance. So knowledge leads to Torah, Torah to repentance, and repentance to God. The logical next step is the prayer for forgiveness, the sign of return. God forgives sin; God is gracious and forgiving. Once we discern what we have done wrong through the guidance of the Torah, we therefore seek to be forgiven. It is sin that leads to suffering. Suffering stands at the beginning of the way to God; once we have taken that way, we ask for our suffering to end; we beg for redemption. We ask for healing, salvation, a blessed year. Healing without prosperity means we may suffer in good health or starve in a robust body. So along with the prayer for healing goes the supplication for worldly comfort.

The individual's task is done. But what of the community? Health and comfort are not enough. The world is unredeemed. Jews are enslaved and in exile. At the end of days a great shofar, or ram's horn, will sound to herald the Messiah's coming. This is now begged for. Israel at prayer asks first for the proclamation of freedom, then for the ingathering of the exiles to the Promised Land. In establishing the messianic kingdom, God needs also to restore a wise and benevolent government, good judges, good advisers and loving justice. Meanwhile Israel finds itself maligned. As The Prayer sees things, the arrogant, hating Israel, hate God as well. They should be humbled. And the pious and righteous, the scholars, the faithful converts, the whole House of Israel that trusts in God, should be rewarded and sustained. Above all, God is asked to remember Jerusalem; to rebuild the city and dwell there; to set up Jerusalem's messianic king, David, and make him prosper. These are the themes of the daily prayer: personal atonement, good health and good fortune; collective redemption, freedom, the end of alienation, good government and true justice; and the final and complete salvation of the Land and of Jerusalem by the Messiah. At the end comes a prayer that prayer may be heard and found acceptable; then an expression of thanksgiving, not for what may come, but for the miracles and mercies already enjoyed morning, noon and night. And at the end is the prayer for peace, a peace that consists of wholeness for the sacred community.

Aleinu

The third component of communal worship, *Aleinu* draws the community outwards into the world. When Jews complete any service of worship, they mark the conclusion by making a statement concerning themselves in the world: the corporate community looking outwards. Like the Exodus, the moment of the congregation's departure becomes a celebration of Israel's God, a self-conscious, articulated rehearsal of Israel's peoplehood. But now it is the end, rather than the beginning, of time that is important:

It is our duty to praise him, Lord over all the world;
Let us acclaim him, author of all Creation.
He made our lot unlike that of other peoples;
He assigned to us a unique destiny.
We bend the knee, worship and acknowledge
The King of kings, the Holy One, praised is he.
He unrolled the heavens and established the earth;
His throne of glory is in the heavens above;
His majestic Presence is in the loftiest heights.
He and no other is God and faithful King.
Even as we are told in his Torah:
Remember now and always, that the Lord is God;
Remember, no other is Lord of heaven and earth.
We, therefore, hope in you, O Lord our God,
That we shall soon see the triumph of your might,
That idolatry shall be removed from the earth,
And false gods shall be utterly destroyed.
Then will the world be a true kingdom of God,
When all mankind will invoke your name,
And all the earth's wicked will return to you.
Then all the inhabitants of the world will surely know
That to you every knee must bend,
Every tongue must pledge loyalty.
Before you, O Lord, let them bow in worship,

Let them give honor to your glory.
May they all accept the rule of your kingdom.
May you reign over them soon through all time.
Sovereignty is yours in glory, now and for ever.
So it is written in your Torah:
The Lord shall reign for ever and ever.[6]

Difference becomes destiny. Israel thanks God that it enjoys a unique destiny. But the community asks that he who made their lot unlike that of all others will soon rule as sovereign over all. The secular difference, which stands for Israel's unique destiny, is for the time being only. When the destiny is fulfilled, there will be no further difference. The natural eye beholds a social group with some particular cultural characteristics defining that group. The story of peoplehood transforms difference into destiny.

The premise of obligatory public worship is simple. The existence of the natural group means little, except as testimony to the sovereignty of the God who shaped the group and rules its life. The unique, the particular, the private now are no longer profane matters of culture, but become testimonies of divine sovereignty, pertinent to all people, all groups. The particularism of the group is for the moment alone; the will of God is for eternity. When that will be done, then all people will recognize that the unique destiny of Israel was intended for everyone. The ordinary facts of sociology no longer predominate. Theology takes over, in the narrative form, the story of eternal truths, to be realized in time when God responds to Israel's presence, established through assembly for prayer.

Studying the Torah

Judaism maintains that humanity finds God in books through the act of learning. So far we have examined encounters with God that correspond to those afforded by other religions, for rites connected with eating and public worship are commonplace. But it is not ordinary for religions to equate prayer with reading and discussing books, and Judaism does just that. Torah-study brings about an encounter with God that differs from the meeting with God at prayer (including grace after meals). The difference is readily captured in the saying, 'When I pray, I speak to God. When I study the Torah, God speaks to me.' Torah-study (in Hebrew, *talmud Torah*) in the here and now recapitulates the encounter at Sinai. That is meant concretely: when Israel assembles for the study of the Torah, God is present. Do not confuse Torah-study with an academic exercise of intellectual enlightenment. It is not simply a quest for information. Learning itself constitutes an act of worship, so that knowledge acquired for the purpose of knowing God's will and word for Israel sanctifies the person who has attained it.

Piety is a prerequisite to learning from the Torah; and 'an ignorant person cannot be pious'. But is it not an exaggeration to compare learning to praying as occasions of divine encounter? On the contrary, 'God joins Israelites in their act of learning',[7] whether in community or alone. The most explicit statement in the entire rabbinic canon of where and how Israel meets God in the Torah is this:

Among ten who sit and work hard on Torah-study the Presence comes to rest, as it is said, 'God stands in the congregation of God' (Psalm 82:1) [and 'congregation' means ten people].

And how do we know that the same is so even of five? For it is said, 'And he has founded his vault upon the earth' (Amos 9:6) [sense obscure].

And how do we know that this is so even of three? Since it is said, 'And he judges among the judges' [a court being made up of three judges] (Psalm 82:1).

And how do we know that this is so even of two? Because it is said, 'Then they that feared the Lord spoke with one another, and the Lord hearkened and heard' (Malachi 3:16).

And how do we know that this is so even of one? Since it is said, 'In every place where I record my name I will come to you and I will bless you' (Exodus 20:24) [and it is in the Torah that God has recorded his name].[8]

Here is an explicit claim that Torah-study, like prayer, engages Israel with God in the here and now. The Torah encompasses not only Scripture but the oral tradition that begins at Sinai and continues down to the newest teaching of a contemporary master of the Torah. Torah studied in a holy book in the community of Israel qualifies. In ordinary practice, all Torah-study begins in one or another of the received texts, ordinarily the Pentateuch (with the authoritative commentary of Rabbi Solomon ben Isaac), the Mishnah, a passage of the Talmud, or a document of equivalent authority and sanctity. Studying under the guidance of a learned rabbi is recommended but not required to qualify as Torah-study. So one text or another qualifies, and in them all Israelites relive the encounter at Sinai and make it their own.

Whether the passage sets forth law, narrative, prophecy or theology, it will recapitulate some episode or other from the master narrative. A fresh encounter with the words of the Torah makes the story happen again at the moment of retelling, as the explicit claim of the Passover ceremony makes clear. Each person, we recall, through telling the story is as though present at the liberation; each Israelite through all time is present at Sinai. So too, in the engagement with the Torah, at public worship for example, Israel recapitulates the moment that it became Israel, having been chosen from all the peoples of the world.

That view of the Torah as the embodiment of the encounter with God at Sinai, not just the memorial and monument to what happened then but the model of what happens always, comes to concrete expression every time an Israelite is called to read the Torah and recite the blessing during a service: 'Blessed are you, Lord our God, ruler of the world, who has chosen us from all peoples by giving us the Torah. Blessed are you, who gives the Torah.' And at the end of the reading of the Torah, the Israelite invokes yet another chapter in the master narrative, the resurrection of the dead; regarding the truth of the Torah as the guarantee of life eternal: 'Blessed are you, Lord our God, ruler of the world, who has given us an authentic Torah, planting in our midst life eternal. Blessed are you, who gives the Torah.' Here is the affirmation of Israel at worship: the Torah marks our election as God's first love; the Torah guarantees to us life eternal. These are the acts of grace that take place when Israel encounters God in the Torah.

Torah-study links the master narrative to the concrete world of everyday Israel by taking a text and digressing from it to the present context, from the words of the Torah to the world beyond. Torah-study ordinarily commences with a direct citation and explanation of a received document of rabbinic learning, whether Scripture or the words of the current generation of masters of the Torah. And then the teacher and students allow their imagination to run free, their sensibility to encompass within the framework of the Torah passage at hand the here and now of their own experience as they discuss the text. (A wise master said, 'The ideal way to study the Torah is to cite a text, and then digress.') In the process of Torah-study, therefore, the issues brought *to* the Torah by the disciples possess authority too. These issues, drawn from the immediate affairs of the workaday world, come under the scrutiny of Sinai. They find their place within the story told by the Torah, the laws set forth, the theology portrayed, the prophecy pronounced therein. So Torah-study opens the outer limits of the narrative set forth in Scripture and the oral Torah, in such a way that the disciples of the Torah find in their own lives and circumstances the echoes of the Torah's story.

In Torah-study the faithful bring to Scripture the questions of contemporary circumstance. In contemporary Judaism, for example, Job serves as the medium for confronting the problem of evil: how a loving, all-powerful God can permit evil in the world. Isaiah's prophecy of the suffering servant (Isaiah 53–4) self-evidently speaks of the Jewish people in the crucible of the twentieth century. Ezekiel's vision of the resurrection of the dry bones (Ezekiel 37) strikes many as an obvious reference to what has happened to the Jewish people after the Holocaust in the restoration of the State of Israel after nearly two thousand years of Israel's exile. These represent cases in which those that study the Torah today find their deepest concerns within its text. And that is not a new or innovative approach. Torah-study as a process of discovery of the present in the revelations of the past characterizes Judaism through its entire history. It is the counterpart, in the act of learning, to identifying oneself with those that were saved by God from Egyptian bondage. In the fifth century CE the rabbinic sages found in the book of Genesis, from more than a thousand years earlier, an account of the very world that they confronted centuries after Sinai. Their interpretation is recorded in *Genesis Rabbah* ('Genesis amplified'), which was completed *c.* 450, about a century after Christianity, long persecuted and suppressed, had become the state religion of the Roman Empire. Because that event challenged Judaism at its foundations, the rabbinic sages and their disciples looked in the record of the beginning of their world, as set forth in Genesis, for guidance on how to respond to events of their own day.

The Christians claimed that they, not Judaism, possessed and understood the Israelite Scriptures. That challenge turned acute when the Christians further pointed to the establishment of Christianity by the

Roman Empire as evidence that Christ really is the Messiah. In response to these challenges to the integrity and truth of the Torah as they read it, the rabbinic sages turned to Scripture and studied it. In *Genesis Rabbah* they produced a systematic account of the meaning of the events of their own time, and a fine model of what Torah-study means and how its recapitulation of Israel's master narrative supplies the energy and dynamism that sustain Judaism. It is a verse-by-verse reading of the present in light of the past. The entire narrative of Genesis shown to point towards the sacred history of the community of Israel: its slavery and redemption; its coming Temple in Jerusalem; its exile and salvation at the end of time. The powerful message of Genesis in *Genesis Rabbah* proclaims that the world's creation commenced a single, straight line of events, leading in the end to the salvation of Israel and through Israel all humanity. Israel's history constitutes the counterpart of Creation, and the laws of Israel's salvation form the foundation of Creation. Therefore a given story out of Genesis, about Creation, the events from Adam to Noah and Noah to Abraham, the domestic affairs of the patriarchs, or Joseph, will bear a deeper message about what it means to be Israel, and what in the end of days will happen to Israel. The tradition of theological study required the sages to search in Scripture for the meaning of their own circumstances.

The single most important proposition of *Genesis Rabbah* is that in the story of the beginnings of Creation, humanity and Israel we find the message of the meaning and end of the life of the Jewish people. The deeds of the founding fathers supply signals for their descendants about what is going to come in the future. The biography of Abraham, Isaac and Jacob also constitutes a protracted account of the history of Israel later on. If the sages could announce a single proposition and argue it systematically, this is the one upon which they would insist.

I said that Torah-study involves 'digression', that is, moving from the text of the Torah to the world of those that are its living disciples. So how exactly did the rabbis' study of Genesis solve the problem represented by the Christianization of Rome? Their attention was focused on the sequence of world empires to which, among other nations, Israel had been or was now subjugated: Babylonia, Media, Greece, and above all Rome. What would happen next? The sages maintained that beyond the rule of Rome lay the salvation of Israel:

'And it came to pass in the days of Amraphel, king of Shinar' (Genesis 14:1) refers to Babylonia.

'Arioch, king of Ellasar' (Genesis 14:1) refers to Greece.

'Chedorlaomer, king of Elam' (Genesis 14:1) refers to Media.

'And Tidal, king of Goiim [nations]' (Genesis 14:1) refers to the wicked government [Rome], which conscripts troops from all the nations of the world.

Said Rabbi Eleazar bar Abina, 'If you see that the nations contend with one another, look for the footsteps of the king-messiah. You may know that that is the case, for lo, in the time of Abraham, because the kings struggled with one another, a position of greatness came to Abraham.'[9]

Here study of the Torah yields a striking reading of Genesis 14:1, since it links the events of the life of Abraham to the history of Israel and even ties the whole to the messianic expectation. History flows in both directions. Abraham's actions prefigured those of his heirs, Israel. But what they did later on reciprocally imposed limitations on Abraham. Time and again events in the lives of the patriarchs prefigure the four empires, among which the fourth, last, and most intolerable was Rome.

Torah-study still finds in Scripture counterparts to contemporary heroes and villains. For example, when in the years from 1933 onward, Jews in Germany observed Purim (the festival that celebrates the story in the book of Esther of how the Jews were saved from Haman's plan to murder all of them), no one had to be reminded of how the Torah portrayed their own difficult times. German secret police supervising Jewish worship in the Nazi period heard 'Haman', but the congregation of Israel heard 'Hitler'. In the fourth and fifth centuries, the rabbinic sages found Rome in Scripture in Israel's counterpart and opposite, Jacob's brother and enemy, Esau. Esau claimed a common ancestry with Jacob just as, in their Old Testament, Christianity (now identified with Rome) claimed possession of the Hebrew Scriptures that Judaism knew as the Torah.

'[When the boys grew up,] Esau was a skilful hunter [a man of the field, while Jacob was a quiet man, dwelling in tents]' (Genesis 25:27).

He hunted people through snaring them in words [as the Roman prosecutors do]: 'Well enough, you did not steal. But who stole with you? You did not kill, but who killed with you?'

Rabbi Abbahu said, 'He was a trapper and a fieldsman, trapping at home and in the field.

'He trapped at home: "How do you tithe salt?" [which does not, in fact, have to be tithed at all!]

'He trapped in the field: "How do people give tithe for straw?" [which does not, in fact, have to be tithed at all!]'

Rabbi Hiyya bar Abba said, 'He treated himself as totally without responsibility for himself, like a field [on which anyone tramples].'[10]

The rabbis' point is, Rome rules, but its rule is illicit and temporary. When matters are rightly done, Rome (Esau) will give way to Israel (Jacob), which possesses the birthright. But the urgent question was, what would happen after Esau's reign?

'And Jacob sent messengers before him' (Genesis 32:3).

To this one [Esau] whose time to take hold of sovereignty would come before him [Jacob; since Esau would rule, then Jacob].

Rabbi Joshua ben Levi said, 'Jacob took off the purple robe and threw it before Esau, as if to say to him, "Two flocks of starlings are not going to sleep on a single branch" [we cannot rule at the same time].'[11]

Torah-study has a powerful dynamism, which is due to the active, contentious character of learning in Judaism. The examples we have looked at do not replicate the principal trait of the religious activity of Torah-study: it is an activity of real people, living ordinary lives, people who like to argue. Torah-study requires sustained, rigorous argument, which yields well-reasoned results. God himself is compelled by these arguments and by exercises in applied reason and practical logic. So in Torah-study, Israelites enter into the very mind of God. The Talmud of Babylonia presents a story that shows how the great masters engaged in vigorous argument, and how God followed the discussion and responded to it by accepting the compelling quality of their reasoning. The debate concerns the status, as to susceptibility to cultic uncleanness, of a certain kind of oven when it is dismantled and so no longer suitable for use. One authority holds it is then rendered useless and so unsusceptible to uncleanness. The other, the sages, who form the majority and so decide the law, maintain that the oven is potentially useful and so remains a susceptible object. Argument does not suffice, so the besieged rabbi invokes nature. The sages reject miracles, maintaining that reason alone dictates what is true:

There we have learned in the Mishnah: If one cut [a clay oven] into parts and put sand between the parts,

Rabbi Eliezer declares the oven broken-down and therefore insusceptible to uncleanness.

And sages declare it susceptible [Mishnah-tractate *Kelim* 5:10] . . .

On that day Rabbi Eliezer produced all of the arguments in the world, but they did not accept them from him. So he said to them, 'If the law accords with my position, this carob tree will prove it.'

The carob was uprooted from its place by a hundred cubits, and some say, four hundred cubits.

They said to him, 'There is no proof from a carob tree.'

So he went and said to them, 'If the law accords with my position, let the stream of water prove it.'

The stream of water reversed flow.

They said to him, 'There is no proof from a stream of water.'

So he went and said to them, 'If the law accords with my position, let the walls of the yeshiva prove it.'

The walls of the yeshiva tilted toward falling.

Rabbi Joshua rebuked them, saying to them, 'If disciples of sages are contending with one another in matters of law, what business do you have?'

They did not fall on account of the honour owing to Rabbi Joshua, but they also did not straighten up on account of the honour owing to Rabbi Eliezer, and to this day they are still tilted.

Nature's miracles do not suffice. But heaven, meaning God himself, witnessing the argument will now be asked to intervene:

So he went and said to them, 'If the law accords with my position, let the Heaven prove it!'

An echo came forth, saying, 'What business have you with Rabbi Eliezer, for the law accords with his position under all circumstances!'

Rabbi Joshua stood up on his feet and said, ' "It [the Torah] is not in heaven" (Deuteronomy 30:12).'

What is the sense of, 'It is not in heaven?'

Said Rabbi Jeremiah, '[The sense of Joshua's statement is this:] For the Torah has already been given from Mount Sinai, so we do not pay attention to echoes, since you have already written in the Torah at Mount Sinai, ''After the majority you are to incline'' (Exodus 23:2).' [So the sages declare the law of the Torah, and God can no longer intervene. Logic overcomes the authority even of heaven.]

Rabbi Nathan came upon [the prophet] Elijah [whom we last met at the covenant of the circumcision, and who is everywhere all the time] and said to him, 'What did the Holy One, blessed be he, do at that moment?'

He said to him, 'He laughed and said, ''My children have overcome me, my children have overcome me!'' '[12]

In that phrase, always quoted in accounts of Torah-study, the energy and dynamism of Torah-study illuminate the hour. God affirms the right of humanity to engage in exercises of reason, and logic pierces mountains. God rejoices when humanity argues its views and overcomes even his, God's, own announced view.

The final point draws us back from the sublime to ordinary life with God. Who, in fact, engages in Torah-study? Ordinary Jews study the Torah, when and as best they can. It is not an activity for a Mandarin class of elite, professional scholars but for everybody; not just masters and disciples in yeshivas (talmudic academies), but ordinary people. Torah-study is the métier of millions of simple Jews who practise Judaism, represented by the tens of thousands who fill Madison Square Garden in New York City, one of the world's great venues for mass meetings, every three years to celebrate the conclusion of a period during which all of them have studied the entire Talmud of Babylonia.

Pious Jews come to morning worship on weekdays and spend a few minutes studying a passage of Scripture or the Mishnah, then go to their jobs and their businesses and live out their day. These humble folk, Israel's true elite, hear the words of the Torah and remember them. And as the day unfolds, sometimes something that happens reminds them of some words that they have learned in Torah-study. And at that moment of realization, as the rabbinic sage Rabbi Halafta says, God comes to that person and bestows a blessing.

6

The Story of the Good Life: Judaism's Ethical Imperatives

The main point of the Torah, stated simply, is this: the Torah, written and oral, aims at transforming Adam into Israel, and Israel into God's image, after God's likeness, which was God's original plan. But God created all humanity 'in our image, after our likeness', and the qualities that in humanity replicate God's traits cannot, therefore, be set forth in language particular to Israel. Ethical imperatives are addressed by God in the Torah to Israel, but they pertain to all humanity, defining what it means to be a human being. The Talmud phrases what is at stake in simple sayings such as, 'The All-Merciful wants the heart', 'The commandments were given only to purify humanity', and the like. Scripture itself is explicit: 'You shall not hate your brother in your heart, but you shall reason with your neighbour, lest you bear sin because of him. You shall not take vengeance or bear any grudge against the sons of your own people, but you shall love your neighbour as yourself: I am the Lord' (Leviticus 19:17–18), which some authorities, in particular Hillel, the great Pharisaic master of the turn of the first century, identify as the most important law of the Torah.

'. . . but you shall love your neighbour as yourself: I am the Lord':
  Rabbi Akiva says, 'This is the encompassing principle of the Torah.'
  Rabbi ben Azzai says, ' "This is the book of the generations of Adam" (Genesis 5:1) is a still more encompassing principle [because that verse proves all humanity shares a common ancestry and forms a single family].'[1]

Right takes priority over rite, as the prophets make clear, and saving a life trumps all other religious obligations and commandments. These sayings, with their insistence on right attitude, one in which the heart of the human being willingly accedes to the will of God, stand no great distance from the story of Adam and Eve in Eden and Israel at Sinai, rebelling against God while Moses was yet on the mountain.

As far as the weight of Judaic teaching, from Scripture onwards, is concerned what matters most is ethical conduct towards one's fellow human being. That is at the heart of Judaism's story of the good life. A famous story leaves no question that right action towards other people is how the entire Torah is best summed up:

There was the case of a gentile who came before Shammai [the colleague and opponent of Hillel]. He said to him, 'Convert me on the stipulation that you teach me the entire Torah while I am standing on one foot.' He drove him off with the measuring rod that he had in his hand.

He came before Hillel: 'Convert me.'

He said to him, ' "What is hateful to you, don't do to your fellow." That's the entire Torah; all the rest is commentary. Now go, study.'[2]

Hillel is paraphrasing Leviticus 19:17–18; since the rest of the Torah elaborates that point, one should go and study the Torah to learn what is required in order to keep this golden rule.

More often than not, the highest virtue is goodwill, which encompasses every other social virtue of generosity, foresight, neighbourliness, and the rest. The worst vice is not envy, bad neighbourliness or defaulting on a loan, but ill-will, which generates all other vices:

[Rabbi Yohannan ben Zakkai, the rabbinic sage] said to them, 'Go and see what is the straight path to which someone should stick.'

Rabbi Eliezer says, 'A generous spirit.'

Rabbi Joshua says, 'A good friend.'

Rabbi Yosé says, 'A good neighbour.'

Rabbi Simeon says, 'Foresight.'

Rabbi Eleazar says, 'Goodwill.'

He said to them, 'I prefer the opinion of Rabbi Eleazar ben Arakh, because in what he says is included everything you say.'

He said to them, 'Go out and see what is the bad road, which someone should avoid.'

Rabbi Eliezer says, 'Envy.'

Rabbi Joshua says, 'A bad friend.'

Rabbi Yosé says, 'A bad neighbour.'

Rabbi Simeon says, 'Defaulting on a loan.'

(A loan owed to a human being and a loan owed to the Omnipresent, blessed be he, are the same, as it is said, 'The wicked person borrows and cannot pay back, but the righteous person is generous and gives' [Psalm 37:21].)

Rabbi Eleazar says, 'Ill will.'

He said to them, 'I prefer the opinion of Rabbi Eleazar ben Arakh, because in what he says is included everything you say.'[3]

The sage Rabbi Yohanan ben Zakai sees goodwill as the source of all specific virtues because in his view attitude and intention in the end define the human being: we are what we want to be; the world is what we want to make of it. The entire message of the Torah for the virtuous man and woman is summed up in that conviction, which, furthermore, is embodied in the law of Judaism governing the social order.

Virtue

But what God really admires is acts of selflessness. That is because these form the opposite of arrogance. The highest virtue of all, so far as the Torah is concerned, is the act that God cannot coerce but very much yearns for, which is the act of love that transcends the self. That is the point of the Shema when it says, 'You shall love the Lord your God with all your heart, and with all your soul, and with all your might', the commandment of love. But love cannot be commanded, it can only be given freely. That is why virtue begins in sincere obedience to the Torah, but reaches its pinnacle through deeds beyond the strict requirements of obedience, and even the limits of the law altogether.

A set of sublime stories convey that principle. To understand the basis for the rabbinic sages' view, we have to keep in mind two facts. First, they believed that God hears and answers prayer, and that if God answers prayer, it is a mark of his favourable recognition of the one who says it. Therefore if someone has the reputation of saying prayers that are answered, the sages want to know why. Second, they believed that Torah-study defined the highest ideal that a man could attain, and they maintained that God wanted them to live a life of Torah-study. But in these stories, they discover people who could pray with effect in ways that the sages themselves could not. And they further discovered that some people win God's favour not by lifelong devotion to divine service but by doing a single remarkable action. So the sages themselves tell us stories about how one enormous deed can outweigh a life of Torah-study. The first story concerns a poor man who asked for charity:

A certain man came before one of the relatives of Rabbi Yannai. He said to him, 'Rabbi, attain *zekut* through me [by giving me charity].'

He said to him, 'And didn't your father leave you money?'

He said to him, 'No.'

He said to him, 'Go and collect what your father left on deposit with others.'

He said to him, 'I have heard concerning property my father deposited with others that it was gained by violence [so I don't want it].'

He said to him, 'You are worthy of praying and having your prayers answered.'[4]

The word *zekut* means 'merit' or 'source of divine favour'. It is the language that is used by the beggar to the donor: you will gain merit by an act of philanthropy to me. This is self-evidently a reference to the possession of entitlement to God's favour, and it is gained, we see, through deeds that the law of the Torah cannot require but must favour: what one does of one's own volition, beyond the measure of the law. Here we see the opposite of sin. A sin is what one has done of one's own volition beyond all limits of the law. So an act that generates *zekut* for the individual is the counterpart and opposite: what one does of one's own volition that also is beyond all requirements of the law.

A more complex body of meritorious actions is set forth in the following story, which captures the entire range of virtues that Judaism values most highly:

A pious man from Kefar Imi appeared [in a dream] to the rabbis. He prayed for rain and it rained. The rabbis went up to him. His householders told them that he was sitting on a hill. They went out to him, saying to him, 'Greetings', but he did not answer them.

He was sitting and eating, and he did not say to them, 'You break bread too.'

When he went back home, he made a bundle of faggots and put his cloak on top of the bundle [instead of on his shoulder].

When he came home, he said to his household [wife], 'These rabbis are here [because] they want me to pray for rain. If I pray and it rains, it is a disgrace for them, and if not, it is a profanation of the Name of Heaven. But come, you and I will go up [to the roof] and pray. If it rains, we shall tell them, "We are not worthy to pray and have our prayers answered." '

They went up and prayed and it rained.

They came down to them [and asked], 'Why have the rabbis troubled themselves to come here today?'

They said to him, 'We wanted you to pray so that it would rain.'

He said to them, 'Now do you really need my prayers? Heaven already has done its miracle.'

They said to him, 'Why, when you were on the hill, did we say hello to you, and you did not reply?'

He said to them, 'I was then doing my job. Should I then interrupt my concentration [on my work]?'

They said to him, 'And why, when you sat down to eat, did you not say to us "You break bread too"?'

He said to them, 'Because I had only my small ration of bread. Why would I have invited you to eat by way of mere flattery [when I knew I could not give you anything at all]?'

They said to him, 'And why when you came to go down, did you put your cloak on top of the bundle?'

He said to them, 'Because the cloak was not mine. It was borrowed for use at prayer. I did not want to tear it.'

They said to him, 'And why, when you were on the hill, did your wife wear dirty clothes, but when you came down from the mountain, did she put on clean clothes?'

He said to them, 'When I was on the hill, she put on dirty clothes, so that no one would gaze at her. But when I came home from the hill, she put on clean clothes, so that I would not gaze on any other woman.'

They said to him, 'It is well that you pray and have your prayers answered.'[5]

The pious man enjoys the recognition of the sages by reason of his claim upon God, able as he is to pray and bring rain. What has so endowed him with *zekut*? Acts of punctiliousness of a moral order: concentrating on his work, avoiding an act of dissimulation, integrity in the disposition of a borrowed object, his wife's concern not to attract other men and her equal concern to make herself attractive to her husband. None of these stories refers explicitly to *zekut*; all of them tell us about what it means to enjoy not an entitlement by inheritance but a claim accomplished by one's own supererogatory acts of restraint.

But the climax is yet to come. In all three embodiments of virtue that follow, defining what the individual must do to gain *zekut*, the point is that the deeds of the heroes of the story make them worthy of having their prayers answered, which is a mark of the working of *zekut*. It is deeds beyond the strict requirements of the Torah, and even the limits of the law altogether, that transform the hero into a holy man, whose holiness served just like that of a rabbinic sage, holy due to his knowledge of the Torah. The following stories should not be understood as expressions of the mere sentimentality of the rabbis concerning the lower orders, for they deny in favour of a single action of surpassing power the sages' lifelong devotion to what they held to be the highest value, knowledge of the Torah.

A certain ass driver appeared before the rabbis [the context requires: in a dream] and prayed, and rain came. The rabbis sent for him and said, 'What is your trade?'

He said to them, 'I am an ass driver.'

They said to him, 'And how do you conduct your business?'

He said to them, 'One time I rented my ass to a certain woman, and she was weeping on the way, and I said to her, "What's the matter?" and she said to me, "The husband of that woman [me] is in prison [for debt], and I wanted to see what I can do to free him." So I sold my ass and gave her the proceeds, and I said to her, "Here is your money, free your husband, but do not sin [by becoming a prostitute to raise the necessary funds]." '

They said to him, 'You are worthy of praying and having your prayers answered.'[6]

The ass driver clearly has a powerful claim on God, so that his prayers are answered, even while those of others are not. What he did for it? He did what no law could demand: impoverished himself to save the woman from a 'fate worse than death'.

In a dream of Rabbi Abbahu, Mr Pentakaka ['Five Sins'] appeared, who prayed that rain would come, and it rained. Rabbi Abbahu summoned him. He said to him, 'What is your trade?'

He said to him, 'Five sins does that man [meaning himself] do every day [for I am a pimp]: hiring whores, cleaning up the theatre, bringing home their garments for washing, dancing, and performing before them.'

He said to him, 'And what sort of decent thing have you ever done?'

He said to him, 'One day that man [I] was cleaning the theatre, and a woman came and stood behind a pillar and cried. I said to her, "What's the matter?" And she said to me, "That woman's [my] husband is in prison, and I wanted to see what I can do to free him," so I sold my bed and cover, and I gave the proceeds to her. I said to her, "Here is your money, free your husband, but do not sin."'

He said to him, 'You are worthy of praying and having your prayers answered.'[7]

This man has done everything sinful that one can do, and, more to the point, he goes on doing it every day. So the singularity of the act of *zekut*, which suffices if done only once, encompasses its power to outweigh a life of sin: once again, an act of *zekut* is shown to be the mirror-image and opposite of sin. The one-time act of self-sacrifice of the ignorant man outweighs a whole life of Torah-learning.

Zekut forms a measure of one's own relationship with God, as the power of one person, but not another, to pray and so bring rain attests. What sort of relationship does *zekut*, as the opposite of sin, then posit? It is not one of coercion, for God cannot force us to do those types of deeds that yield *zekut*, and that, story after story suggests, is the definition of a deed that generates *zekut*: doing what we ought to do but do not have to do. But then, we cannot coerce God to do what we want done either, for example by carrying out the commandments. These are obligatory, but do not obligate God. *Zekut* pertains to deeds of a supererogatory character, to which God responds by deeds of a supererogatory character.

The simple fact that rabbis cannot pray and bring rain, but a simple ass driver can, tells the whole story. The relationship measured by *zekut*, God's response by an act of uncoerced favour to a person's uncoerced gift contains an element of unpredictability. So while I cannot coerce God, I can through *zekut* gain acts of favour from God, by doing what God cannot require of me. An act of pure selflessness – giving the woman his means of livelihood – is what gains for a man God's deepest interest. The ultimate act of virtue turns out to be an act of pure grace, to which God responds with pure grace. The extraordinary person is the one who sacrifices for the other in an act of selfless love, and that can be anybody, at any time, anywhere. That is why, for Judaism, the great commandment is one of love: 'You shall love the Lord your God with all your heart, and with all your soul, and with all your might,' as the creed of Judaism maintains. The one thing one person cannot command of another person is love. That, by definition, is freely given, or not given at all. Then virtue consists in doing on one's own what God yearns for but cannot impose, which is, to love God. That defines the goal of the Torah, and whether attained in a lifetime of study or in a single instance makes no difference.

Sin

The master narrative encompasses not only virtue but also sin. Defined by the first sin, the one committed by man in Eden, sin is an act of rebellion against God. Rebellion takes two forms. As a gesture of omission, sin embodies the failure to carry out one's obligation to God set forth in the Torah. As one of commission, it constitutes an act of defiance. In both cases sin comes about by reason of man's intention to reject the will of God, set forth in the Torah. However accomplished, whether through omission or commission, an act becomes sinful because of the attitude that accompanies it. That is why man is responsible for sin, answerable for it to God in particular, who may be said to take the matter personally, just as it is meant. The consequence of sin is death for the individual, exile and estrangement for holy Israel, and disruption for the world.

Since sin represents an act of rebellion against God, God has a big stake in the matter. It follows that sin in public is worse than sin in private, since in public one's sin profanes God's name:

Said Rabbi Abbahu in the name of Rabbi Hanina, 'It is better for someone to transgress in private but not profane the Name of Heaven in public: "As for you, house of Israel, thus says the Lord God: Go, serve every one of you his idols, now and hereafter, if you will not obey me; but my holy name you shall not profane" (Ezekiel 20:39).'

Said Rabbi Ilai the Elder, 'If someone sees that his impulse to sin is overpowering him, he should go somewhere where nobody knows him and put on ordinary clothing and cloak himself in ordinary clothing and do what he wants, but let him not profane the Name of Heaven by a public scandal.'[8]

The extraordinary advice of Ilai the Elder catches our attention. He does not mean to justify sin. What he is saying is, there are gradations of sin. A man should not sin, but if he is coerced by his impulse to do evil, he should at least take responsibility for not shaming God. The worst kind is a sin that shames heaven, that profanes the name of God. That is to be avoided at all costs. Sin therefore defines one important point at which God and man meet and the world order is affected. The just arrangement of matters that God has brought about in Creation can be upset by man's intervention, for man alone has the will and freedom to stand against God's plan and intention for Creation.

What has been said about sin as an act of rebellion implies that an act may or may not be sinful, depending upon the attitude of the actor. In fact only a few actions are treated as sinful in and of themselves – chiefly murder, fornication and idolatry. Under all circumstances a man must refrain from committing such absolute sins, even at the cost of his own life:

Another matter: 'For the earth is filled with violence' (Genesis 6:13):

Said Rabbi Levi, 'The word for violence refers to idolatry, fornication and murder.

'Idolatry: "For the earth is filled with violence" (Genesis 6:13).

'Fornication: "The violence done to me and to my flesh be upon Babylonia" (Jeremiah 51:35). [The word for "flesh" refers to incest, as at Leviticus 18:6].

'Murder: "For the violence against the children of Judah, because they have shed innocent blood" (Joel 3:19).

'Further, the word for "violence" stands for its ordinary meaning as well.'[9]

Since these were the sins of the men of the generation of the Flood that so outraged God as to bring about mass destruction, they form a class of sin by themselves. All the children of Noah, not only the children of Israel, must avoid these sins at all costs. But there is a sin that Israel may commit that exceeds even these cardinal sins. Even those three are forgivable, but rejection of the Torah is not:

Rabbi Huna and Rabbi Jeremiah in the name of Rabbi Samuel bar Rabbi Isaac: 'We find that the Holy One, blessed be he, forgave Israel for idolatry, fornication, and murder. [But] for their rejection of the Torah he never forgave them.'

What is the scriptural basis for that view?

It is not written, 'Because they practised idolatry, fornication and murder', but rather, 'And the Lord said, "Because they have forsaken my Torah" (Jeremiah 9:13).'

Said Rabbi Hiyya bar Ba, 'If they were to forsake me, I should forgive them, for they may yet keep my Torah. For if they should forsake me but keep my Torah, the leaven that is in [the Torah] will bring them closer to me.'

Rabbi Huna said, 'Study Torah [even if it is] not for its own sake, for, out of [doing so] not for its own sake, you will come [to study it] for its own sake.'[10]

We find ourselves looking at a mirror of virtue: attitude and intention are reflected back. God does not object to insincerity when it comes to study of the Torah, because the Torah itself contains the power to reshape the will of man (as stated succinctly by the rabbinic sages elsewhere – 'God demands the heart',[11] and similar formulations). The very jarring intrusion, 'If they were to forsake me, I should forgive them, for they may yet keep my Torah', underscores that conviction. God can forgive Israel for forsaking him, because if they hold on to the Torah, they will find their way back. The Torah will reshape Israel's heart. And then, amplifying that point but moving still further from the main proposition, comes Rabbi Huna's sentiment that studying the Torah does not require proper intentionality, because the Torah in due course will effect the proper intentionality.

As to the importance of intention, the rabbinic sages maintain that it is better to sin sincerely than to perform a religious duty hypocritically. It would be difficult to state in more extreme language the view that all things are relative to attitude or intentionality than to recommend sincere sin over hypocritical virtue.

Said Rabbi Nahman bar Isaac, 'A transgression committed for its own sake, in a sincere spirit, is greater in value than a religious duty carried out not for its own sake, but in a spirit of insincerity.

'For it is said, "May Jael, wife of Heber the Kenite, be blessed above women, above women in the tent may she be blessed" (Judges 5:24).

'Now who are these women in the tent? They are none other than Sarah, Rebecca, Rachel and Leah.' [The murder Jael committed gained more merit than the matriarchs' great deeds.]

This assertion shocks and is immediately challenged:

> But is this really true, that a transgression committed for its own sake, in a sincere spirit, is greater in value than a religious duty carried out not for its own sake, but in a spirit of insincerity? And did not Rabbi Judah say that Rav said, 'A person should always be occupied in study of the Torah and in practice of the commandments, even if this is not for its own sake [but in a spirit of insincerity], for out of doing these things not for their own sake, a proper spirit of doing them for their own sake will emerge'?
>
> It is equivalent to doing them not for their own sake.

Now we revert to the view that insincere Torah-study and practice of the commandments still have the power to transform a man; but there follows a concrete case of blatant insincerity's producing a reward; the Messiah himself is the offspring of an act of hypocrisy on the part of Balak, king of Moab and ancestor of Ruth, from whom the scion of David, the Messiah, will descend:

> For as a reward for the forty-two offerings that were presented by the wicked Balak to force Balaam to curse Israel, he was deemed worthy that Ruth should descend from him.
>
> For said Rabbi Yosé ben Rabbi Hanina, 'Ruth was the granddaughter of Eglon, the grandson of Balak, king of Moab.'[12]

So intentionality is everything; and sincerity in sin exceeds in merit hypocrisy in virtue.

In a system that resolves conflict by appealing to the theory that things ultimately complement one another, no explanation of sin can stand on its own, any more than any definition of sin can ignore the context in which sin takes place. All things are relative to one relationship: humility versus arrogance. Specific sins, such as adultery, are placed into the larger context of a failure of right attitude. Adultery is an expression of arrogance, and so too is jealousy. A larger theory of sin and virtue then takes over this topic, among many others: sin is an expression of arrogance, and virtue, of humility. The marital bond expresses that same faithfulness that is required of Israel in relationship to God. Sin contrasts with faithfulness, since the opposite of faithfulness is arrogance, the opposite of sin, humility.

Then the question presses, why do people rebel against God? The answer is, due to their arrogance, and that has to be accounted for. Specifically, they become arrogant when they are prosperous; then they trust in themselves and take it for granted that their own power has secured abundance. They forget that it is God who, by his act of will, has given them what they have got. Prosperity and success have their own threatening consequences in the change of man's attitude that they may well bring about. So arrogance comes from an excess of good fortune, but it is the absence of humility that accounts for the wrong attitude:

['So Jeshurun grew fat, and kicked – you grew fat and gross and coarse – then he forsook the God who made him, and spurned the Rock of his salvation. They incensed him with alien things, vexed him with abominations. They sacrificed to demons which were no gods, to gods they had never known, to new gods that had come in of late, whom your fathers had never dreaded. You neglected the Rock that begot you, and forgot the God who gave you birth' (Deuteronomy 32:15–18).]

'So Jeshurun grew fat, and kicked':

Out of satiety people rebel.

So you find in connection with the people of the generation of the Flood, that they rebelled against the Holy One, blessed be he, only from an abundance of food, drink and prosperity.

What is said in their regard?

'Their houses are safe, without fear' (Job 21:9).

So you find in connection with the people of the generation of the Tower [of Babel], that they rebelled against the Holy One, blessed be he, only from prosperity.

What is said in their regard?

'And the whole earth was of one language' (Genesis 11:1).

A. So you find in connection with the people of Sodom, that they rebelled against the Holy One, blessed be he, only from abundance of food.

What is said in their regard?

'As for the earth, it produces bread' (Job 28:5).

And so for the rest.

And thus Scripture says, 'As I live, says the Lord God, Sodom, your sister, has not done . . .' (Ezekiel 16:48).

Next we move from the gentiles to Israel, showing that the Israelites too rebel by reason of prosperity:

So you find in connection with the people of the wilderness, that they rebelled only out of an abundance of food.

For it is said, 'And the people sat down to eat and drink and rose up to make merry' (Exodus 32:6).

What then is stated in their regard? 'They have turned aside quickly out of the way . . .' (Exodus 32:8).[13]

Considering the dire consequences of disobeying God's will (both nature and history respond to Israel's misconduct with disastrous results), why in the world would anyone rebel? People forget the precariousness of their existence in times of prosperity. How is it that man's will does not correspond with, but rebels against, the will of God? Here man's free will requires clarification. Man and God are possessed of free will. Man's free will encompasses the capacity to rebel against God because innate in man's will is the impulse to do evil, *yeser hara* in Hebrew. So man corresponds to God but is complex, comprised as he is of conflicting impulses, where God is one and unconflicted.

That impulse within man to do evil struggles with man's impulse to do good, *yeser hattob*. The struggle between the two impulses in man corresponds with the cosmic struggle between man's will and God's word. But Creation bears within itself the forces that ultimately will resolve the struggle. That struggle will come to an end in the world to come, which itself comes about by an act of divine response to human regeneration, as we shall see in due course. The impulse to do evil in this world having perished in the regeneration brought about by man, the impulse to do evil in the world to come will be slain by God.

Here is the crux of the matter: man by nature is sinful, and only by encounter with the Torah knows how to do good. That explains why the gentiles, with idolatry in place of the Torah, in the end cannot overcome their condition but perish, while Israel, with the Torah as the source of life, will be judged and enter eternal life. The key to man's regeneration lies in the fact that Israel, while part of humanity and by nature sinful, possesses the Torah. Herein lies the source of hope. Gentiles enjoy this world but, rejecting God in his self-manifestation in the Torah, have no hope of regeneration in the world to come.

From the definition of sin, both public and personal, we turn to its consequences, once more noting the correspondence between the costs of sin to the individual and those exacted from holy Israel all together. In both cases sin exacts a double-edged penalty. The sinner, acting out of arrogance, is diminished; and, defying God, is cut off from God. This applies to both the private person and all Israel. So what the person sought, aggrandizement through rebellion against God's will, he does not gain, but what he did not want, diminution, is what he gets:

Rabbi Ishmael taught on tannaite authority, 'Before a man has sinned, people pay him reverence and awe. Once he has sinned, they impose on him reverence and awe.

'Thus, before the first man had sinned, he would hear [God's] voice in a workaday way. After he had sinned, he heard the same voice as something strange. Before he had sinned, the first man heard God's voice and would stand on his feet: "And they heard the sound of God walking in the garden in the cool of the day" (Genesis 3:8). After he had sinned, he heard the voice of God and hid: "And man and his wife hid" (Genesis 3:8).

'Before the Israelites sinned, what is written in their regard? "And the appearance of the glory of the Lord was like a consuming fire on the top of the mountain before the eyes of the children of Israel" (Exodus 24:17).'

Said Rabbi Abba bar Kahana, 'There were seven veils of fire, one covering the next, and the Israelites gazed and did not fear or take fright.

'But when they had sinned, even on the face of the intercessor [Moses] they could not look: "And Aaron and all the children of Israel feared . . . to come near" (Exodus 34:30).

'Before the deed of David [with Bathsheba] took place, what is written? For David: "The Lord is my light and my salvation, of whom shall I be afraid?" (Psalms 27:1).

'But after that deed took place, what is written? "I will come upon him while he is weary and discouraged" (2 Samuel 17:2).

'Before Solomon sinned, he could rule over demons and demonesses: "I got for myself . . . Adam's progeny, demons and demonesses" [a version of Ecclesiastes 2:8].

'But after he had sinned, he brought sixty mighty men to guard his bed: "Lo, the bed of Solomon, with sixty mighty men around it, all of them holding a sword and veterans of war" (Song of Solomon 3:7−8).

'Before Saul had sinned, what is written concerning him? "And when Saul had taken dominion over Israel, he fought against all his enemies on every side, against Moab, against the Ammonites, against Edom, against the kings of Zobah, and against the Philistines; wherever he turned he put them to the worse'' (1 Samuel 14:47).

'After he had sinned what is written concerning him? ''And Saul saw the camp of the Philistines and was afraid'' (1 Samuel 28:5).'[14]

These cases validate the proposition that sin weakens the sinner; prior to sin, various figures are shown to have been strong, but afterwards, weak.

The Costs of Sin and the Rewards of Virtue

In the context of the master narrative, the heaviest cost exacted by sin is neither individual nor communal but cosmic. Sin separated God from man. Man's arrogance, his exercise of his will to confront the will of God, brought about sin and ultimately exiled Israel from the Land of Israel. That same attitude estranges God from Israel. If sin cuts the individual off from God and diminishes him in the world, then the sin of all Israel produces the same result. The costs of sin to Israel have proved catastrophic. Just as Israel was given every advantage by their acceptance of the Torah, so by rejecting the Torah death, exile and suffering took over. When Israel accepted the Torah, death, exile and suffering and illness no longer ruled them. When they sinned, they incurred all of them. That is because God himself went into exile from the Temple, the city, and the Land. We begin with the penalty of alienation from God, marked by the advent of death:

'Yet the harvest will flee away' (Isaiah 17:11).

You have brought on yourselves the harvest of the foreign governments, the harvest of violating prohibitions, the harvest of the angel of death.

For Rabbi Yohanan in the name of Rabbi Eliezer, son of Rabbi Yosé the Galilean, said, 'When the Israelites stood before Mount Sinai and said, ''All that the Lord has said we shall do and we shall be obedient'' [Exodus 24:7], at that very moment the Holy One, blessed be he, called the angel of death and said to him, ''Even though I have made you world ruler over all of my creatures, you have no business with this nation. Why? For they are my children.'' That is in line with the following verse of Scripture: ''You are the children of the Lord your God'' (Deuteronomy 14:1).'[15]

At Sinai, for the brief moment from the mass declaration, 'We shall do and we shall be obedient', death died. Israel then compared to Adam and Eve before the fall. But when Israel rebelled as Moses tarried on the mountain, sin took over, and the process of alienation from God got under way. Death, exile, suffering and illness do not belong to the order of nature; they have come about by reason of sin. Israel was exempt from them all when they accepted the Torah. But when they sinned, they returned to the condition of unredeemed man. A basic rationality then explains the human condition: people bring about their own fate. They possess the power to dictate their own destiny, by giving up the power to try to coerce God.

But beyond this is the cosmic charge cost of sin. Here the narrative of Israel and its loss of the Temple, Jerusalem and the Land takes over. Since God now finds himself alienated, he has abandoned not only Israel but the Temple, the City, the Land, the world altogether. The estrangement of God from Israel becomes a series of departures. This is set forth in a set of remarkably powerful statements, narratives of profound theological consequence. In one version, God's presence departed in ten stages, as God abandoned the people of Israel and they were estranged from him:

The divine presence [Shekhinah] made ten journeys [in leaving the Land and people of Israel prior to the destruction of the first Temple]. That is, 'The Divine Presence left Israel by ten stages' [this we know from] Scripture. And corresponding to these [stages], the Sanhedrin was exiled [successively to ten places of banishment]. [This we know from] tradition.

The divine presence [Shekhinah] made ten journeys [in leaving the people, Israel, prior to the destruction of the first Temple]. [This we know from] Scripture:

(1) from the ark-cover to the cherub;
(2) and from the cherub to the threshold [of the Holy-of-Holies];
(3) and from the threshold to the [Temple-]court;
(4) and from the court to the altar;
(5) and from the altar to [Temple-]roof;
(6) and from the roof to wall;
(7) and from the wall to the city;
(8) and from the city to the mountain;

(9) and from the mountain to the wilderness;

(10) and from the wilderness it ascended and dwelled in its place [in heaven], as it is said [Hosea 5:15]: 'I will return again to my place, [until they acknowledge their guilt and seek my face].'

We are now given the evidence from Scripture to back up each point:

(1) From the ark-cover to the cherub;

(2) and from the cherub to the threshold [of the Holy-of-Holies], as it is written [Exodus 25:22, proving that the original location of the divine presence was above the ark-cover]: 'There I will meet with you, and [from above the ark-cover, from between the two cherubim that are upon the ark of the testimony], I will speak with you.' And [showing that, later, the divine presence had moved to the cherub] it is written [II Samuel 22:11]: 'He rode on a cherub and flew.' And [proving that the divine presence then moved to the threshold] it is written [Ezekiel 9:3]: 'Now the glory of the God of Israel had gone up from the cherubim on which it rested to the threshold of the house.'

(3) And from the threshold to the [Temple-]court, as it is written [Ezekiel 10:4]: 'And the house was filled with the cloud, and the court was full of the brightness of the glory of the Lord.'

(4) And from the court to the altar, as it is written [Amos 9:1]: 'I saw the Lord standing beside the altar.'

(5) And from the altar to [Temple-]roof, as it is written [Proverbs 21:9]: 'It is better to live in a corner of the housetop [than in a house shared with a contentious woman].'

(6) And from the roof to wall, as it is written [Amos 7: 7]: 'Behold, the Lord was standing beside a wall built with a plumb line.'

(7) And from the wall to the city, as it is written [Micah 6:9]: 'The voice of the Lord cries to the city.'

(8) And from the city to the mountain, as it is written [Ezekiel 11:23]: 'And the glory of the Lord went up from the midst of the city and stood upon the mountain which is on the east side of the city.'

(9) And from the mountain to the wilderness, as it is written [Proverbs 21:19]: 'It is better to live in a land of wilderness [than with a contentious and fretful woman].'

(10) And from the wilderness it ascended and dwelled in its place [in heaven], as it is said [Hosea 5:15]: 'I will return again to my place, [until they acknowledge their guilt and seek my face].'

The systematic proof, deriving from Scripture, shows how God moved by stages from the inner sanctum of the Temple; but the climax comes at the end, pointing towards the next stage in the unfolding of the theology of the oral Torah: the possibility of reconciliation and how this will take place.

The next part of this document expands on that point: God hopes for the repentance of Israel, meaning its freely given acceptance of God's will, demonstrated by a statement expressing a change in attitude and, specifically, regret for its act of arrogance:

For six months, the divine presence waited on Israel [the people] in the wilderness, hoping they might repent. When they did not repent it said, 'May their souls expire.' [We know this] as it says [Job 11:20]: 'But the eyes of the wicked will fail; all means of escape will elude them, and their [only] hope will be for their souls to expire.'[16]

God's progressive estrangement in heaven finds its counterpart in the sequence of exiles that Israel's political institutions suffered, embodying the exile of all Israel from the Land. In the interim, God has abandoned the holy place. He too has gone into exile, just like Israel. That means God has accepted the condition of uncleanness, leaving the Temple where cleanness prevailed.

'In the midst of which I dwell:'

So precious is Israel that even though the people suffer uncleanness, the Presence of God is among them, as it is said, 'Thus he shall make atonement for the holy place, because of the uncleanness of the people of Israel . . . and so he shall do for the tent of meeting [where God met Moses in the wilderness tabernacle], which abides with them in the midst of their uncleannesses' (Leviticus 16:16).

And Scripture says, 'Through their imparting uncleanness to my tabernacle, which is in their midst' (Leviticus 15:31).

And Scripture says, 'That they not make their camp unclean' (Numbers 5:3).

And Scripture says, 'You shall not defile the land in which you live' (Numbers 35:33).

Rabbi Nathan says, 'So precious is Israel that, wherever they have been carried away into exile, the Presence of God is with them.

'They were carried into exile to Egypt, the Presence of God was with them, as it is said, "Thus the Lord has said, I exiled myself with the house of your father when they were in Egypt subject to the house of Pharaoh" (1 Samuel 2:27).

'When they went into exile to Babylonia, the Presence of God was with them, as it is said, "On your account I was sent to Babylonia" (Isaiah 43:14).

'When they went into exile to Elam, the Presence of God was with them, as it is said, "And I will set my throne in Elam, and destroy their king and princes" (Jeremiah 49:38).

'When they went into exile to Edom, the Presence of God was with them, as it is said, "Who is this that comes from Edom, in crimsoned garments from Bozrah, he that is glorious in his apparel, marching in the greatness of his strength" (Isaiah 63:1).

For the rabbinic sages, this last-exile also represents their own situation, under Roman occupation. The return from exile, to take place when the Messiah brings back the Israelites to the Land of Israel as part of the cosmic restoration to Eden, will encompass God as well:

And when they return, the Presence of God will return with them, as it is said, 'Then the Lord your God will restore your fortunes and have compassion upon you, and he will gather you again from all the peoples where the Lord your God has scattered you. If your outcasts are in the uttermost parts of heaven, from there the Lord your God will gather you, and from there he will fetch you; and the Lord your God will bring you into the land which your fathers possessed, that you may possess it' (Deuteronomy 30:3–5). The word that is used is not, 'restore', but 'the Lord your God will return'.[17]

In an analysis of God's estrangement from the created world (rather than from Israel in particular) his progress is seen in seven movements (corresponding to the fixed stars or visible planets, which are deemed to represent seven layers or firmaments) – moving out of, and back into, the world – the implication is that the present condition of Israel also comes about as a result of sin and will be remedied through attainment of *zekut*:

What is written is not, 'I have come into the garden', but rather, 'I have come back to my garden'. That is, 'to my canopy'.

That is to say, to the place in which the principal [presence of God] had been located to begin with.

The principal locale of God's presence had been among the lower creatures, in line with this verse: 'And they heard the sound of the Lord God walking about' (Genesis 3:8).

. . . the principal locale of God's presence had been among the lower creatures, but when the first man sinned, it went up to the first firmament.

The generation of Enosh came along and sinned, and it went up from the first to the second.

The generation of the Flood [came along and sinned], and it went up from the second to the third.

The generation of the dispersion [came along] and sinned, and it went up from the third to the fourth.

The Egyptians in the time of Abraham our father [came along] and sinned, and it went up from the fourth to the fifth.

The Sodomites [came along] and sinned, and it went up from the fifth to the sixth.

The Egyptians in the time of Moses came along and sinned, and it went up from the sixth to the seventh.

Now God returns to the world through the founders of Israel:

And, corresponding to them, seven righteous men came along and brought it back down to earth:

Abraham our father came along and acquired merit, and brought it down from the seventh to the sixth.

Isaac came along and acquired merit and brought it down from the sixth to the fifth.

Jacob came along and acquired merit and brought it down from the fifth to the fourth.

Levi came along and acquired merit and brought it down from the fourth to the third.

Kohath came along and acquired merit and brought it down from the third to the second.

Amram came along and acquired merit and brought it down from the second to the first.

Moses came along and acquired merit and brought it down to earth.

Therefore it is said, 'On the day that Moses completed the setting up of the Tabernacle, he anointed and consecrated it' (Numbers 7:1).[18]

God yearns for Israel, but Israel is estranged as a result of the sins of one generation after another. Then the merit of successive generations of Israel brought God back to the world. So Israel's story in everyday life is intertwined with Israel's corporate story in history.

The Master Narrative and the Ethical Imperatives

The upshot is clear. Once more, Judaism emerges as story: story before it is anything else, story after it is everything else, as Father Greeley says in the quotation that began this book. Here we see how Judaism cannot speak of virtue and sin outside the framework of the master narrative. Both the question and the answer derive from that sustaining story, which yields the ethical system. The two accounts – God leaves the world as a result of man's sin, is brought back through Israel's saints; God leaves the world as a result of Israel's sin but can be restored to the world by Israel's act of repentance – match. They conform to the theory of Israel as the counterpart to Man, the other Adam; the Land as counterpart to Eden; and now we see, the exile of Israel as counterpart to the fall of Man. Both stories are necessary for a complete statement of the theology.

The chapter of the master narrative that concerns Adam and Eve in Eden, and therefore Israel in the Land of Israel, contributes the ethical principles of virtue and vice. God's traits of justice, equity, love and compassion form the model for God's creatures: 'You shall be holy, for I the Lord your God am holy' (Leviticus 19:1). Moreover, the Torah knows humanity as the children of Adam via Noah to Abraham. As soon as we introduce the names of Adam and Eve, created by God 'in our image, after our likeness' (Genesis 1:26), the matter of virtue finds its context in their relationship with God. That relationship was disrupted by their disobedience to God's commandment, an act of rebellion brought on by arrogance. Consequently, virtue stands for those traits that bring about reconciliation between Adam and Eve and God, and vice represents those that disrupt the relationship. So the working system of the Torah finds its dynamic in the struggle between God's plan for Creation, to create a perfect world of justice, and the free will of humanity. All virtuous traits then find their place within that encompassing vision that explains who we are by telling the story of Creation culminating in Adam,

Eve, and Eden. That is to say, in Judaism 'we' stand for humanity (Adam and Eve fallen from Eden), and are represented by Israel dispossessed of the Land by its own sins. In a word, virtue embodies the regeneration of humanity for restoration to Eden: humility and self-denial are therefore the most important virtues.

The rabbinic sages had the notion that the most ignorant people, who devote their lives to sin, can through a single action accomplish what a life devoted to Torah-study cannot achieve. And that brings us back to our starting point, the merit of the act of selfless love, the act God cannot compel or coerce but craves of humanity. The commandments to love God, 'You shall love the Lord your God with all your heart, and with all your soul, and with all your might' (Deuteronomy 6:5) and to love other people, 'You shall love your neighbour as yourself' (Leviticus 19:18) meet and form a single statement of what God aspires to for us, but what he cannot impose upon us. God can command love, but not coerce it, favour but not force it. But then God responds to an act of selfless generosity with an act of grace, precisely that act that humanity for its part cannot compel or coerce out of God, cannot cajole from God, but can only beseech.

Israel's Story in
   Theology and Law

7
The Theology of Judaism:
Revealing the Rationality of Being

Theology and law (in Hebrew, *aggadah* and *halakhah*) set forth the system that sustains the story. They turn Judaism's story into a rational, cogent system for the Israelite cultural and social order. That comprehensive composition of the whole, showing the coherence of the parts, comes to full expression in the two complementary systems of theology and law, the one systematizing rules of attitude, the other making the same statement through norms of action. In each medium is expressed the governing logic that animates the telling of Israel's tale, because they turn facts into insight, and insight into God's truth. These systems encompass in a coherent construction the theological propositions and the legal consequences of the various chapters of Israel's story. Working with the facts provided by Scripture and their own observations of nature, history and society, the rabbinic sages cobbled together an account of the world, embedded in the written part of the Torah itself, that realized the ideal of a world order of reason, balance, proportion, equity and reliability.

What we see in theology and law is how the story is translated into norms of belief and behaviour. Then the narrative emerges as the medium of a well-composed theological statement, all the parts of which hold together in fixed logical order. And in the legal code the story demonstrates proper actions and transactions, and thus the rules for Israel's social order: how, in accord with the will of God, people are not only to believe, but to behave in God's kingdom. In this chapter I retell Israel's story by reading religious stories philosophically, that is, in quest of the logic of the whole. In the next chapter, I compose Judaic laws into a construction that, in its way, recapitulates in social norms the point of the stories that Judaism tells about Israel.

Justice: The Rationality of Being

The theology embodied in the aggadic narratives and scriptural exegeses of Scripture (found in the two Talmuds and various midrash compilations) sets forth a world of reason, where all things cohere to a single inner logic and so are to be explained in an orderly way. The foundation of this world order is embodied in the conviction of the justice and mercy of the Creator of the universe, who through the Torah has made known to humanity himself and his plan for creation. Read rightly, the Torah reveals God's merciful justice. Justice defines the logic of being. It is what guarantees that whatever happens makes sense, and finds a rational explanation in accordance with reliable principles of order and balance. Whatever happens is for good and sufficient cause. Each action produces an equal and opposite reaction, a perfect match, a mirror of a human deed in God's responsive deed. This perfect world of universal reason and self-evident rationality is in a steady state: do this and that will happen; do not do this and that will not happen. The principle of measure for measure prevails in all matters, meaning an exact balance between a sin and its punishment, and an act of virtue and its reward. Then the task of intellect is to discover in the Torah how all things are to be justified, meaning, *shown to be just to begin with.*

Justice means that principles of order describe the final outcome of all transactions and all relationships. Well-ordered nature finds its match in the well-constructed society of humanity. The very traits of humanity correspond to those of nature. The same law that rules the tree rules me, so the orderly mind maintains. The *telos*, the ultimate end and goal of all things, is present at the outset and explains and governs what happens; nothing can happen that violates this rational rule. The acorn grown up has not changed but has only realized its end. Teleology then takes the place of history as a mode of organizing existence. In such a world the future is present even now, the oak in the acorn. Inertia and stasis characterize this universe, in accordance with the rules that dictate cause and effect. Proportion and balance mark the well-ordered world. They should then characterize the relationships between people and nations. The destiny meted out to each by the purposeful intellect that has made things just so, is what God accomplishes.

In such a purposeful realm rationality yields compelling explanations for all things. A single logic, an integral rationality or *logos*, commands. Before the cosmic intellect that has conceived all things in a single reasonable, purposeful way there are no mysteries, neither about the past and what lies hidden, nor about the present and what comes into view, nor even about what lies over the distant horizon of the future. Since rules of justice govern, reason suffices to explain the past, understand the present, and dictate what is going to come about in the future. Not only public history but private life conforms to the same reasonable laws: do this, and that will happen. The well-examined lives of people match the rules of reason, so private lives correspond to those same principles of justice and order. All things come under the one orderly law of reason: for every thing its place, for every person a calling, for every event a purpose. And that is why those who master the givens of reality and reflect reasonably about them make sense of all existence and events.

In line with the inner logic of the whole, time and change do not, or at least ought not, mar this Eden, where perfection consists in stability in proper balance and proportion. And when change (not just fulfilment of the innate *telos*) marks time, change is a problem that requires explanation. In this domain of contemplation of what is, or can be made, perfect, people know the rules and how they work and are applied. Consequently, through knowing the regularities of eternity that supersede the random moments of time, the past yields its secrets of how things really work. The present rehearses the rules in the here and now. The future promises only more of that same regularity and certainty. The categories, past, present and future lose all currency.

Events take place, but history does not happen. Events now stand not for that which disrupts, but that which embodies rules or actualizes potentials, much as the well-conceived experiment in the laboratory allows the testing of hypotheses. And the same rules govern nations, families, and even individuals. Public affairs and private ones match in conforming to the governance of order, purpose and reason. These virtues of the well-constructed intellect not only account for history and the course of nations in the unfolding of time but also prevail in the street and marketplace and household. Fairness and a balanced exchange in the transactions of the village marketplace match in structure and proportion the workings of applied reason and practical logic in the relations of people and nations. In this philosophers' Eden, all things allow of reasoned explanation, and there are no mysteries. Here then we discern the remarkable, hopeful vision, the fantasy-world of intellectuals who conceive that ideas make all the difference, that minds command and reason governs.

That is the world portrayed by the rabbinic sages in their presentation of the Torah. The writings, read all together as a single coherent statement, portray the reason why things are now as they are (in the fifth century when the sages were writing). And they show the logic of that reason, revealing its integrity in the working of justice throughout. The Torah as interpreted and amplified by the rabbinic sages lays heavy emphasis upon the perfection of the timeless, flawless Creation that God forms and governs in accordance with wholly rational and accessible rules. If everything fits together and works coherently, it is because, as philosophers maintain in their realm of reflection, a single, unitary logic or logos, the logic of monotheism comprised by the one just, therefore reasonable and benevolent, God prevails.

What is primary is the governing conception of a prevailing logic, a governing reason articulated endlessly out of a few simple propositions of order and coherence. Throughout, a highly articulated system of classification is at work, one that rests on a deep theoretical foundation. The basic method involves a search for abstraction out of concrete data. A variety of cases deriving from Scripture is subjected to generalization, and the whole is then set forth in the form of a generalization sustained by numerous probative cases. The generalization, moreover, is itself elaborated. Cases that validate the generalization are selected not at random but by appeal to common traits of classification, and then the generalization not only derives from the cases but from a very specific aspect of them. These cases are all characterized by sudden and supernatural intervention in a crisis. Or a set of kindred propositions is established through a series of cases; no effort is made to order the cases in a compelling sequence. It is adequate to state the generalization and then adduce probative cases out of Scripture.

The whole represents the systematization of Scripture's evidence on a given topic, and it is the systematization of the data that yields a generalization. Scripture's facts are organized and sorted out in such a way as to present a generalization. Generalizations are to be formulated through that same process of collecting kindred facts and identifying the implication that all of them have in common. But Scripture may also be asked to provide illustrative cases for principles that are formulated autonomously, as the result of analytical reasoning distinct from the sorting out of Scriptural precedents. Then Scripture is asked only to define in concrete terms what has been said abstractly. Successive propositions organize and rationalize a vast body of data, all of the facts pointing to the conclusions that are proposed as generalizations. The proof then lies once more in the regularity and order of the data that are collected. The balance and coherence of the laws yield the looked-for generalizations. The method would have been familiar to elementary students of natural history or simple logic in the schools of certain ancient philosophical traditions.

So the rabbinic sages set forth the rational rules contained within the narratives of Scripture: Creation and its flaws; Eden and the loss of Eden. But their logic, involving as it did the insistence on a perfect and unchanging world, sought out what complements and completes an account (modes of thought that will occupy us later on). Thus they also taught how Eden is to be recovered. Adam and his counterpart, Israel, are seen in the cosmic drama acted out every day, here and now, in the humble details of Israel's ordinary life: unflawed Creation, spoiled by humanity's act of will, is restored by Israel's act of repentance. The rationality of the orderly and balanced world set forth in rabbinic Judaism comes to full realization in the match of Eden and the Land of Israel, Adam and the community of Israel, the paradise and paradise lost, with one difference. Adam had no Torah, Israel does. Adam could not regain Eden, but Israel can and will regain the Land. And that is where the halakhah takes over, defining for Israel the society that will restore Eden.

The Moral Order: Reward and Punishment

In the rabbinic sages' view the will of the one, unique God, made manifest through the Torah, governs and, further, God's will for both private life and public activity is rational. That is to say, within a mortal's understanding of reason, God's will is just. And by 'just', the sages understood the commonsense meaning: fair, equitable, proportionate, commensurate, bound by reasonable rules and not arbitrary. In place of fate, impersonal destiny, chance, or simply irrational, inexplicable chaos, God's plan and purpose come to realization everywhere. So Judaism identifies God's will to do justice in a merciful manner as the active and causative force in the lives of individuals and nations.

How did the sages know that God's will is realized in the moral order of justice, involving reward and punishment? They turned to Scripture for the pertinent facts; that is where God makes himself manifest. But of the various types of scriptural evidence – explicit commandments, stories, prophetic admonitions – that they had available to show how the moral order prevailed in all being, they preferred those that demonstrated an exact match between sin and punishment. Here was their starting point; from here all else flows smoothly and in orderly fashion. Their world order was best demonstrated by examples where sin is punished and merit rewarded.

The body of evidence that Scripture supplied recorded human action and divine reaction on the one hand, and meritorious deed and divine response and reward on the other. It was comprised of examples drawn from both private and public life, to underscore the sages' insistence on the match between the personal and the public; that all things were subject to the same simple rule. The demonstration of not only the principle but the precision of measure for measure, deriving from Scripture's own record of God's actions permeates the sages' system and frames its prevailing modes of explanation and argument. The principle that all existence conforms to rules, and that these rules embody principles of justice through exact punishment of particular sins and precise reward of singular acts of virtue defined the starting point of all rational thought and the entire character of the sages' theology.

This was despite the contrary evidence of contemporary reality, beginning with Israel's own situation, subordinated as it was to Rome after its defeat in two rebellions in the first and second centuries. The sages deemed it a fact that humanity lived in a world in which good is rewarded and evil punished. Since the world in which they lived knew better, and since the sages framed a system that coheres solely as an explanation of why, though justice is supposed to prevail, present matters are chaotic, we may take it for granted that the sages too knew better, so far as their secular knowledge was concerned. It was their theology, the logic of

God, systematically expounded, that taught them to see matters as they did.

Here is the sages' account of God's justice, which is always commensurate, both for reward and punishment, in consequence of which the present permits us to peer into the future with certainty of what is going to happen. What we note is their identification of the precision of justice, the exact match of action and reaction, each step in the sin, each step in the response, and, above all, the immediacy of God's presence in the entire transaction. They draw general conclusions from the specifics of the law that Scripture sets forth, and that is where systematic thinking about takes over from exegetical learning about cases, or, in our own categories, philosophy from history.

By that same measure by which a man metes out [to others], do they mete out to him:

She primped herself for sin, the Omnipresent made her repulsive.

She exposed herself for sin, the Omnipresent exposed her.

With the thigh she began to sin, and afterward with the belly, therefore the thigh suffers the curse first, and afterward the belly.

But the rest of the body does not escape [punishment].[1]

The reaction of a woman accused of adultery to drinking the bitter water that is supposed to produce one result for the guilty, another for the innocent, is described in Scripture in this language: 'If no man has lain with you . . . be free from this water of bitterness that brings the curse. But if you have gone astray . . . then the Lord make you an execration . . . when the Lord makes your thigh fall away and your body swell; may this water . . . pass into your bowels and make your body swell and your thigh fall away' (Numbers 5:19–22). This is amplified and expanded, extended to the entire rite, where the woman is stripped in stages; then the order, thigh, belly, shows the perfect precision of the penalty. What Scripture describes as a particular instance, the sages transform into a generalization, so making Scripture yield governing rules.

The Political Order: Israel and the Torah

Politics marks the starting point of this encompassing account of Creation ordered by justice that, in my view, the rabbinic sages systematically formulate through all of their documents. The theory of the political order that is set forth in the documents of the aggadah rests on a simple logic of balanced relationships. The stories of Israel retold in Chapters 1 and 2 show that all humanity is divided into two distinct groups, those who know God through the Torah, and those who do not know God at all but instead worship idols. The former are called Israel, the latter, the gentiles. God rules as sovereign over all mankind, but these two subdivisions compete and one, the gentiles, was currently dominating the other, Israel. It follows that to make sense of – to justify – the political order, the sages had to find the rational principle that accounted for the two political entities and their relationships. The power relationships between the two responded to three rules. First, as the sages' theory of world order maintained in its definition of justice, each action provokes an equal and commensurate reaction. Second, God responds to the attitude as much as to the action of the human actor, especially prizing humility over arrogance. Third, God's special relationship to those who know him through the Torah may require him to use the gentiles to penalize Israel for disobedience, in order to encourage their return to a proper attitude and consequent actions. For the theology of Judaism, the political order of mankind plays itself out within those three rules. In combination, they respond to the critical issue of Israel's public life: why do the gentiles prosper while Israel languishes? Where is the justice in the political order of mankind?

The sages' doctrine of the political order of the world is comprised by these convictions. First, because Israel accepted the Torah God loves Israel. The Torah therefore defines Israel's life and governs Israelites' welfare. Second, in genus Israel does not differ from the gentiles, deriving from the same ancestry, sharing the same origin backward from Abraham. In species, forward from Abraham, matters are otherwise. Distinguished by the Torah, Israel is alone in its category (*sui generis*), which is proved by the fact that what is a virtue to Israel is a vice to other nations; what is life-giving to Israel is poison to the gentiles. Third, Israel's condition of weakness comes about as a result of its own sin, which God justly and reasonably punishes through, among others, political means. Still, fourth, if Israel sins, God forgives that sin, having punished the nation on account of it. Such a process has yet to come to an end, but it will and in time is going to culminate in Israel's complete regeneration and consequently the restoration of Eden. Meanwhile, fifth, Israel's assurance of God's love lies in the many expressions of his special concern, in his provision of numerous commandments for Israel to carry out for its own sanctification.

The Holy One, blessed be he, wanted to give occasions for attaining merit to Israel.

Therefore he gave them abundant Torah and numerous commandments,

as it is said, 'It pleased the Lord for his righteousness' sake to magnify the Torah and give honour to it' (Isaiah 42:21).[2]

The means for Israel's sanctification extend to even the humblest and most ordinary aspects of national life: the food the nation eats and the sexual practices by which it procreates. These life-sustaining, life-transmitting activities draw God's special interest, as a mark of his general love for Israel. Israel then is supposed to achieve its life in conformity with the marks of God's love. That, in theory, forms the moral order that justifies Israel's existence through all time.

What about Israel's sin? That question brings us to the centre of the structure built upon God's choice of Israel and carries within itself the answer to the anomaly of Israel's condition in the world. God's response to Israel's sin demonstrates his love for Israel and his capacity to bear with, even to forgive Israel. Israel tested God ten times, and God forgave them ten times:

Ten trials did our ancestors impose upon the Holy One, blessed be he: two at the shore of the sea, two in the water, two in regard to the manna, two in regard to the quail, one in regard to the [golden] calf, one in the wilderness of Paran.[3]

Scripture yields ample evidence of God's unlimited capacity to forgive Israel, so that the relationship between God and Israel is shaped by the principles of love and forbearance, shown by God through all time.

This brings us to the theology of politics contained within the image of 'the kingdom of heaven', which is located not in the future but everywhere and always. It is realized when Israel does God's will. Here and now Israel forms the realm of God in this world, where God takes up his presence, in synagogues and yeshivot, where prayers are recited and the Torah studied, respectively. God's kingdom, unlike the kingdoms of this world and this age, has no geographical location, nor is it tangible. It is a kingdom that one enters by right attitude, through accepting the government and laws of that King and undertaking to obey his rules, the commandments. To be Israel in the sages' model means to live in God's kingdom, wherever one is located and whenever, in the sequence of the ages, one enjoys this-worldly existence. God's kingdom forms the realm of eternity within time. Death marks not an end but an interruption in the life with God; the individual is restored to life at the end, within that larger act of restoration of Adam to Eden, meaning Israel to the Land, that Israel's repentance will bring about. Various religious activities represent a taste even now of what is coming: the sabbath, for example, affords a sixtieth of the taste of the world to come. Embodying God's kingdom by obeying God's will, Israel was created to carry out religious duties and perform good deeds. These are what differentiate Israel from the gentiles, meaning the idolators.

What this means, concretely, is that God rules now, and those who acknowledge and accept his rule, performing his commandments and living by his will, live under God's rule. We recall the observation that, to single out Israel, God sanctified the people by endowing them with numerous commandments. Carrying out these commandments, then, brings Israel into the kingdom of heaven, as they acknowledge the dominion of God. That merging of politics and theology emerges in the language of the formula for reciting a blessing before carrying out a commandment or religious duty, 'Blessed are you, Lord our God, king of the world, who has sanctified us by his commandments and commanded us to . . .' That is the formula that transforms an ordinary deed into an act of sanctification, a gesture of belonging to God's kingdom.

The Political Order: The Gentiles and Idolatry

Gentiles by definition are idolaters because, unlike Israelites, they do not worship the one, true God, who has made himself known in the Torah. That is the difference, the only consequential distinction, between Israel and the gentiles. Why does idolatry define the boundary between Israel and everybody else? Idolatry, or rebellious arrogance against God is central to the entire Torah. The religious duty to avoid idolatry is primary; if someone violates that single religious duty, he violates the entire Torah. Violating the prohibition against idolatry is equivalent to transgressing all Ten Commandments:

'But if you err and do not observe [all these commandments which the Lord has spoken to Moses]' (Numbers 15:22).

'But if you err and do not observe':

Scripture speaks of idolatry.

Now, as they commonly do, the rabbinic sages test the proposition by proposing other readings of the evidence besides the one offered as normative:

You maintain that Scripture speaks of idolatry. But perhaps Scripture refers to any of the religious duties that are listed in the Torah?

Scripture states, '. . . then if it was done unwittingly without the knowledge of the congregation' (Numbers 15:24) Scripture thereby has singled out a particular religious duty unto itself, and what might that be? It is the prohibition against idolatry.

You maintain that Scripture speaks of idolatry. But perhaps Scripture refers to any of the religious duties that are listed in the Torah?

Scripture states, 'But if you err and do not observe', indicating that all of the religious duties come together to give testimony concerning a single religious duty.

Just as if someone violates all of the religious duties, he thereby throws off the yoke [of the commandments] and wipes out the mark of the covenant and so treats the Torah impudently, so if someone violates a single religious duty, he thereby throws off the yoke [of the commandments] and wipes out the mark of the covenant and so treats the Torah impudently.

And what might that single religious duty be? It is idolatry, for it is said [in that regard], 'to violate his covenant' (Deuteronomy 17:2). [Thus the covenant refers in particular to the rule against idolatry, which then stands for the whole.]

'Covenant' moreover refers only to the Torah, as it is said, 'These are the words of the covenant' (Deuteronomy 29:1).[4]

The gentiles hate Israel and therefore hate God. What accounts for the logic that links these two ideas? The answer to that question fully spells out the doctrine of the gentiles that the theology of Judaism constructs. What defines the gentiles – the lack of the Torah – explains also why their very character requires them to hate Israel, the people of the Torah. The gentiles' hatred of Israel came about because of the revelation of the Torah at Sinai. Israel accepts the Torah and gentiles reject it; everything follows from that single fact. Israel knows God and gentiles deny him, and relations between the two sectors of humanity are determined by that fact.

But how can justice be thought to order the world if the gentiles rule? That formulation furthermore forms the public counterpart to the private perplexity: how is it that the wicked prosper and the righteous suffer? The two challenges to the conviction of the rule of moral rationality – gentile hegemony and the prosperity of wicked people – are parallel. Having established that idolaters subject themselves to God's hatred by reason of their attitudes and consequent actions, the question of fairness becomes urgent: how has this catastrophic differentiation come about between Israel and the gentiles, a differentiation which means that the gentiles, for all their glory in the here and now, win for themselves the grave, while Israel, for all its humiliation in the present age, inherits the world to come? And the answer is self-evident: the gentiles reject God, whom they could and should have known in the Torah. They rejected the Torah, and all else followed. The argument goes as follows:

(1) Israel differs from the gentiles because Israel possesses the Torah and the gentiles do not;

(2) because they do not possess the Torah, the gentiles also worship idols instead of God; and

(3) therefore God rejects the gentiles and identifies with Israel.

The gentiles deprived themselves of the Torah because they rejected it, and they rejected the Torah because the Torah deprived them of the very practices or traits that they deemed characteristic and essential to their being. The gentiles' own character, the shape of their conscience then, now and always, accounts for their condition which, by an act of will (choosing to convert to Judaism) they can change. What they did not want, that of which they were by their own word unworthy, is denied them. And what they do want condemns them. So when each nation is judged for rejecting the Torah, the indictment of each is spoken out of its own mouth; its own self-indictment forms the core of the matter. The circularity that characterized the gentiles' original rejection also describes how things always are; it is not historical but philosophical.

This theory of the gentiles sees all of humanity as divided between those who accept God's dominion and those who reject God altogether. It derives not from observations of how people really behave but a theory of matters based on the logic of monotheism. For monotheism, the belief that there is only one God, who is all-powerful and loving, makes no compromise with polytheism and does not tolerate the representation of God in the form of idols that people create and then worship. The prophets time and again caricature polytheism and idolatry in just that way. What the rabbis of the oral Torah contributed is the concretization of the prophetic view in their story of how the gentile nations were offered the Torah and rejected it due to their own character. We recall the story (quoted in Chapter 1) of how each nation, first Rome, then Persia, and onward through humanity, found in the Torah the prohibition of precisely those things that it most valued. This account of matters rests on the fact that Israel at this time found little or no competition in setting forth monotheism as revealed in the Torah. But in medieval and modern times, Judaism would come to grips with the advent of two more monotheisms, Christianity and Islam. The rather one-sided and implacable rejection of the gentiles because of their idolatry and rejection of God would give way to a more nuanced conception of them, with special reference to Islam and Christianity. The racist anti-Semitism and anti-Judaism evinced in medieval and modern times by Christianity and in modern times by Islam did not prevent the rabbinic authorities of later times from recognizing the difference between pagan and Christian Rome, or between pagan and Muslim Arabia.

Given what we know about the definition of Israel as those destined to live for ever, and gentiles as those destined to remain in the grave, we realize that the issue concerns the end of days, not the here and now. At that time, prophecy teaches and Israel prays, the gentiles will recognize that the Lord is God alone, and all will acknowledge his unity and dominion and enter the community of Israel. Those who deny God's rule and thus remain outside Israel will not enter into the life eternal that the restoration of Eden brings about.

The Ultimate Anomaly: Private Lives

There is an obvious obstacle to the belief that God orders the world
through justice accessible to human reason: justice prevails in the world
only now and then. Humanity's fate rarely accords with the fundamental
principle of a just order but mostly challenges it. But if the human
condition embodied in Israelites' individual lives defies the smooth explanations that serve to justify the condition of Israel in the abstract, then
the entire logic of the Torah fails. To discern grounds for doubt, the
rabbinic sages only had to walk out of their yeshiva and consider the
condition of their neighbours – indeed or to contemplate their own
lives. They devoted themselves to the study of the Torah, ordinarily in
conditions of poverty, while round about Israelites who neglected the
Torah prospered. How could they justify the lives ordinary people had
to live when even their own lives of Torah study seemed to go unre-
warded? The good fall, the wicked rise, the ignorant or the arrogant
exercise power, and even rabbinic sages can merely rant and cavil, so
where is that orderly world of reason infused with justice?

If, through their theology of Israel and the gentiles, the sages could
account for gentile rule over Israel, explaining private lives required a
more complex and diverse philosophy. The thin, one-dimensional
assertion that the gentiles serve God's will in ruling Israel, thereby
punishing Israel for its sin, but will themselves give way to Israel at the
end of the world, served nicely as a solution to that theological challenge.
But when it came to everyday life, the anomaly represented by a random,
not a just, fate, encompassed many cases, each with its own special traits,
and none easily resolved by appeal to a single overriding principle of
reward and punishment. And the cases pressed in, near at hand, in the
next house, the next room. So the human condition presented its own
anomalies to the rule of the just order: suffering, illness and death come
to all, the wicked and the righteous alike.

Can we invoke the same explanation for private lives that serves in
accounting for the public condition of all Israel? The answer is affirmative,
but with important qualifications. The fundamental affirmation, pertaining
to public Israel and private Israelite alike, maintains that exact justice
governs. No anomalies will persist past the resurrection, the Last Judge-

ment, and the world to come. But the application of that principle yields far more diversity in the range of explanation than in the case of the condition of Israel subjugated by the gentiles.

Private matches public. If the gentiles are responsible for their condition, so is Israel, and so are the Israelites. Everything begins with the insistence that people are responsible for what they do, and therefore for what happens to them. Justice reigns, whatever happens. The reason that people are responsible for their own actions is that they enjoy free will. They are constantly subject to divine judgement; they have free choice, hence they can sin. God judges the world in a generous way; but judgement does take place: 'Everything is foreseen, and free choice is given. In goodness the world is judged. And all is in accord with the abundance of deeds.'[5]

God may foresee what is to happen, but humanity still exercises free will. A person's attitude and intentionality make all the difference. Because a person is not coerced to sin, nor can someone be forced to love God or even obey the Torah, an element of uncertainty affects every life. That is the point at which Adam's will competes with God's. It follows that where humanity gives to God what God wants but cannot coerce, or what God wants but cannot command – love or generosity, for instance – there, the theology of Judaism alleges, God responds with an act of uncoerced grace. But in all, one thing is reliable: the working of just recompense for individual action. The contrast between the expectation of a just reward or punishment and actuality precipitates all thought on the rationality of private life: what happens is supposed to make sense within the governing theology of a just order.

Then how to account for the injustice realized in private lives and in Israel's corporate existence? At this point in our encounter with Judaism's story, the answer is blatant, as we saw in our inquiry into the sources of sin. The human being bears a single trait that makes him most like God: his possession of free will. In his act of will God makes just rules, and in his, Adam wilfully breaks them. When God asks, 'Have you eaten of the tree of which I commanded you not to eat?' Adam replies, 'The woman whom thou gavest to be with me, she gave me the fruit of the tree, and I ate.' Then Eve claims, 'The serpent beguiled me, and I ate.' What is at stake is responsibility: who bears responsibility for deliberately violating the law. Each blames the next, and God sorts things out, responding to each in accord with the facts of the case: whose intentionality matches the actual deed? 'The Lord God said to the serpent, "*Because you have done this* . . ."' (Genesis 3:11–14). The ultimate responsibility lies with the one who acted deliberately, not under constraint or as a result of deception or misinformation, as did Adam because of Eve, and Eve because of the serpent. True enough, all are punished, but the punishment is differentiated. Those who were duped are distinguished from the one who acted wholly on his own: the serpent himself is cursed; the woman is subjected to pain in childbearing, which ought to have been pain-free; and because of Adam, the earth is cursed – a diminishing scale of penalties, each in accordance with the level of intentionality or free, uncoerced will, involved in the infraction.

Restoring World Order: Repentance and Atonement in Theological Context

We come to the key to the entire normative theological system: repentance, which plays an equally critical role in the halakhic or legal structure. The logic of repentance is simple and (in context) predictable. If sin is what introduces rebellion and change, and the will of the human being is what causes sin and so constitutes the variable in disrupting Creation, then the theology of Judaism makes provision for restoration through the free exercise of a person's will. That requires an attitude of remorse, a resolve not to repeat the act of rebellion, and a true effort at reparation; in all, transformation from rebellion against to obedience to God's will. So with repentance we come once more to an exact application of the principle of measure for measure, here, will for will, each comparable to and corresponding with the other. World order, disrupted by an act of will, regains perfection through an act of will that complements and corresponds to the initial, rebellious one. That is realized in an act of wilful repentance (Hebrew: *teshuva*).

According to the Torah, repentance effects the required transformation of humanity and inaugurates reconciliation with God. Through a matched act of will, now in conformity with God's design for Creation, repentance restores the balance upset by a human being's act of will. So the act of repentance, and with it atonement, takes its place within the theology of perfection, disruption and restoration around which the world of Creation is ordered. It is a logic that appeals to the balance and proportion of all things.

An apology or a changed attitude does not suffice; an atoning act also is required. That is why repentance is closely related to atonement and is integral to the Day of Atonement. Although by repenting, a person has ceased to sin, he must also atone for the sin and gain God's forgiveness, in order to be no longer deemed a sinner. Finally, there comes a test of this change of heart or will (where feasible): entering a situation in which the original sin is possible but is not repeated. Then the statement of remorse and voluntary change of will is confirmed by an act of omission or commission, as the case requires.

Followed by atonement, therefore, repentance commences the work of closing off the effects of sin: history, time, change, inequity. It marks the beginning of the labour of restoring Creation to Eden: the perfect world as God wants it and creates it. Since the Hebrew word, *teshuva*, is built out of the root for return, the concept is generally understood to mean returning to God from a situation of estrangement. The turning is not only from sin but towards God, for sin serves as an indicator of a deeper pathology, which is utter estrangement from God, humanity's will alienated from God's.

Repentance then involves not humiliation but reaffirmation of the self in God's image. It forms a theological category encompassing moral issues of action and attitude — wrong action and arrogant attitude in particular. The penitent needs to correct the damage he has done to someone else. But apart from reparations, the act of repentance is simply a change in attitude, specifically substituting feelings of regret and remorse for the arrogant intention that led to the commission of the sin. So it is through the will and attitude of the sinner that the act of repentance is realized; the entire process is carried on beyond the framework of religious actions, rites or rituals. The power of repentance overcomes sins of the most heinous and otherwise unforgivable character.

Restoring Private Lives: Resurrection

The restoration of world order, which completes the demonstration of God's justice, encompasses both private life and the community of Israel. For both, restorationist theology provides eternal life; to be Israel means to live. So far as the individual is concerned, beyond the grave, at a predetermined moment, the Israelite rises from the grave in resurrection, is judged, and then enjoys the world to come. For the entirety of Israel, congruently: all Israel participates in the resurrection (which takes place in the Land of Israel), is judged and enters the world to come. Death does not mark the end of the individual human life, nor exile the last stop in the journey of Holy Israel. Israelites will live in the world to come, all Israel in the Land of Israel.

The last things are to be known from the first. In the just plan of Creation Adam, representing the human race, was meant to live in Eden, and Israel in the Land of Israel in time without end. The restoration will bring about that long and tragically postponed perfection of the world order, sealing the demonstration of the justice of God's plan for Creation. Risen from the dead, having atoned for their sins through death, each individual will be judged in accord with his or her deeds. Israel for its part, when it repents and conforms its will to God's, recovers its Eden. So the consequences of rebellion and sin having been overcome, the struggle of humanity's will and God's word having been resolved, God's original plan will be realized at the last. The simple, global logic of the system, with its focus on the world order of justice established by God but disrupted by the human being, leads inexorably to this eschatology of restoration, the restoration of balance, order, proportion, eternity.

The belief in the resurrection of the dead is stated in prayer, theology and law: at the end of days, death will die. The certainty of resurrection derives from a simple fact of restorationist theology: God has already shown that he can do it.

You find that everything that the Holy One, blessed be he, is destined to do in the age to come he has already gone ahead and done through the righteous in this world. The Holy One, blessed be he, will raise the dead, and Elijah raised the dead.[6]

That God will raise the dead leads to the ultimate question: whom does he raise from the dead? And the answer is, 'All Israel, with some few exceptions.' Thus by 'Israel' is meant those who are raised from the dead, and to practise Judaism, to keep the Torah, is to choose life eternal, in line with Moses' admonition in Deuteronomy 30:19, 'Therefore choose life'. That definition of who is the Israelite and what Israel is – the one who will rise from the grave, the people destined for life eternal in heaven – removes the entire Judaic way of life from the realm of the merely ethnic or the this-worldly.

All Israelites have a share in the world to come,

   as it is said, 'Your people shall all be righteous; they shall possess the land for ever, the shoot of my planting, the work of my hands, that I might be glorified' (Isaiah 60:21).[7]

Restoring the Public Order: The World to Come

Resurrection concerns the individual Israelite, with some further implications for the whole of Israel. The world to come encompasses all Israel; the entire holy community is redeemed, and the only part of mankind that remains is Israel. But what, exactly do the rabbinic sages mean by *olam ha-ba*, 'the world or the age that is coming'? The world or the age to come completes, and necessarily forms the final chapter, of the theology of the Torah. The age that is coming will find Adam's successor in Eden's replacement – resurrected, judged and justified Israel, comprising nearly all Israelites who ever lived, now eternally rooted in the Land of Israel.

When the sages speak of the world to come, their language signifies a final change in the relationship between God and humanity, a model of how God and humanity relate that marks the utter restoration of the world order as originally contemplated. Israel's master narrative yields this account of matters: Adam loses Eden; Israel, the new Adam, loses the Land twice; then Israel repents, the dead are raised, Israel is restored to the Land, and eternal life follows. So here the story that commences with God's creation of a perfect world defined by a just order comes full circle. That world is not perfect due to the character of humanity. But the world will be restored to perfection (requiring, then, eternity), humanity to Eden, Israel to the Land of Israel, through Israel's act of repentance and reconciliation with God. That act of reconciliation, prepared for in countless lives of virtue and acts of merit, is realized in the world or age to come.

What makes the rabbinic sages so sure of themselves? To them, what gives Israel hope even now (when they were exiled from Jerusalem, and the Temple had been destroyed for the second time) is that the prophetic warnings about punishment for sin have come true, so the prophetic consolation about God's response to Israel's repentance also will come true. That is, for them, a natural result of a theology that finds perfection in balance, order, proportion, and above all complementarity. Just as the prophets warned that Israel would be punished for its rebellion against God, so they insisted that Israel would attain reconciliation through its repentance to God. Now that the first of the two elements of the equation, punishment for arrogant sin, has been realized, the sages find solid ground for certainty in the ultimate fulfilment also of the promise of reconciliation. The condition of the world today, the sages held, contains within itself not only the past and its consequence but, as a matter of certainty, also the future and its consolation. All are present in the here and now, as the Torah says, 'Today, if you want'.

'For Mount Zion which lies desolate; jackals prowl over it' (Lamentations 5:18).

Rabban Gamaliel, Rabbi Joshua, Rabbi Eleazar ben Azariah and Rabbi Akiva went to Rome. They heard the din of the city of Rome from a distance of a hundred and twenty miles.

They all begin to cry, but Rabbi Akiva began to laugh.

They said to him, 'Akiva, we are crying and you laugh?'

He said to them, 'Why are you crying?'

They said to him, 'Should we not cry, that idolators and those who sacrifice to idols and bow down to images live securely and prosperously, while the footstool of our God has been burned down by fire and become a dwelling place for the beasts of the field? Shouldn't we cry?'

He said to them, 'That is precisely the reason that I was laughing. For if those who outrage him he treats in such a way; those who do his will all the more so!'

There was the further case of when they were going up to Jerusalem. When they came to the Mount of Olives they tore their clothing. When they came to the Temple Mount and a fox came out of the house of the Holy of Holies, they began to cry. But Rabbi Akiva began to laugh.

'Akiva, you are always surprising us. Now we are crying and you laugh?'

He said to them, 'Why are you crying?'

They said to him, 'Should we not cry, that from the place of which it is written, "And if anyone else [not a member of a priestly tribe] comes near, he shall be put to death" (Numbers 1:51) a fox comes out? So the verse of Scripture is carried out: "for Mount Zion which lies desolate; jackals prowl over it".'

He said to them, 'That is precisely the reason that I was laughing. For Scripture says, "And I will got reliable witnesses, Uriah the priest and Zechariah the son of Jeberechiah, to attest for me" (Isaiah 8:2).

'Now what is the relationship between Uriah and Zechariah? Uriah lived in the time of the first temple, Zechariah in the time of the second!

'But Uriah said, "Thus says the Lord of hosts: Zion shall be plowed as a field; Jerusalem shall become a heap of ruins" (Jeremiah 26:18).

'And Zechariah said, "Old men and old women shall again sit in the streets of Jerusalem, each with staff in hand for old age" (Zechariah 8:4).

'And further: "And the streets of the city shall be full of boys and girls playing in its streets" (Zechariah 8:5).

'Said the Holy One, blessed be he, "Now lo, I have these two witnesses. So if the words of Uriah are carried out, the words of Zechariah will be carried out, while if the words of Uriah prove false, then the words of Zechariah will not be true either."

'I was laughing with pleasure because the words of Uriah have been carried out, and that means that the words of Zechariah in the future will be carried out.'

They said to him, 'Akiva, you have given us consolation. May you be comforted among those who are comforted.'[8]

And that is exactly what the sages intended: to console and hearten Israel, for God's sake. That has remained the task of rabbinic sages down the ages. With this compelling theology of one just God called to account for all things, the sages have sustained Israel with a sufficiency of reasoned hope through the ages. And they still do, even – I should say, *especially* – in the aftermath of the Holocaust.

Kabbalah: Esoteric Doctrine and Experience

So much for the story told by the public theology of Judaism. But Judaism contains another theological story, an esoteric one, made up of secret doctrines called kabbalah.[9] Identifying God and the Torah as one, the kabbalistic tradition concerns itself with the inner personality of God. The whole of Scripture is seen as revealing the story of God. So this esoteric tradition dealt with who and what God is, whereas the exoteric tradition of Scripture, as interpreted by the Mishnah, the Talmuds and the scriptural exegeses, with what God wants and what God did and does.

The esoteric tradition also provided a narrative of God and humanity, to which, in this survey of Judaism's theological story, we briefly turn. The principal document for conveying Judaism's story in mystical form was the *Zohar*, 'the book of Splendour, Radiance, Enlightenment',[10] a medieval work of immense proportions and commensurate influence. It was written as a multi-layered commentary to the Pentateuch and the Five Scrolls (Esther, Ruth, Song of Songs, Qoheleth – in the Christian Bible, Ecclesiastes – and Lamentations). It is an anthology of texts composed and edited over a long period of time, from the latter part of the thirteenth century into the fourteenth century. The main, but not the sole, author was Moses de Leon, who worked in Spain between 1281 and 1286. We can speak of a completed book of the *Zohar* only from the sixteenth century, when kabbalists began to prepare the manuscripts for printing; it is more accurate to think in terms of 'Zoharic literature', until that time.

We cannot be surprised that the *Zohar* speaks in the name of important second-century rabbinic sages. For the mystics before and after the *Zohar* took for granted that their doctrines were tradition, even part of the Torah, and derived from the same authorities who gave them the Mishnah and other parts of the oral Torah.

The *Zohar* is made up of diverse writings, most of them interpretations, scriptural passages, short sayings or longer disquisitions, many of them attributed to the second-century rabbinical authority Simeon bar Yohai and his disciples. Hidden meanings of Scripture are spelled out. These include the story of the Creation and the cosmos that unfolds in the structure of the ten emanations (sefirot) of God. These provide the paradigmatic plan of all that unfolds from the supreme deity, called the 'Ein Sof', or infinity. So the *Zohar* provides another way of telling the story of Creation, registering its theological points through narrative. A single passage suffices to show how this is done:

'And God said, Let there be light, and there was light' (Genesis 1:3):

This is the primal light that God made. It is the light of the eye. This light God showed to Adam, and by means of it he was enabled to see from end to end of the world. This light God showed to David, and he, beholding it, sang forth his praise, saying, 'Oh, how abundant is thy goodness, which thou hast laid up for them that fear thee' (Psalms 31:19). This is the light through which God revealed to Moses the Land of Israel from Gilead to Dan. Foreseeing the rise of three sinful generations, the generation of Enoch, the generation of the Flood, and the generation of the Tower of Babel, God put away the light from their enjoyment. Then he gave it to Moses in the time that his mother was hiding him, for the first three months after his birth. When Moses was taken before Pharaoh, God took it from him, and did not give it again until he stood upon the mount of Sinai to receive the Torah. Thenceforth Moses had it for his until the end of his life, and therefore he could not be approached by the Israelites until he had put a veil upon his face [Exodus 34:33].[11]

On the surface, we are given an account of the primordial light and how it was preserved. The doctrine of the disposition of that light and its cosmic meaning is hinted at but hardly articulated. The upshot is that the Torah is 'cosmic law, a blueprint of Creation. The *Zohar* illuminates the cosmic aspect of Torah . . . the literal sense is sanctified, but readers are urged to "look under the garment of Torah".'[12] For the unenlightened there is a rift between the plain sense and the mystical sense, exoteric and esoteric, but the enlightened can see through the veil of Scripture and understand that the deep meaning is the mystical meaning. But if all the garments are removed, there is nothing to see, since the ultimate reality of the Torah is the infinite light of God, that in and of itself has no form.

Indeed, the main concept of mystical Judaism is that God is very real; he is accessible in the scriptural interpretations that the kabbalists made and the desire of the mystic is 'to feel and to enjoy Him; not only to obey but to approach Him'; so says Abraham J. Heschel, the great theologian of Judaism in the twentieth century, who goes on: 'They want to taste the whole wheat of spirit before it is ground by the millstones of reason. They would rather be overwhelmed by the symbols of the inconceivable than wield the definitions of the superficial.'[13] What, then, is the mystic doctrine of God in Judaism? According to Heschel,

God is not a concept, a generalization, but a most specific reality . . . But He who is 'the Soul of all souls' is 'the mystery of all mysteries.' While the cabalists speak of God as if they commanded a view of the Beyond, and were in possession of knowledge about the inner life of God, they also assure us that all notions fail when applied to Him, that He is beyond the grasp of the human mind and inaccessible to meditation. He is the *En Sof*, the Infinite, 'the most Hidden of all Hidden.' While there is an abysmal distance between Him and the world, He is also called All. 'For all things are in Him and He is in all things . . . He is both manifest and concealed. Manifest in order to uphold the all and concealed, for He is found nowhere. When He becomes manifest He projects nine brilliant lights that throw light in all directions. So, too, does a lamp throw brilliance in all directions, but when we approach the brilliance we find there is nothing outside the lamp. So is the Holy ancient One, the Light of all Lights, the most Hidden of all Hidden. We can only find the light which He spreads and which appears and disappears. This light is called the Holy Name, and therefore All is One.'

The basic point is, the Torah is God and all of the life, study and practice of Judaism serves as a means of attaining conjunction with God, to overcome the separation of the self from the source.

Thus, the 'Most Recondite One Who is beyond cognition does reveal of Himself a tenuous and veiled brightness shining only along a narrow path which extends from Him. This is the brightness that irradiates all.' The *En Sof* has granted us manifestations of His hidden life: He had descended to become the universe; He has revealed Himself to become the Lord of Israel. The ways in which the Infinite assumes the form of finite existence are called *Sefirot*. These are various aspects or forms of Divine action, spheres of Divine emanation. They are, as it were, the garments in which the Hidden God reveals Himself and acts in the universe, the channels through which His light is issued forth.[14]

The mystery or paradox is that the revelation of the Ein Sof through the emanations (sephirot) is at the same time a concealment of the Ein Sof.

Obviously, in so fresh and original a system, all the antecedent symbols and conceptions of Judaism are going to be revised and given new meanings. The single most striking revision is in the very definition of 'Torah'. We know that for classical Judaism Torah means revelation, and revelation is contained in various documents – some of them written down and handed on from Sinai, others transmitted orally, also from Sinai. But here 'Torah' takes on an altogether different meaning, being regarded as an emanation from God. It is clear that the mystic finds in the Torah meanings and dimensions not perceived elsewhere. In many ways the mysterious power of the mystic is to see what lesser eyes cannot perceive. Thus, Torah for the kabbalist came to include both the literal meaning of the words and the deeper or symbolic meaning, the level of meaning far more profound than meets the eye: God talking about God.

How widespread was kabbalistic learning, and what was its influence on the rabbinic tradition from the advent of the *Zohar* to the present? Many of the greatest sages of the Torah mastered the *Zohar* and other kabbalistic writings, and interpreted the Torah in line with those writings. The greatest models of piety sought God in the way in which the kabbalah taught. The most vital movements in Judaism from the advent of the *Zohar* to the nineteenth century – Hasidism for example – made concrete and specific the doctrines of the *Zohar* and the succession of writings that carried forward kabbalistic speculation. So in Europe, North Africa, and the Near and Middle East, kabbalistic books entered into the mainstream of Judaic theology and worship and reshaped Judaism.

8
The Law of Judaism

The halakhah, or law, of Judaism translates the Torah's master narrative into the design for Israel's social order by articulating the implicit lessons that Scripture's stories yield and framing those lessons in terms of public policy and conduct. Through its details shines the vision of the halakhah: here is how God's dominion is embodied in everyday actions and patterns of behaviour by faithful Israelites forming a holy community. They find in the laws narrated by the Torah the pattern of deeds that actualize belief. And these always are intended to acknowledge God's rule. Asked why not eat pork or why love one's neighbour as oneself, the pious Israelite responds, 'I want to eat pork, I do not want to keep the sabbath or to love my neighbour as myself, but my Father in heaven has decreed these things, and what can I do about it?' The correct motive for carrying out the acts of commission and omission required by the halakhah is to do God's will in the here and now.

The acts specified by the halakhah match the attitudes described in the aggadah, and the way of life and world-view set forth in those two principal parts of the Torah render holy Israel God's kingdom on earth. When, specifically, the faithful Israelite recites the Shema and so proclaims God's unity – a matter of theology – he or she also accepts the 'yoke of the kingdom of heaven'; God's rule in the everyday world of concrete conduct. Accordingly, Judaism defines itself through both theology and law: aggadah and halakhah, attitude and action, conviction and conduct.

The halakhah, Scripture makes clear, aims at the sanctification of Israel in accord with God's holiness. That is made explicit. When God commands Moses to tell Israel, 'You shall be holy, for I the Lord your God am holy', he immediately spells out the details of holiness, and these turn out to involve ethical conduct and concrete deeds: 'Every one of you shall revere his mother and his father, and you shall keep my sabbaths . . . Do not turn to idols or make for yourselves molten gods . . .'[1]

The rabbinic sages translated the principles set forth in the written Torah into concrete, exemplary cases. They are not the source of the law of the Torah that embodies the covenant between God and Israel. Moses is, on God's instructions. Here is how they amplify the climactic statements of Leviticus 19:18: 'You shall not take vengeance or bear any grudge . . . but you shall love your neighbour as yourself':

'You shall not take vengeance or bear any grudge' (Leviticus 19:18):

  To what extent is the force of vengeance?

  If one says to him, 'Lend me your sickle,' and the other did not do so.

  On the next day, the other says to him, 'Lend me your spade.'

  The one then replies, 'I am not going to lend it to you, because you didn't lend me your sickle.'

  In that context, it is said, 'You shall not take vengeance.'

  '. . . or bear any grudge':

  To what extent is the force of a grudge?

  If one says to him, 'Lend me your spade,' but he did not do so.

  The next day the other one says to him, 'Lend me your sickle,' and the other replies, 'I am not like you, for you didn't lend me your spade [but here, take the sickle]!'

  In that context, it is said, 'or bear any grudge'.

  '. . . but you shall love your neighbour as yourself: [I am the Lord]':

  Rabbi Akiva says, 'This is the encompassing principle of the Torah.'[2]

Christian critics of Judaism have supposed that the laws form a burden, turn people into robots, and define piety as a form of book-keeping ('I give so you give'). But that misses the point of the halakhah, which is to translate the imperatives of the Torah and the teachings of the prophets, beginning with Moses, into concrete actions shaping the entire social order of Israel. If in its details the halakhah realizes the Torah's theological principles, the details should cohere into a cogent whole, a statement of theology through law. This conception of the halakhah was set forth by Rabbi Simelai, who showed how the 613 distinct commandments that God gave Moses cohere within a few large theological and moral principles:

Six hundred and thirteen commandments were given to Moses, 365 negative ones, corresponding to the number of the days of the solar year, and 248 positive ones, corresponding to the parts of man's body.

David came and centred them upon eleven: A Psalm of David [Psalm 15]: 'Lord, who shall sojourn in thy tabernacle, and who shall dwell in thy holy mountain? (i) He who walks uprightly and (ii) works righteousness, (iii) speaks truth in his heart, (iv) has no slander on his tongue, (v) does no evil to his fellow, (vi) does not take up a reproach against his neighbour, (vii) in whose eyes a vile person is despised, but who (viii) honours those who fear the Lord. (ix) He swears to his own hurt and changes not. (x) He does not lend on interest. (xi) He does not take a bribe against the innocent.'

Isaiah came and centred them upon six: '(i) He who walks righteously and (ii) speaks uprightly, (iii) he who despises the gain of oppressions, (iv) who shakes his hands lest they hold a bribe, (v) who stops his ear from hearing of bloodshed (vi) and shuts his eyes from looking upon evil, he shall dwell on high' (Isaiah 33:15–16).

Micah came and centred them upon three: 'It has been told you, man, what is good, and what the Lord demands from you, (i) only to do justly and (ii) to love mercy, and (iii) to walk humbly with God' (Micah 6:8).

Isaiah came again and centred them upon two: 'Thus says the Lord, (i) "Keep justice and (ii) do righteousness" ' (Isaiah 56:1).

Amos came and centred them upon a single one, as it is said, 'For thus says the Lord to the house of Israel: "Seek Me and live" ' (Amos 5:4).

Habakkuk further came and based them on one, as it is said, 'But the righteous shall live by his faith' (Habakkuk 2:4).[3]

Living by one's faith should not be misunderstood. Simelai does not take Habbukuk to mean by 'faith' one's personal opinions or beliefs, nor to be commending the individual who stands against the world as a result of personal conviction. Faith is not a matter of holding particular beliefs – that God is one, for example, though that forms a principal part of Judaic theology. By 'faith' Simelai understands Habakkuk to mean 'faithfulness'; that is, trust in God and loyalty to him. 'The righteous shall live by his faith' means, 'by confidence in God's providence'. That accords with Amos's 'Seek me and live', and Micah's recommendation to 'walk humbly with God'. Naturally, faithfulness to God also yields adherence to justice and mercy.

The Halakhah of the Written Torah

The first and principal source of the halakhah in rabbinic Judaism is the Pentateuch, with the laws on the tabernacle – its design, layout and furnishings – in Exodus 29–40; the rules of Temple offerings, the maintenance of the priesthood and the purity of the Temple in Leviticus; diverse topics and special problems in Numbers; and a survey of the social laws of holy Israel in Deuteronomy. These laws form the foundation of the halakhic system and are subject to later clarification, interpretation and extension by the rabbinic sages.

For example, Scripture states, as a principle of justice, 'An eye for an eye'. Does that mean literally removing the eye of one who has blinded someone else? In response, the later rabbinic masters state:

'An eye for an eye' (Exodus 21:24), might I not say that it means an eye literally?

Perish the thought! For it has been taught on tannaite authority: Might one suppose that if someone blinded a person's eye the court should blind his eye? Or if he cut off his hand, then the court should cut off his hand, or if he broke his leg, the court should break his leg? Scripture states, 'He who hits any man . . . and he who hits any beast' – so just as if someone hits a beast, he is assigned to pay monetary compensation, so if he hits a man, he is required to pay monetary compensation.

And if you prefer, then note the following: 'Moreover you shall accept no ransom for the life of a murderer, who is guilty of death' (Numbers 35:31) – for the life of a murderer you shall take no ransom, but you shall take a ransom for the major limbs, which will not grow back.[4]

Two proofs are offered. First, an analogy is drawn to a comparable case, namely, damaging someone's property. Monetary compensation is paid, and Scripture is explicit on that point. So fair damages are also paid to a human being, not inflicted in a vengeful manner. A second proof is offered, this one based on a close reading of a pertinent passage. 'You shall accept no ransom for the life of a murderer' is taken to exclude other cases of damage, where one should take a ransom. The murderer is put to death for the murder, but one who inflicts damage on another pays monetary compensation.

A survey of the Pentateuch yields a sizeable corpus of laws that pertain to Israel's social order: civil and criminal laws; rules governing the marking of holy time (which we looked at in Chapter 1); rules on the conduct of the life cycle (see Chapter 2); and rules on purity and impurity in the holy place – originally the tabernacle, later the Temple in Jerusalem. But these rules, viewed together, tend to be episodic and particular. They are not organized in large-scale, coherent categories. For example, Leviticus 19:1–4 deals with sanctification, honouring your parents, the sabbath, and not making idols. The Ten Commandments in Exodus 20:1– 14 include not worshipping idols; not swearing falsely by God's name; the sabbath; honouring your parents; and the prohibition of murder, adultery, stealing, bearing false witness and coveting. Some of these we may call moral rules, others are matters of civil legislation, and still others entail acts of omission or commission of a religious character. The Ten Commandments do form a coherent body of halakhah for holy Israel. But Scripture provides other cases that require restatement as rules: it does not set forth the halakhah in a clear and coherent set of well-organized topics.

While, therefore, Scripture sets forth the foundations of the halakhah, it leaves two further tasks, which complement one another, incomplete: how to transform Scripture's episodic rules into laws that cover cases beyond those specified by Scripture itself; and how to organize the cases of Scripture into large-scale, coherent constructions, which form a systematic account of the social order and its cultural categories. The first involves amplifying and extending the laws, covering cases and problems that appear over time as Israelite society grows more complex and enters circumstances not encompassed by the initial revelation of the Torah. The second entails the systematization and organization in large, rational categories of the detailed and diverse laws set forth in the Torah. A survey of the specific cases mentioned in Deuteronomy 12–26, for example, covers a vast range of topics exhibiting no clear programme of organization. Most of the rules are particular to an occasion, for example,

You shall not see your brother's ass or his ox fallen down by the way, and withhold your help from them; you shall help him to lift them up again.

A woman shall not wear anything that pertains to a man, nor shall a man put on a woman's garment; for whoever does these things is an abomination to the Lord your God.

If you chance to come upon a bird's nest, in any tree or on the ground, with young ones or eggs and the mother sitting upon the young or upon the eggs, you shall not take the mother with the young . . .

When you build a new house, you shall make a parapet for your roof . . .

You shall not sow your vineyard with two kinds of seed . . .

You shall not plough with an ox and an ass together.

You shall not wear a mingled cloth combining wool and linen.

You shall make yourself tassels on the four corners of your cloak . . .[5]

This miscellany yields no generalizations and the details do not cohere; there is little more to be learned from the repertoire of rules than the rules themselves. They do not yield a large-scale design of how society is to conduct its affairs.

The task of the later rabbinic sages is clear. They had to take the details of scriptural cases and carefully reframe them into general rules. They therefore looked at each case and decided whether it gave rise to general rules or not. Their systematic and reasoned reading of the Torah turned Scripture into what we now know as the orderly and encompassing halakhic code.

But the task of recasting the miscellaneous laws of Scripture into an orderly account of Israel's society and culture went far beyond the interpretation and clarification of the Pentateuchal laws. To see how the rabbinic masters reorganized the halakhah into a rational, topical exposition by cogent categories, rather than case by case, we turn to the most important source of the halakhah besides Scripture, which is the Mishnah. The whole of the halakhah derives explicitly or by interpretation from God's revelation to Moses at Mount Sinai. But only part of it was transmitted in the written Torah we know as the Pentateuch. The other part of the Torah of Sinai, its principles and details, was transmitted orally, via the memories of masters and disciples from generation to generation until it was ultimately collected and organized as the Mishnah, a law code that was completed *c.* 200 CE under the sponsorship of Rabbi Judah the Patriarch, the recognized ruler, under the Romans, of the Jews of the Land of Israel.

The Halakhah of the Oral Torah

The philosophical law code of the Mishnah constitutes the first and most important document of the halakhah after Scripture. It set out categories under which the law was organized, yielding coherent principles that transformed cases into laws, and laws into jurisprudence. Over the next four centuries, *c.* 200–600, the Mishnah's authoritative organization and articulation of the halakhah was supplemented and systematically criticized. The first document after the Mishnah was a complementary compilation of halakhah, the Tosefta ('Supplements') of *c.* 300. The halakhah underwent a further systematic analytical process aimed at creating a completely coherent, principled legal system. That process yielded two Talmuds, or commentaries on the Mishnah: the Talmud of the Land of Israel of *c.* 400, and the Talmud of Babylonia of *c.* 600. The former is a clarification and exposition of the laws, while the latter not only presents a commentary on the Mishnah but sets forth the authoritative presentation of the halakhah and the aggadah in a single work. These expositions of the halakhah in an orderly, analytical manner represent a vast corpus of law and legal inquiry. But the presentation of the halakhah did not end in 600. Over the following centuries, right down to the present day, the process of making law codes, commentaries and answers to particular questions has continued, so that a continuous legal tradition has taken shape from Sinai onward. The goal of education in the received traditions of Judaism is to turn out informed, experienced, pious theologian-lawyers. All of this rests on the twin pillars of Scripture and the Mishnah, the former the source of the laws, the latter the recapitulation and organization of them into law, with the continuation-documents, particularly the two Talmuds, transforming law into jurisprudence.

A Talmudic story narrates the origin of the law of the Mishnah in a process of oral formulation and oral transmission beginning with God to Moses:

What is the order of Mishnah teaching? Moses learned it from the mouth of the All-Powerful. Aaron came in, and Moses repeated his chapter to him and Aaron went forth and sat at the left hand of Moses. His sons came in and Moses repeated their chapter to them, and his sons went forth. Eleazar sat at the right of Moses, and Itamar at the left of Aaron.

Then the elders entered, and Moses repeated for them their Mishnah chapter. The elders went out. Then the whole people came in, and Moses repeated for them their Mishnah chapter. So it came about that Aaron repeated the lesson four times, his sons three times, the elders two times, and all the people once.

Then Moses went out, and Aaron repeated his chapter for them. Aaron went out. His sons repeated their chapter. His sons went out. The elders repeated their chapter. So it turned out that everybody repeated the same chapter four times.

On this basis said Rabbi Eliezer, 'A person is liable to repeat the lesson for his disciple four times. And it is an argument a fortiori: if Aaron, who studied from Moses himself, and Moses from the Almighty – so in the case of a common person who is studying with a common person, all the more so!'

Rabbi Akiva says, 'How on the basis of Scripture do we know that a person is obligated to repeat a lesson for his disciple until he learns it [however many times that takes]? As it is said, "And you teach it to the children of Israel" (Deuteronomy 31:19). And how do we know that that is until it will be well ordered in their mouth? "Put it in their mouths" (Deuteronomy 31:19). And how on the basis of Scripture do we know that he is liable to explain the various aspects of the matter? "Now these are the ordinances which you shall put before them" (Exodus 21:1).'[6]

This stress on a chain of oral tradition from Moses at Sinai forward is explicitly linked to the Mishnah. The Mishnah sets forth much of the halakhah in mnemonic patterns, grouping constructions by threes or by fives, the latter corresponding to the number of fingers. It is therefore very easy to memorize. The process of memorization continued into the early centuries of the Common Era, when the Mishnah was finalized pretty much as we know it (there were some variations in manuscript versions of the Mishnah, before printing standardized the text in the early sixteenth century).

The links of oral tradition are not only formal but doctrinal. The connection of the Mishnah to Sinai is set forth in the opening statement of *Pirke Avot*, a supplement to the Mishnah, which makes two points. First, it establishes a chain of tradition from Sinai to the Mishnah's own specific authorities, Shammai and Hillel and their heirs, whose sayings mark the earliest named authorities of the Mishnah itself. It begins:

Moses received the Torah at Sinai and handed it on to Joshua, Joshua to the elders, and the elders to the prophets.

And the prophets handed it on to the men of the great assembly.

They said three things: 'Be prudent in judgement. Raise up many disciples. Make a fence for the Torah.'[7]

The chain eventually concludes by mentioning Hillel, Shammai, Gamaliel and his son. Hillel and Shammai are the masters of the Houses of Shammai and Hillel, cited very frequently in the Mishnah, and Gamaliel is the ancestor of none other than Judah the Patriarch, the sponsor of the Mishnah.

Second, *Pirke Avot* claims that the specific teachings of the rabbinic sages in the chain of tradition are deemed to form part of the Torah. This means that the Torah encompasses not only the laws of Scripture but also the teachings and traditions of those who stand in the chain of tradition from Sinai, including the rabbinic sages of this generation. There is no closed canon, no point at which the process is concluded and all one can do is find the law and cite it. The halakhic canon accommodates the rulings of the Torah sages of each successive generation. Recent discussions by contemporary Torah sages, for instance, have focused on human cloning. They have unanimously decided that the Torah permits human cloning, their argument being that immediately after conception what will become the foetus is merely physical; the soul only joins the body on the fortieth day after conception. The greatest halakhic authorities of our own times master contemporary natural science in order to reach informed decisions within the halakhic framework.

So there are important passages of the halakhah that do not derive from Scripture, but that do derive from the traditions of the Torah. The following states that fact in so many words, referring to some areas of the halakhah set forth in the Mishnah's structure that have no foundations in the written Torah, some areas in which the halakhah is elaborate, but the basis in the written Torah sparse, and some in which the Mishnah's statement of the halakhah is fully articulated and rests symmetrically upon the halakhah of Scripture:

The absolution of vows hovers in the air, for it has nothing [in the Torah] upon which to depend.

The laws of the sabbath, festal offerings, and sacrilege – lo, they are like mountains hanging by a string, for they have little Scripture for many laws.

Laws concerning civil litigations, the sacrificial rites, things to be kept ritually clean, sources of ritual uncleanness, and prohibited consanguineous marriages have much on which to depend.

And both these and those [equally] are the essentials of the Torah.[8]

The key is the concluding sentence: all are essential to the Torah, however founded on Scripture.

The Structure and Contents of
the Halakhah of the Oral Torah

The Mishnah is organized by subject area and imposes upon the laws a coherent structure that joins one fact to another in a systematic presentation of generative principles illustrated by particular rules. The later works derived from it – the Tosefta and the two Talmuds – follow the Mishnah's structure. Only many centuries later would other ways of laying out the halakhah come to the fore; even so, from 200 to the present the Mishnah's classifications of the law remain definitive.

Given what we know about Scripture's ad hoc presentation of the halakhah, the Mishnah's systematic and orderly way of accomplishing the same goal is noteworthy. It does not set forth its law as a commentary to that of Scripture, but defines for itself an independent structure, a topical programme based on a logic dictated by the indicative traits of the laws themselves. So while in Deuteronomy, as we have seen, we find this, that and the other thing mixed up together, in the Mishnah all the laws on a given subject are stated in a clear and logical order, from principles to detail.

While this mode of organization may appear to be necessary or 'self-evident' (it is how *we* should have written a law code, is it not?), there are examples of three other modes of organization in the Mishnah, which show us what might have been done. One of these is to collect diverse sayings around the name of a given authority; the whole of the tractate *Eduyyot* is organized in this way. A second way is to express a given basic principle – a fundamental rule which cuts across many areas of law – through all of the diverse types of law through which the principle may be expressed. A third way is to take a striking language pattern and collect sayings on diverse topics which conform to it. But faced with these possible ways of organizing materials, the framers of the Mishnah chose to adhere to a highly disciplined, logical, thematic organization.

The Mishnah is divided into six subject areas: (1) laws governing agriculture (the basis of economic life); (2) laws governing appointed seasons (for example, sabbaths and festivals); (3) laws on the transfer of women and property from one man (father) to another (husband); (4) the system of civil and criminal law (corresponding to what we today should regard as 'the legal system'); (5) laws for the conduct of religious rites and the Temple; and (6) laws on the preservation of ritual purity both in the Temple and under certain domestic circumstances, with special reference to the table and bed.

Let us briefly consider the six components of the Mishnah's whole, closed system for Israel's social order. There are two critical issues in the first division, farming. First, Israel, as tenant on God's holy Land, must maintain the property in the ways God requires, keeping the rules which mark the Land and its crops as holy. Second, the hour at which the sanctification of the Land comes to form a critical mass, namely in the ripened crops, is a moment ponderous with danger and heightened holiness. Israel's will affects the crops, marking a part of them as holy, the rest as available for common use. Human will is determinative in the process of sanctification.

In the second division, what happens in the Land at certain appointed times marks off spaces of the Land as holy in another way. The centre of the Land and the focus of its sanctification is the Temple. There the produce of the Land is received and given back to God, the one who created and sanctified the Land. At these unusual moments of sanctification, the inhabitants of the Land in their villages enter a state of spatial sanctification. That is to say, the village boundaries mark off holy space, within which one must remain during the holy time. This is expressed in two ways. First, the Temple itself observes and expresses the special, recurring holy time. Second, the villages of the Land are brought into alignment with the Temple, forming a complement and completion to the Temple's sacred being. The advent of the appointed times precipitates a spatial reordering of the Land, so that the boundaries of the sacred are matched and mirrored in village and Temple. Like the harvest, the advent of an appointed time is made to express that regular, orderly and predictable sort of sanctification of Israel which the system as a whole seeks.

If for a moment we now leap over the next two divisions, we come to the counterpart of the divisions of agriculture and appointed times. These are the fifth and sixth divisions, namely holy things and purities, which pertain to the Temple. They too deal with issues of sanctification of place and occasion, but of the Temple in Jerusalem rather than the village. The fifth division is about the Temple on ordinary days. The Temple, the locus of sanctification, is to be run in a wholly routine and reliable, punctilious manner. The ritual cleanness defined in the sixth division applies both to the Temple and by analogy to the household, whose table for ordinary meals is compared to the altar of the Temple, where the offerings were sent up in smoke to heaven.

The system of cleanness does not function without the wish and act of a human being. It is inert. Those sources of uncleanness and modes of purification which occur naturally remain inert until human will has intervened – that is, introduced into the system that food, bed, chair or pan which is deemed unclean. The movement from sanctification to uncleanness takes place when human will and work precipitate it.

This now brings us back to the middle divisions, the third and fourth, on women and damages. These show the congruence, within the larger framework of regularity and order, of the human concerns of family, farm, politics and workaday transactions among ordinary people. For without attending to these matters, the Mishnah's system does not encompass what, at its foundations, it is meant to comprehend and order. In the case of women, the third division, attention focuses upon the point of disorder marked by the transfer of that disordering anomaly, woman, from the regular status provided by one man, to the equally trustworthy status provided by another. In the case of the fourth division concerning damages, the Mishnah's paramount interest lies in preventing, as far as possible, the disorderly rise of one person and fall of another, and in sustaining the status quo of the economy of Israel, the holy society in eternal stasis. The necessary concomitant of this is the provision of a system of political institutions to carry out the laws which preserve the balance and steady state of the members of the community.

The Historical Setting in which the
Halakhah of the Oral Torah Took Shape

The categories of the Mishnah defy the political circumstances under which it was composed. With the Temple in ruins and the sacrificial rites suspended, four of its divisions are devoted to tithing, the conduct of sacrifices in the Temple and at festivals, and ritual purity. The Mishnah's formation of the halakhah portrayed the public life of holy Israel not as it was but as it would be in some point in the future, when the ancient paradigm of exile and return would be renewed and Jerusalem restored.

Well over half the Mishnah speaks of the Temple and its rites, priesthood and government. Moreover, it expresses a profoundly priestly conception of sanctification. When we consider that at the time it was composed the Temple lay in ruins, the city of Jerusalem was prohibited to all Israelites, and the Jewish government and administration which had centred on the Temple and based its authority on the holy life lived there were in ruins, the fantastic character of the Mishnah's address to its own catastrophic day becomes clear. Much of the Mishnah speaks of matters not in being in the time in which it was created, because it wishes to make its statement about what really matters.

The pattern of events that produced the Pentateuch – the destruction of the Temple of Jerusalem in 586, the return to Zion after 530 and the subsequent rebuilding of the Temple and restoration of the sacrifices – may have yielded expectations of a recurrence after the destruction of the Second Temple in 70 CE. But the revolt against Rome of 132–5 produced only despair, and the ancient pattern did not apply. The Mishnah preserved an account of an ideal world once lost, then regained, now lost once more, but which could be reconstructed yet again. Just as the Pentateuch responded to the first destruction and reconstruction of the Temple, so the Mishnah responded to its second destruction with a recapitulation of that same Torah, setting forth what Israel had to do this time around to maintain its covenant with God.

In the age beyond catastrophe, the problem was to reorder a world off course and adrift, to gain reorientation for an age in which the sun had come out after the night and the fog. The Mishnah is a document of imagination and fantasy, describing how things 'are' out of the shards and remnants of reality, but, in larger measure, building social being out of beams of hope. The Mishnah's halakhah, resting on Scripture's, tells us something about how things were, but everything about how a small group of men wanted things to be. The document is orderly, repetitious and careful in both language and message. It is small-minded, petty, obvious, dull, routine – everything its age was not. The Mishnah stands in contrast to the world to which it speaks. Its halakhic message is one of small achievements and modest hope. It means to defy a world of large disorders and immodest demands. The heirs of heroes built an unheroic people in the new and ordinary age. The Mishnah's message is that what a person wants matters in important ways. It states that message to an Israelite world which can shape affairs in no important ways, and speaks to people who by no means will the way things now are. The Mishnah therefore lays down a practical judgement in favour of the imagination and will to reshape reality, regain a system, and re-establish that order upon which trustworthy existence is to be built. No wonder then that in the aftermath of the Holocaust of the twentieth century a renewal of, and a rededication to, the halakhic Judaism defined the principal response of the Torah camp of Judaism, as we shall see in Chapter 11.

How Does the Halakhah Carry
Forward the Torah's Story of Israel?

These general remarks about the character and context of the halakhah – where we find it, what it is – convey little of the depth and density of its discourse. The law serves as the principal medium of theology in rabbinic Judaism. Precisely how this works is best set forth in a single concrete case, showing how the Mishnah responds to the written Torah's laws. The example I have chosen is a specific statement that, on the Day of Atonement, 'you shall afflict yourselves' (Leviticus 16:31).

Telling what is done and so indicating the rule governing what should be done, the written Torah presents the offerings of the Day of Atonement as a narrative, mostly in Leviticus 16, concluding with a reference to the requirement of the affliction of the soul in atonement for sin. In the oral

Torah, of the eight chapters on this topic, the first seven provide a narrative, with interpolations, of the sacrificial rite of the Day of Atonement. The eighth does little more, taking up the rules of the affliction of the soul, that is, fasting. But at the end, the oral Torah links atonement to repentance, completely recasting the topic, and it is at this point that the oral Torah does more than make its comment on the written one.

The pertinent verses of Scripture are as follows:

The Lord spoke to Moses after the death of the two sons of Aaron, when they drew near before the Lord and died; and the Lord said to Moses, 'Tell Aaron your brother not to come at all times into the holy place within the veil, before the mercy seat which is upon the ark, lest he die; for I will appear in the cloud upon the mercy seat. But thus shall Aaron come into the holy place: with a young bull for a sin offering and a ram for a burnt offering. He shall put on the holy linen coat and shall have the linen breeches on his body, be girded with the linen girdle, and wear the linen turban; these are the holy garments. He shall bathe his body in water, and then put them on. And he shall take from the congregation of the people of Israel two male goats for a sin offering and one ram for a burnt offering . . .

'It shall be a statute for you for ever that in the seventh month, on the tenth day of the month, you shall afflict yourselves, and shall do no work, either the native or the stranger who sojourns among you; for on this day shall atonement be made for you, to cleanse you; from all your sins you shall be clean before the Lord. It is a sabbath of solemn rest to you, and you shall afflict yourselves; it is a statute for ever. And the priest who is anointed and consecrated as priest in his father's place shall make atonement, wearing the holy linen garments; he shall make atonement for the sanctuary and he shall make atonement for the tent of meeting and for the altar, and he shall make atonement for the priests and for all the people of the assembly. And this shall be an everlasting statute for you, that atonement may be made for the people of Israel once in the year because of their sins.' And Moses did as the Lord commanded him.[9]

This is how the Mishnah and then the Tosefta amplify the matter of 'afflicting one's soul':

On the Day of Atonement it is forbidden to eat, drink, bathe, put on any sort of oil, put on a sandal, or engage in sexual relations. But a king and a bride may wash their faces. 'And a woman who has given birth may put on her sandal', in the words of Rabbi Eliezer; but other sages prohibit.[10]

*

On the Day of Atonement it is forbidden to eat, drink, bathe, anoint, put on
sandals, [and] have sexual relations. [It is not permitted to put on] even felt
shoes. Minors are permitted to do all of them except putting on sandals, for
appearance's sake.[11]

A man should not put on a nail-studded shoe and walk about his house, even
from one bed to another. But Rabban Simeon ben Gamaliel permits. And so did
Rabban Simeon ben Gamaliel say, 'If someone's hands are dirty with mud or
excrement, he may rinse them off in water, so that they will not dirty his clothes.'
[If] he was going to receive his father, master, [or] disciple, he can cross over
the sea or river in the normal way, even up to his neck, and need not scruple.[12]

This shows how the law set forth in the Mishnah is amplified, and how
minority opinion is allowed to register.

Now we turn to the halakhic reprise of the atonement process,
represented only in part by the narrative of Leviticus 16. Here is where
the halakhah takes a position of independence and autonomy of Scripture,
going beyond the limits of the written Torah and imposing a new
perspective upon it:

A sin-offering and an unconditional guilt-offering atone. Death and the Day of
Atonement atone when joined with repentance. Repentance atones for minor
transgressions of positive and negative commandments. And as to serious transgressions, [repentance] suspends the punishment until the Day of Atonement
comes along and atones.[13]

Rabbi Ishmael says, 'There are four kinds of atonement. [If] someone has violated
a positive commandment but repented, he hardly moves from his place before
they forgive him, since it is said, "Return, backsliding children. I will heal your
backsliding" (Jeremiah 3:22).

'[If] he has violated a negative commandment but repented, repentance
suspends the punishment, and the Day of Atonement effects atonement, since it
is said, "For that day will effect atonement for you" (Leviticus 16:30).

'[If] he has violated [a rule for which the punishment is] extirpation or death
at the hands of an earthly court, but repented, repentance and the Day of
Atonement suspend [the punishment], and suffering on the other days of the year
will wipe away [the sin], since it says, "Then will I punish their transgression
with the rod" (Psalms 89:32). But he through whom the Name of Heaven is

profaned deliberately but who repented – repentance does not have power to suspend [the punishment], nor the Day of Atonement to atone, but repentance and the Day of Atonement atone for a third, suffering atones for a third, and death wipes away the sin, with suffering, and on such a matter it is said, "Surely this iniquity will not be forgiven you till you die" (Isaiah 22:14).'[14]

The Mishnah classifies the means of atonement. What the supplement of the Tosefta contributes is the organization of the whole into a dynamic process of forgiveness, including the prophetic doctrines of that process: Rabbi Ishmael introduces Jeremiah, Psalms and Isaiah into his halakhic exposition. The halakhah is no longer a sequence of formal actions, but a response to God's attitude towards the process of atonement and how God guides that process towards the sought-after conclusion, reconciliation (not punishment at all). When the aggadah says, 'All Israel has a portion in the world to come', it depends upon the halakhah of repentance and atonement: specific actions aimed at producing concrete consequences.

Since the halakhah imposes patterns of behaviour, requiring restraint in some things, initiative in others, where is there room for the individual and the exercise of his or her particular intentionality? For, as the aggadic narrative calls to mind, at issue throughout is the regeneration of humanity, the re-education of Adam and Eve through the Torah. Responding to their rebellion against God, when they put their will above God's, the Torah means to purify the heart of human beings, so that Israelites will freely give what God most wants but cannot coerce – each person to love him 'with all your heart, and with all your soul, and with all your might' (Deuteronomy 6:5).

The halakhah demonstrates the centrality of a person's intention to this process by showing that the rites of atonement do not coerce God, who only responds to the *attitude* involved in them. The concluding rule of the Mishnah discusses the possibility of pre-emptive atonement – first atone, then sin – which would turn the rite into a form of magic, by which one may manipulate God. The halakhah insists on the contrary view: one's intent in repenting means everything, and if the intent is to repent in order to sin again, the entire process is null and void:

He who says, 'I shall sin and repent, sin and repent' – they give him no chance to do repentance. 'I will sin and the Day of Atonement will atone' – the Day of Atonement does not atone . . .

This exegesis did Rabbi Eleazar ben Azariah state: ' "From all your sins shall you be clean before the Lord" (Leviticus 16:30) – for transgressions between man and the Omnipresent the Day of Atonement atones. For transgressions between man and his fellow, the Day of Atonement atones, only if the man regains the goodwill of his friend.'

Said Rabbi Akiva, 'Happy are you, O Israel. Before whom are you made clean, and who makes you clean? It is your Father who is in heaven, as it says, "And I will sprinkle clean water on you, and you will be clean" (Ezekiel 36:25). And it says, "O Lord, the hope [mikveh; immersion pool] of Israel" (Jeremiah 17:13) – just as the immersion pool cleans the unclean, so the Holy One, blessed be he, cleans Israel.'[15]

Thus the halakhah stresses that repentance takes effect only if it is honest and sincere. If one treats repentance as a matter of mere ritual, doing its work automatically, repentance produces nothing. It is an expression of the heart, to which God responds in his heart. Also, repentance pertains not only to God but to the person whom one has injured or hurt. The Day of Atonement and its rites pertain to the relationships between God and humanity. But it atones for those between people only when we have repented what we have done to the other person.

The Tosefta's amplification of these matters deepens the discussion considerably. First, the requirement of repentance along with the Day of Atonement itself is articulated:

The sin-offering, guilt-offering, and Day of Atonement all effect atonement only along with repentance since it says, 'But on the tenth day of the seventh month [is the Day of Atonement]' (Leviticus 23:27). If [the sinner] repents, atonement is effected for him, and if not, it is not effected for him. Rabbi Eleazar says, ' "Forgiving [iniquity and transgression and sin]" ' (Exodus 34:7) – he forgives iniquity to penitents, but he does not forgive iniquity to those who do not repent.'

Rabbi Judah says, 'Death and the Day of Atonement effect atonement along with repentance. Repentance effects atonement with death. And the day of death – lo, it is tantamount to an act of repentance.'[16]

Second, the stake of the community is articulated, in the match between zekut/merit and het/sin. If a person leads the community in acts of self-abnegation so that God responds with favour, that person never gets to transgress at all; for the same reason, whoever makes the community sin cannot repent:

Whoever bestows merit on the community – they never suffice him to commit a transgression, lest his disciples [the community] inherit the world [to come] while he descends to Sheol. As it is said, 'For you will not leave my soul in hell' (Psalms 16:10).

Whoever brings sin on the community – they never suffice him to effect repentance, lest his disciples [the community] descend to Sheol [the dwelling-place of the dead], while he inherits the world [to come], as it is said, 'A man who does violence to any person shall flee to the pit, let no man stay him' (Proverbs 28:17).[17]

Note the ubiquitous presence of the belief in the resurrection of the dead, the Last Judgement, and the restoration of Adam and Eve to Eden, corresponding to the restoration of Israel to the Land of Israel.

Third, what of the recidivist? God forgives, but not for ever. There is a point at which a person is marked as incorrigible, and such a person is punished; some few people will not appear at the Last Judgement, but are condemned:

Rabbi Yosé says, '[If] a man sins two or three times, they forgive him. [But on the] fourth, they do not forgive him, as it says, "Forgiving iniquity and transgression and sin, but he will by no means clear the guilty" (Exodus 34:7). Up to this point he clears [him]. From this point forward he will not clear [him], since it says, "For three transgressions of Israel – but for four, I will not revoke the punishment" (Amos 2:6). And it says, "He will deliver his soul from going down into the pit . . . all these things does God do two or three times for a man" (Job 33:28–9).'[18]

On the other hand, sin does not pile up without limit; if one has been forgiven, that does register, and sins for which one has confessed on a prior Day of Atonement do not have to be recapitulated again and again:

Matters concerning which someone has said confession on the preceding Day of Atonement he does not have to include in the confessions of the coming Day of Atonement, unless he did those same transgressions [in the intervening year]. [If] he committed those transgressions, he must include them in the confession. [If] he did not commit those transgressions, but he included them in his confession – concerning such a person the following is said: 'As a dog returns to his vomit, so a fool returns to his folly' (Proverbs 26:11). Rabbi Eliezer ben Jacob says, 'Lo, such a person is praiseworthy, since it is said, "For I acknowledge my transgressions" (Psalms 51:3).'[19]

It is only when we reach the concluding statements of the halakhah on atonement as set forth in the Mishnah and amplified by the Tosefta (and the Talmuds, not cited here) that we move beyond the halakhic reprise of the Torah's narrative. It is at the end that the presentation of the halakhah tells us what is at stake, which is the prophetic reading of Judaism. The rabbinic sages understood the prophets' critique of the Temple sacrifices not as repudiation but as refinement, and in their account of the rites of blood sacrifice they therefore invoke the prophets' norms alongside the Torah's: Jeremiah's call to repentance, Isaiah's reflections on the role of death in the penitential process and God's infinite mercy, and Ezekiel's insistence on purity of spirit. Above all, the rabbinic sages underscore God's explicit promise to purify Israel, the promise set forth in Ezekiel's and Jeremiah's prophecies. So the halakhah recasts the entire category of the Day of Atonement, taking the theme of atonement to require an account of repentance and God's power to forgive and purify from sin. The rites of atonement do not work automatically but are conditional upon the attitude and intention of the Israelite.

Two fundamental messages register. First, the rites atone and so does death — but only when joined with repentance, and repentance reaches its climax in the cleansing effect of the occasion, the Day of Atonement itself. But, second, the entire system realizes its promise of reconciliation with God only on one condition: the Israelite to begin with must have the right attitude, of sincerity and integrity.

The halakhah carries the matter still further when it insists that, in the end, the attitude of the repentant sinner does not complete the transaction; the sinner depends also upon the attitude of the sinned-against. I cannot think of a more eloquent way of saying that the entire condition of Israel depends upon the inner integrity of Israel: the intentionality that motivates its actions, whether in relationship to God or man. The halakhah in this example takes shape within its own logic, which emerges from the dialogue between the written Torah's and the prophets' contrasting but complementary teachings. It is the logic that joins rite to right which was discerned by the sages of the halakhah of the oral Torah.

Holy Israel responded to the Day of Atonement by fixing upon not the sacrificial rite of the high priest in the Temple, but the atonement-celebration of all Israel in the world. What mattered to Moses in Leviticus and to the rabbinic sages in the Mishnah alike was the timeless performance of atonement through the bloody rites of the Temple. But the Day of Atonement that came down through the ages, realized in the halakhah of self-affliction through fasting, prayer and confession, emphasized the personal discipline of atonement through repentance on the Day of Atonement and a life of virtue and Torah-learning on the rest of the days of the year. Israel took that very mysterious rite of atonement that the Day of Atonement called forth out of the Holy of Holies and brought it into the homes and streets of the holy people. The wider vision of the halakhah transformed the presentation the day and its meaning, transcending the limits of the sacrificial rites that the details of its rules focused on. And it was this vision which would prove definitive.

From antiquity to our own day the Day of Atonement has enjoyed the loyalty of holy Israel come what may, gaining the standing of Judaism's single most widely observed occasion. That fact attests to the power of the halakhah and aggadah, working together, to transform a sacerdotal narrative into a medium of the inner, moral sanctification of Israel. The entire dynamism of the halakhah is captured in this single case. It gathers power from its capacity to address the situation of Israel, the holy people, bereft of their Temple, and to translate into the everyday and the here and now the meaning of this 'service of the heart'. The halakhah represents the realization of the covenant of God and Israel at Sinai. It accomplishes the embodiment of that covenantal nomism that is Judaism.

Judaism in Medieval and
Modern Times

9
The Success of Judaism's Story

The Success of Rabbinic
Judaism in Western Civilization

From the completion, in *c.* 600 CE, of the Talmud of Babylonia, which marked the realization of the story told by Judaism as described in Chapters 1 to 8 of this book, Judaism endured in the Christian West as well as in the Muslim East. This was for two reasons: Christianity and Islam permitted it; and Israel, the Jewish people wherever located, wanted it to. The fate of paganism in the fourth century (and of Zoroastrianism and 'Sabeanism' – probably Mandean gnosticism – in the seventh and eighth under Islam) shows the importance of the first of these two factors. It was not the intellectual power of the rabbinic sages alone that secured the long-term triumph of Judaism; it was also due to the character of the Christian emperors' tolerant policy towards Judaism. The religious worship of Judaism was never prohibited. Pagan sacrifice, by contrast, was forbidden in 341; their festivals went on into the fifth century, but the die was cast.

Rabbinic Judaism constructed for Israel a world in which their experience of the loss of political sovereignty and the persistence of their condition of tolerated subordination within Islam and Christendom were seen as evidence of the importance and centrality of Israel in the human situation. The success of Judaism derives from a reciprocal process. First, rabbinic Judaism restated that experience of loss and restoration, death and resurrection that the first Scripture had set out. Second, it pointed to the condition of the Jews, subordinated and exiled, as evidence of the truth of the Torah: they were punished for sin, and just as surely, they would be restored when they repented. So the system reinforced itself. That is how the very situation in which the Jews found themselves attested to the truth of the Torah of Moses and gave hope to the people, a small and not always respected minority. But rabbinic Judaism did more than react, reassure and encourage. It acted upon and determined the shape of matters. For a long time rabbinic Judaism defined the politics and policy of the community. It instructed Israel, the Jewish people, on those attitudes and actions that would produce an Israel that was on the one hand subordinate and tolerated, but also proud and hopeful. Rabbinic Judaism began in the encounter with a successful Christianity and persisted in the face of a still more successful Islam. But for the community of Israel that Judaism persevered because, long after the conditions that originally precipitated the positions and policies that became orthodox, that same Judaism not only reacted to, but also shaped, Israel's condition in the world. Making a virtue of a policy of subordination that was not always necessary or even wise, rabbinic Judaism defined and set the limits to the Jews' condition.

How do we know that rabbinic Judaism has governed the entire world of Judaism from antiquity to our own day? What attests to its power is its capacity to encompass diverse Judaisms, each with its distinctive choice of elements, within the classical system. We see the cogency of the system when we consider the Judaisms that it both precipitated and also accommodated. Over the centuries from the fourth to the present time, derivative systems took shape, restating in distinctive ways the fundamental convictions of rabbinic Judaism, or adding their particular perspective or doctrine to that system. Not only so, but heresies attained heretical status specifically by rejecting important components of the received system. For example, rabbinic Judaism taught that the Torah came in two forms, oral and written. One heresy denied the authority or authenticity of the oral part. Rabbinic Judaism prophesied that the Messiah would be a sage and would observe the Torah. Another heresy rejected that doctrine in favour of the sinning Messiah, who did not need to observe the Torah.

So long as the established Judaism persisted, derivative systems, whether orthodox or heretical, positioned themselves in relationship to the dominant statement of matters. Only when the received Judaism no longer enjoyed virtually unique standing as the self-evidently valid answer to obviously urgent questions did Judaic systems take shape that were utterly out of phase with the one that reached its initial version in the fourth century and its final one in the Talmud of Babylonia.

New Modes of Thought and the
Advent of Philosophical Thinking

The rise of Islam from the seventh century brought important intellectual changes, due to the character of Islamic culture. Muslim theologians, responding to Greek philosophy translated (not uncommonly by bilingual Jews) into Arabic, developed a rigorous, abstract and scientific way of thinking. They had a special interest in Aristotle, founder of the philosophical tradition of criticism. Rabbinic sages in the Islamic world then began to think philosophically about religious data and produced theology; and they engaged with their counterparts in Islam and Christianity and produced a common philosophy of religion as well.

The new thinking and the issues it generated represented a challenge to the received tradition of doctrine and thought. While in ancient times a school of Judaic philosophy in the Greek-speaking Jewish world, represented by Philo of Alexandria, read Scripture in the light of philosophy, the sages of the Talmud did not follow that generalizing and speculative mode of thought. They read Scripture within a different framework altogether. But as the Judaic intellectuals in the Islamic world faced the challenge of Muslim rationalism and philosophical rigour, they read Scripture and the oral Torah in a new way. The task at hand was to reconcile and accommodate the principles of the Torah with the propositions of philosophy. In medieval Islam and Christendom, no Judaic intellectuals could rest easy in the admission that Scripture and science, in its philosophical form, came into conflict.

That is why alongside study of Torah, which meant spending one's life in learning the Babylonian Talmud and later codes, commentaries and rabbinic court decisions, a different sort of intellectual-religious life now flourished in Judaism. It was the study of the tradition through the instruments of reason and the discipline of philosophy. The philosophical enterprise attracted small numbers of elite intellectuals and mainly served their specialized spiritual and intellectual needs. But they set the standard, and those who followed it included the thoughtful and the perplexed, those who took the statements of the tradition most seriously and, through questioning and reflection, intended to examine and then carry them out. The rabbinic philosophers of Judaism, moreover, were not men who limited their activities to study and teaching. They frequently both occupied high posts within the Jewish community and served in the high society of politics, culture and science outside the community as well. Though not numerous, the philosophers exercised considerable influence, particularly over the mind of an age that believed reason and learning, not wealth and worldly power, were what really mattered.

Philosophy flourished in a world of deep religious conviction, a conviction common to the several disparate religious communities. The issues of philosophy were set, not by lack of belief, but by deep faith. Few, if any, denied providence, a personal God, and a holy book revealed by God through his chosen messenger. Everyone believed in reward and punishment, in a Last Judgement, and in a settling of accounts. The Jewish philosopher had to cope with problems imposed not only by the classical faith, but also by the anomalous situation of the Jews themselves. That situation was perceived within the theology of the Torah that told the story of Israel as Adam's counterpart and opposite, covenanted with God. The question of justice loomed large: how was philosophy to account reasonably for the homelessness of God's people, who were well aware that they lived as a minority among powerful, prosperous majorities, Christian or Muslim?

The new context of intellectual competition contributed a new question: if the Torah was true, why did different revelations claiming to be based upon it, but to complete it in different ways, flourish, while the people of the Torah suffered? Why, indeed, ought one to remain a Jew, when every day one was confronted by the success of the daughter religions? Conversion was always a possibility, an inviting one even under the best of circumstances for a member of a despised minority. Life in accordance with the Torah therefore was complicated by the formidable appeal of Greek philosophy to medieval Christian and Islamic civilization. Its rationalism, its openness, its search for pure knowledge challenged all revelations. Philosophy called into question all assertions of truth verifiable not through reason, but only through appeals to a source of truth not universally recognized. Reason thus stood, it seemed, against revelation. Mysterious divine plans came into conflict with allegations of the limitless capacity of human reason. Free inquiry might lead anywhere and so would not reliably lead to the synagogue, church or mosque. And not merely traditional knowledge, but the specific propositions of faith and the assertions of a holy book had to be measured against the results of reason. Faith *or* reason, this seemed to be the choice.

For the Jews, moreover, the very substance of faith – a personal, highly anthropomorphic God who exhibited traits of character not always in conformity with humanity's highest ideals and who in rabbinic hands looked much like a rabbi himself – posed a formidable obstacle. Classical conundrums of philosophy were further enriched by the obvious contradictions between belief in free will and belief in divine providence. Is God all-knowing? Then how can people be held responsible for what they do? Is God perfect? Then how can he change his mind or set aside his laws to forgive people? No theologian in such a cosmopolitan, rational age could begin with an assertion of a double truth or a private, relative one. The notion that something could be true for one party and not for another, or that faith and reason were equally valid and yet contradictory were ideas that had little appeal. And the holy book had to retain the upper hand. Two philosophers represent the best efforts of medieval Judaic civilization to confront these perplexities.

The first is Moses Maimonides (1141–1205), who was a distinguished student of the Talmud and of Jewish law in the classical mode, a community authority, a great physician, and a leading thinker of his day. His achievement was to synthesize a Neoplatonic Aristotelianism with scriptural revelation. His *Guide to the Perplexed*, published in 1190, was intended to reconcile the believer to the philosopher and the philosopher to faith. For him philosophy was not alien to religion but identical with it, for truth was, in the end, the sole issue. Faith is a form of knowledge; philosophy is the road to faith. His proof for the existence of God was Aristotelian. He argued from creation to Creator, but accepted the eternity of the world. God becomes, therefore, an 'absolutely simple essence from which all positive definition is excluded'.[1] One can say nothing about the attributes of God. He is purged of all sensuous elements. One can say only that God is God, nothing more, for God can only be *known* as the highest cause of being.

What then of revelation? Did God not say anything about himself? And if he did, what need for reasonings such as these? For Maimonides, prophecy, like philosophy, depends upon the active intellect. Prophecy is a gift bestowed by God upon man. The Torah and commandments are clearly important, but are not ultimately beyond question or reasonable inquiry. They do, however, survive the inquiry unimpaired. The Torah fosters a sound mind and body. The greatest good, however, is not to study the Torah in the sense described earlier, but rather to know God – that is, to worship and love him. Piety and knowledge of the Torah serve merely to prepare people for this highest achievement. Study of the Torah loses its character as an end in itself and is rendered into a means to a philosophical goal. This constituted Maimonides' most striking transformation of the old values.

Maimonides provided a philosophical definition of Judaism, a list of articles of faith he thought obligatory for every faithful Jew: (1) the existence of God; (2) his unity; (3) his incorporeality; (4) his eternity; (5) the obligation to worship him alone; (6) prophecy; (7) Moses as the greatest of the prophets; (8) the divine origin of the Torah; (9) the eternal validity of the Torah; (10) God's knowledge of man's deeds; (11) his promise to send a Messiah; and (12) his promise to resurrect the dead. These are now sung in synagogue worship, so the words of the philosopher have been transformed into a message of faith, at once sufficiently complex to sustain critical inquiry according to the canons of the day and simple enough to bear the weight of the faith of ordinary people and to be sung. The 'God without attributes' is still guide, refuge and stronghold. It is a strange and paradoxical fate for the philosopher's teachings.

Judah Halevi (1080–1141) represents those who found the philosophers presumptuous, inadequate, and incapable of investigating the truths of faith. But the critics of 'philosophy' were themselves philosophers. Halevi produced a set of imaginary dialogues between a king, the king of the Khazars (a kingdom which had, in fact, considered Islam and Christianity and then adopted Judaism several centuries earlier), in search of true religion, and the advocates of the several religious and philosophical positions of the day, including Judaism. Judah Halevi, poet and mystic, objected to the indifference of philosophy to the comparative merits of the competing traditions. In philosophy's approach, religion is recommended, but which religion does not matter much. For the majority religions in the West, Islam and Christianity, such an indifference may have been tolerable, but not for a minority destined any day to meet a challenge to their faith. In 1096 the Jews in the Rhineland were subjected to martyrdom or forced conversion to Christianity, and many communities chose suicide rather than apostasy. But, the critics of philosophical rationalism argued, martyrdom, such as Jews faced, will not be evoked by the unmoved mover, the God anyone may reach either through revelation or through reason. Only for the God of Israel will a Jew give up his or her life. By its nature, philosophy is insufficient for the religious quest. It can hardly compete with, let alone challenge, the *history* of the Jewish people, a history recording extraordinary events starting with revelation. What has philosophy to do with Sinai, with the Land, with prophecy? On the contrary, the Jew, expounding religion to the king of the Khazars, begins not like the philosopher with a disquisition on divine attributes, not like the Christian who starts with the works of Creation and expounds the Trinity, nor like the Moslem who acknowledges the unity and eternity of God, but as follows:

I believe in the God of Abraham, Isaac, and Israel, who led the Israelites out of Egypt with signs and miracles; who fed them in the desert and gave them the Land, after having made them traverse the sea and the Jordan in a miraculous way; who sent Moses with His Torah and subsequently thousands of prophets, who confirmed His law by promises to those who observed and threats to the disobedient. We believe in what is contained in the Torah, a very large domain.[2]

The king then asks the Jew why he did not say he believed in the creator of the world and in similar attributes common to all creeds? The Jew responds that the evidence for Israel's faith is *Israel*, the people, this history and endurance, and not the kinds of reasonable truths offered by other traditions. The *proof* of revelation is the testimony of those who were *there* and wrote down what they heard, saw, and did. If so, the king wonders, what accounts for the despised condition of Israel today? The Jew compares Israel to the dry bones of Ezekiel, 'these bones, which have retained a trace of vital power and have once been the seat of a heart, head, spirit, soul, and intellect, are better than bones formed of marble and plaster, endowed with heads, eyes, ears, and all limbs, in which there never dwelt the spirit of life.'[3] God's people are Israel; he rules them and keeps them in their present status:

Israel amid the nations is like the heart amid the organs: it is the most sick and the most healthy of them all . . . The relationship of the Divine power to us is the same as that of the soul to the heart. For this reason it is said, 'You only have I known among all the families of the earth, therefore I will punish you for all your iniquities' (Amos 3:2) . . . Now we are oppressed, while the whole world enjoys rest and prosperity. But the trials which meet us serve to purify our piety, cleanse us, and to remove all taint from us.[4]

The pitiful condition of Israel is, therefore, turned into the primary testimony and vindication of Israel's faith. That Israel suffers is the best assurance of divine concern. The suffering constitutes the certainty of coming redemption. In the end, the Jew parts from the king in order to undertake a journey to the Land of Israel. There he seeks perfection with God. To this the king objects. He thought the Jew loved freedom, but the Jew finds himself in bondage by imposing obligatory duties, including residing in the Land of Israel. The Jew replies that the freedom he seeks is from the service of men and the courting of their favour. He seeks the service of one whose favour is obtained with the smallest effort. He, therefore, turns to Jerusalem to seek the holy life. Here we find no effort to identify Judaism with rational truth, but rather the claim that the life of the pious Jew stands above, indeed constitutes the best testimony to, truth.

The source of truth is scriptural revelation. Halevi argued that revelation took place in public. It was complete. It was known to large numbers of witnesses. It was an historical event. History, not philosophy, testifies to the truth and in the end constitutes its sole criterion. Philosophy claims reason can find the way to God. Halevi says only God can show the way to God, and he does so through revelation, and therefore in history. The philosopher seeks to know God. For Halevi, God is the source of knowledge: God reveals himself, thus is the subject of knowledge And Israel has a specifically religious faculty which mediates the relationship with God, as suggested in the reference to the role of Israel among the nations as similar to the role of the heart among the limbs. Halevi seeks to explain the supernatural status of Israel. The religious faculty is its peculiar inheritance and makes it the core of humanity. But while the rest of humanity is subject to the laws of nature, Israel is subject to supernatural, divine providence, manifested in reward and punishment.

The very condition of the Jews, in that God punishes them, verifies the particular and specific place of Israel in the divine plan.

While they were much like the Muslim and Christian intellectuals in mentality, the Jewish philosophers had more in common with the Talmudic rabbis than with gentile philosophers. The rabbis accepted scripture and the Talmud as 'the whole Torah', and so did the Jewish philosophers. Both groups devoted themselves to the articulation of the role of Torah in the life of Israel, to the meaning of the fate of Israel, and to the effort to form piety and shape faith. And for both, applied reason and practical logic provided the means of reaching into the Torah, of recovering and achieving truth. Both agreed that words could contain and convey the sacred, and therefore reason, the examination of the meaning of words and what they stand for, was the golden rule. They differed only in the object of their reasoning: the rabbinic sages studied law, the philosophers, philosophy. Yet Maimonides, the complete and whole Jew, studied both and made a lasting impact upon the formation not only of both sorts of Judaic tradition, but also of the pious imagination of the ordinary Jew. That is because he translated his philosophical and theological principles and convictions into his presentation of concrete, practical law.

Hasidism

Not only did rabbinic Judaism draw strength from new modes of thought, it also accommodated emphases in piety that placed a higher value on direct encounter with God and on spiritual gifts than upon knowledge of the Torah.[5] Beginning in the mid eighteenth century in the Ukraine and Poland and continuing to this day as a bastion of true belief and realized Torah-piety, Hasidism, a mystical movement drawing upon the resources of the kabbalah, began with emphases quite at variance with those of rabbinic Judaism. What distinguished Hasidism from the standard rabbinic Judaism was its focus on holy men as conduits of divine grace. These holy men, called *zaddikim*, righteous men, or *rebbes*, some of them endowed with profound learning in the Torah, were all exemplars of purity and piety. The groups that took shape around these charismatic personalities favoured direct encounter with God by holy men over meeting God in the Torah. But one Hasidic circle, today known as Habad (an acronym of the initials of the Hebrew words for wisdom, understanding and knowledge), and centred around the Hasidic dynasty deriving from the town of Lubavich, ultimately found a central place in its piety for Torah-study. Many other Hasidic groups preserved the value of Torah-study as a means of mystical experience, through meditation on the shape of the Hebrew letters. What made Habad special was the emphasis they put on Torah-study in an early stage in Hasidic development, and on Hasidic theology, not only practice.

The mystic circles in the Ukraine and Poland in the eighteenth century among whom Hasidism developed carried on certain practices that marked them as different from other Jews – special prayers, distinctive ways of observing certain religious duties, and the like. The first of the ecstatics, Israel ben Eliezer, also known as Baal Shem Tov or Besht (c. 1700–1760), worked as a popular healer. From the 1730s on he undertook travels and attracted to himself circles of followers in Podolia (Ukraine), Poland, Lithuania, and elsewhere. When he died he left behind no more than a small, unformed group of disciples and admirers. One of his prominent disciples, Rabbi Dov Baer (c. 1700–1773), the Maggid of Mezhirich, succeeded him as leader of this group. It was during his time that the group became a mass movement. During the last year of his activity, the first anti-Hasidic reactions took place. When he died, he left disciples who organized the movement in various centres in south-eastern Poland and Lithuania. Dov Baer inaugurated the institution of the Hasidic court and dispatched disciples beyond Podolia to establish courts on their own. Most of the major Hasidic circles originate in his disciples, one of whom was Rebbi Shneur Zalman of Liadi, the founder of Habad Hasidism. Leadership of the movement passed to a succession of holy men, about whom stories were told and preserved. In the third generation, from the third quarter of the eighteenth century into the first of the nineteenth, the movement spread and took hold. Diverse leaders, called Zaddikim, charismatic figures, developed their own standing and doctrine.

Given the controversies that swirled about the movement, we should expect that many of the basic ideas would have been new. But that was hardly the case. The movement drew heavily on available mystical books and doctrines, which from medieval times had won a place within the faith as part of the Torah. Emphasis on the distinctive doctrines of Hasidic thinkers should not obscure the profound continuities between the modern movement and its medieval sources. To take one example of how the movement imparted its own imprint on an available idea, Menahem Mendel of Lubavich notes that God's oneness, surely a given in all Judaisms, means more than that God is unique. It means that God is all that is:

There is no reality in created things. This is to say that in truth all creatures are not in the category of something or a thing as we see them with our eyes. For this is only from our point of view, since we cannot perceive the divine vitality. But from the point of view of the divine vitality which sustains us, we have no existence and we are in the category of complete nothingness like the rays of the sun in the sun itself . . . From which it follows that there is no other existence whatsoever apart from his existence, blessed be he. This is true unification . . .[6]

Since all things are in God, the suffering and sorrow of the world cannot be said to exist. So to despair is to sin.

Hasidism laid great stress on joy and avoiding melancholy. It further maintained that the right attitude must accompany the doing of religious deeds: the deed could only be elevated when carried out in a spirit of devotion. The doctrine of Hasidism moreover held that,

In all things there are 'holy sparks' waiting to be redeemed and rescued for sanctity through man using his appetites to serve God. From this idea stems the early Hasidic doctrine that in the material world are divine sparks, so even a material act can be a spiritual action for revealing the divine light, if it is carried out by a Tsaddik or Rebbe who acts with such an intention. The very taste of food is a pale reflection of the spiritual force which brings the food into being . . .[7]

What followed from this doctrine was that before carrying out a religious deed, the Hasidic Jew would recite the formula, 'For the sake of the unification of the Holy One, blessed be he, and his *shekhinah* [presence in the world].' They were criticized for thus adding to the prayers that everyone said, and reshaping their meaning. But the fundamental pattern of life, the received world-view contained in the holy canon of Judaism, defined the issues that Hasidism addressed. Hasidism therefore was distinctive, yet in its major traits so closely related to rabbinic Judaism as to be indistinguishable except in trivial details. But one of these mattered a great deal, and that was the doctrine of zaddikism: the *zaddik*, or holy man, had the power to carry the prayers of his followers up to heaven, and so to work miracles for them. The *zaddik* was the means through which grace reached the world, the one who controlled the universe through his prayers. The *zaddik* would bring humanity nearer to God and God closer to humanity. The Hasidim were well aware that this doctrine of the *zaddik*, the pure and elevated soul that could reach to that realm of heaven in which only mercy reigns, represented an innovation. Hasidism postulated that Israelites should cling to God (*devekut*), through mystical experience. But even in its early stages, the Hasidic leadership realized that not everyone is capable of realizing that ideal. The doctrine of the *zaddik* solved the problem. The *zaddik* clings to God, and the common Hasid is connected to the *zaddik* and thus through him to God. Each Hasid had to find the *zaddik* that suited his own personality, and the *zaddikim* afforded a variety of nuances in the Hasidic message.

By the end of the eighteenth century a powerful opposition, led by the most influential figures of East European Judaism, characterized Hasidism as heretical. The ecstasy, visions, and the *zaddikim*'s miracles it laid stress on were seen as delusions, and the veneration of the *zaddik* was interpreted as worship of a human being. The stress on prayer to the detriment of study of the Torah likewise called into question the legitimacy of the movement. In the war against Hasidism the movement found itself anathematized, its books burned, its leaders vilified. They were forced to leave their communities and were denied lodgings elsewhere – very severe penalties. The faithful were forbidden to do business with them. No one could marry into their group or participate in their burial. Under these circumstances, the last thing anyone anticipated was that Hasidism would find a place for itself within what would at some point be deemed Orthodoxy. But it did. By the 1830s the original force of the movement had run its course, and Hasidism now defined the way of life of the Jews in the Ukraine, Galicia and central Poland, with offshoots in White Russia (Belarus) and Lithuania on the one side, and Hungary on the other. The waves of emigration from the 1880s onward carried the movement to Western Europe and, in the aftermath of the Second World War, to the USA and the Land of Israel as well. Today the movement forms a powerful component of Orthodox Judaism, demonstrating the capacity of rabbinic Judaism to find strength by naturalizing initially alien modes of thought and piety. Rabbinic Judaism possessed the inner resources to make its own what began as a movement of criticism and radical reform of that same Judaism.

Rabbinic Judaism Defines its
Heretics: Karaism and Sabbateanism

The heresies generated by rabbinic Judaism present still more striking evidence of the power of the received system to thrive during the long epoch in which, with no competition, that Judaism defined the norm (this lasted from the fourth to the nineteenth century in Christendom, and to the mid twentieth century in the Muslim world.) For rabbinic Judaism in its ascendancy also defined the character and limits of heresy, imposing its values and its emphases upon the contrary-minded statements of the age. It so predominated, so defined the issues, that opposition framed itself around the critical doctrines of rabbinic Judaism, rather than taking an entirely new approach and framing a system utterly incongruent with the dominant Judaic system. If two doctrines characterized standard rabbinic Judaism they were the doctrine of the dual Torah, written and oral, the oral mediating the written; and the conviction that the Messiah would be a great master of the Torah and would (it hardly needed saying) embody its theology and its law.

Karaism denied that God revealed to Moses at Sinai more than the written Torah, and explicitly condemned belief in an oral one. Karaism rested on four principles: the literal meaning of the scriptural text; the consensus of the community; the conclusions derived from Scripture by the method of logical analogy; and knowledge based on human reason and intelligence. It advocated a return to Scripture and a rejection of tradition, including rabbinic tradition. The sect originated in Babylonia in the eighth century, following the formation of the Talmud of Babylonia and the rise of Islam. The movement itself claimed to originate in scriptural times and to derive its doctrine from the true priest, Zadok, King David's chief priest. The founder of the movement, Anan ben David, reinstated the original Torah, imposed rules concerning food that were stricter than those of the rabbis, and in other ways legislated a stricter version of the law than the Talmudic authorities admitted. The basic principle was that Scripture was to be studied freely, independently, and individually. No uniformity of view could then emerge. Given the stress of rabbinic Judaism on the authority of the Talmud and related canonical documents, we could not expect a more precise statement of the opposite view.

What is important about the Sabbatean movement, a seventeenth-century Judaic Messianic movement organized around the figure of Shabbetai Zevi, 1626–76, is that it defined the Messiah not as a sage who kept and embodied the law, but as the very *opposite*: a holy man who violated the law in letter and in spirit. In positing a Messiah in the mirror-image of the sage-Messiah of rabbinic Judaism, the Sabbatean movement, like Karaism, paid its respects to the received system. Shabbetai Zevi and his followers depicted him as the Messiah – the embodiment of God and the fulfilment of the Torah. Faith in him was portrayed as faith in God incarnate, which is the essence or spirit of the law. But his enemies did not see matters that way. On this matter, Professor Elliot Wolfson commented to me, 'While there is clearly an antinomian dimension to Shabbatianism, it seems more accurate to speak of his breaking of the law as the fuller expression of the law.'

Shabbetai Zevi, born in Smyrna (now Izmir, in Turkey) in 1626, mastered Talmudic law and lore and enjoyed respect for his learning even among his opponents. He was what we would today recognize as manic-depressive. During his manic periods he deliberately violated religious law, in what were called, in the doctrine of his movement, 'strange or paradoxical actions'.[8] In depressed times he chose solitude 'to wrestle with the demonic powers by which he felt attacked and partly overwhelmed'.[9] During a period of wandering in Greece and Thrace, he placed himself in active opposition to the law, declaring the commandments to be null and saying a benediction 'to Him who allows what is forbidden'.[10]

In this way he distinguished himself even before his meeting in 1665 with the disciple who organized his movement, Nathan of Gaza. When the two met, Nathan announced to Shabbetai that the latter was the true Messiah. This confirmed Shabbetai's own messianic dreams. In May 1665 Shabbetai announced himself as the Messiah, and various communities, hearing the news, split in their response to that claim. Leading rabbis opposed him, others took a more sympathetic view. Nathan proclaimed that the time of redemption had come. In September 1666 the grand vizier of the Ottoman Empire offered Shabbetai Zevi the choice of accepting Islam or imprisonment and death. He converted to Islam.

Nathan of Gaza explained that this apostasy marked the descent of the Messiah to the realm of evil, outwardly to submit to its domination but actually to perform the last and most difficult part of his mission by conquering that realm from within. The Messiah was engaged in a struggle with evil, just as in his prior actions in violating the law, he undertook part of the labour of redemption. The apostate Messiah would then form the centre of the messianic drama, meant to culminate, soon enough, in triumph. Up to his death in 1676 Shabbetai Zevi carried out his duties as a Muslim and also observed Jewish ritual. He went through alternating periods of illumination and depression and, in the former periods, founded new festivals and taught that accepting Islam involved 'the Torah of grace', as against Judaism, 'the Torah of truth'. The Sabbatean heresy found its focus and definition in its opposition to the rabbinic dogma that the Messiah would qualify as a great sage, like Moses, who was called 'our Rabbi' by the sages.

So much for the success of rabbinic Judaism, able as it was to accommodate intellectual, emotional and moral challenge in the forms of philosophy and Hasidism. A truly great political leader so defines matters that the shape of the opposition is cast in his or her image, and so too with a successful religion.

But thus far classical Judaism has formed a story that reserves no chapter for that half of holy Israel constituted by women. To represent the story Judaism tells as a story told only by men and about men would distort the truth, which is that Judaism in its classical documents portrayed 'Israel' as androgynous. Let me explain why Israel's androgyny forms an essential chapter in the larger story recounted in these pages, and how that chapter forms the bridge between olden times and the modern age.

10
Women in the Aggadah and the Halakhah

When it comes to the portrait and treatment of women within Judaism, its native categories – aggadah, theology, and halakhah, law – guide my description. Each makes its statement autonomous of the other, but together they lay down a single judgement. When it comes to women, the rabbis, all of them male until the last quarter of the twentieth century, set forth an essentially patriarchal system. But it is patriarchy with a difference, because, as we shall see, they recommend for themselves the adoption of virtues they deem feminine. And, when it comes to the law, they provide a fair and equitable position for women. They see Israel as God's bride, and they mean to secure for the this-worldly counterpart of the bride, namely their own wives and daughters, the protections that they as Israel require for a life of dignity and piety.

Feminine and Masculine in the Aggadah

The rabbis of classical Judaism present their system in an androgynous way, with Israel portrayed as feminine now, but masculine in the world to come. In telling its tale, Judaism in its classical documents joins traits explicitly marked as male to those explicitly classified as female and insists upon both in the formation of models of virtue. It therefore may be classified as androgynous, exhibiting the traits of both sexes as the religion itself defines those gender qualities. Women's capacity for devotion, selfless faith and loyalty defines the model of what is required of Israel in this world in order for the Messiah to come.

The rabbinic sages who wrote the Mishnah, Talmud and midrash thought in terms of the holy community, not isolated individuals. Gender roles formed part of the larger statement that the sages crafted concerning the coherent life of the community overall. Their doctrine of feminine virtue, therefore, makes sense only within its larger systemic context. The dual Torah, from beginning to end, taught that the Israelite was to exhibit the moral virtues of subservience, patience, endurance and hope. These would translate into the commendable traits of humility and forbearance, yielding the social virtues of passivity and conciliation. The hero was one who overcame impulses, and the truly virtuous person one who reconciled others by giving way before their opinions. All of these acts of self-abnegation and self-denial, accommodation rather than rebellion, required to begin with the right attitudes, sentiments, emotions and impulses, and the single most dominant motif of the rabbinic writings is its stress on the right attitude leading to the right action, the correct intentionality producing the sought-after decision; and above all, to adapting in one's heart to what could not be changed by one's action. And that meant, the world as it was. The sages prepared Israel for the long centuries of subordination and alienation by inculcating attitudes that best suited people who could govern little more than how they felt about things. As we shall now see, the sages themselves classified the sought-after virtues as feminine, and they proposed to feminize Israel, the holy people.

When I speak of virtues as feminine and masculine, it is not to perpetuate contemporary stereotypes, but to pay close attention to the rabbinic sages' own judgement of matters. In the classical writings we have several systematic exegeses that focus on women and therefore permit us to characterize the sages' conception of women's virtues, and it will follow, the virtues they classify as feminine. Their reading of the scriptural books of Ruth and Esther and their treatment of Miriam the prophetess and other scriptural prophetesses reveal their thinking on what characterizes the virtuous woman.

None of their exegeses more reliably records the sages' conception of the feminine and of the feminine in relationship to the masculine than *Song of Songs Rabbah*, a writing contemporary with the Talmud of Babylonia, *c.* 600. There, in reading the Song of Songs as a statement of the relationship between God and Israel, Israel is identified as the female beloved, God as the male lover. Because of the critical place of *Song of*

Songs Rabbah in the representation of androgynous Judaism and, in particular, the definition of the feminine component of the androgyny, I quote representative passages at considerable length.

The first point is the most telling. The relationship of Israel to God is the same as the relationship of a wife to the husband:

'I am my beloved's, and his desire is for me':

There are three yearnings:

The yearning of Israel is only for their Father who is in heaven, as it is said, 'I am my beloved's, and his desire is for me.'

The yearning of a woman is only for her husband: 'And your desire shall be for your husband' (Genesis 3:16).

The yearning of the Evil Impulse is only for Cain and his ilk: 'Its [sin's] desire is for you' (Genesis 4:7).[1]

Here gender relationships are explicitly characterized, and with them the traits associated with the genders. The sages turn to everyday experience, the love of husband and wife, for a metaphor for God's love for Israel and Israel's love for God. Israel is assigned the feminine role and the feminine virtues. It is difficult to identify a more extravagant form of praise for women's virtue, their capacity to love generously and in an act of unearned grace. Then, when Solomon's song says, 'O that you would kiss me with the kisses of your mouth! For your love is better than wine' (Song of Songs 1:2), the rabbinic sages think of how God kissed Israel.

What is important here is not the doctrinal message of *Song of Songs Rabbah*, but its implicit and tacit affirmations. The document does not set forth a great many explicit doctrines, but delivers its message through the description of attitudes and emotions. And our particular interest lies in the identification of the system's designation of clearly defined attitudes and emotions as feminine and masculine. The writers mean to paint word-pictures, evoke feelings – speak empathetically, rather than only sympathetically. *Song of Songs Rabbah* tells Israelites how to think and feel, forming sensibility by inspiring a heart at one with God.

No account of feminine virtue can accomplish its goals without cataloguing masculine virtue as well, represented by God in *Song of Songs Rabbah*:

'My beloved has gone down to his garden, to the beds of spices, [to pasture his flock in the gardens, and to gather lilies]':

Said Rabbi Yosé ben Rabbi Hanina, 'As to this verse, the beginning of it is not the same as the end, and the end not the same as the beginning.

'The verse had only to say, "My beloved has gone down to pasture in his garden", but you say, "in the gardens"!

'But "my beloved" is the Holy One, blessed be he;

' "to his garden" refers to the world;

' "to the beds of spices" refers to Israel;

' "to pasture his flock in the gardens" refers to synagogues and yeshivot;

' "and to gather lilies" speaks of picking [taking away in death] the righteous that are in Israel.'[2]

'My beloved' is God; the choice part of the garden, which is the world, is Israel, its synagogues and houses of study. Israel is now the faithful beloved, waiting patiently for her lover, always trusting in his faithfulness.

'Set me as a seal upon your heart, as a seal upon your arm; for love is strong as death, jealousy is cruel as the grave. Its flashes are flashes of fire, a most vehement flame.'

'For love is strong as death': as strong as death is the love with which the Holy One, blessed be he, loves Israel: ' "I have loved you," says the Lord' (Malachi 1:2).

'Jealousy is cruel as the grave': that is when they make him jealous with their idolatry: 'They roused him to jealousy with strange gods' (Deuteronomy 32:16) . . .

Another explanation of 'for love is strong as death': as strong as death is the love with which a man loves his wife: 'Enjoy life with the wife whom you love' (Ecclesiastes 9:9).

'Jealousy is cruel as the grave': the jealousy that she causes in him and leads him to say to her, 'Do not speak with such-and-so.'

If she goes and speaks with that man, forthwith: 'The spirit of jealousy comes upon him, and he is jealous on account of his wife' (Numbers 5:14).[3]

The virtues of wives are loyalty and submission: a wife's trust in her husband is the mark of the perfect wife. Israel follows wherever Moses, on behalf of God, leads; Israel trusts in God the way a woman who has accepted marriage trusts her husband:

'Then Moses led Israel onward from the Red Sea' (Exodus 15:22):

He led them on from the sin committed at the sea.

They said to him, 'Moses, our lord, where are you leading us?'

He said to them, 'To Elim, from Elim to Alush, from Alush to Marah, from Marah to Rephidim, from Rephidim to Sinai.'

They said to him, 'Indeed, wherever you go and lead us, we are with you.'

The matter is comparable to the case of one who went and married a woman from a village. He said to her, 'Arise and come with me.'

She said to him, 'From here to where?'

He said to her, 'From here to Tiberias, from Tiberias to the tannery, from the tannery to the upper market, from the upper market to the lower market.'

She said to him, 'Wherever you go and take me, I shall go with you.'

So said the Israelites, 'My soul clings to thee' (Psalms 63:8).[4]

Israel's feminine virtue must exceed even a wife's trust in her husband's protection. Israel also must care only for God, the way a wife's entire desire is solely for her husband. The point is unmistakable and critical. Israel is subject to an oath to wait patiently for God's redemption, not to rebel against the gentile nations on its own; that is the concrete social politics meant to derive from the analogy of Israel's relationship to God as a wife's relationship to her husband: perfect submission, and also perfect trust. Rebellion against the gentiles stands for arrogance on Israel's part, an act of lack of trust and therefore lack of faithfulness. Implicit in this representation of the right relationship, of course, is the promise that feminine Israel will evoke from masculine God the response of commitment and intervention: God will intervene to save Israel, when Israel makes herself into the perfect wife of God.

The upshot is, Israel must fulfil the vocation of a woman, turn itself into a woman, serve God as a wife serves a husband. The question then follows: is it possible that the Judaism that has treated the present document as canonical asks men to turn themselves into women? And the answer is, that demand is stated in so many words. Here we find a full statement of the feminization of the masculine. The two brothers, Moses and Aaron, are compared to Israel's breasts, a reversal of gender classifications that can hardly be more extreme or dramatic:

'Your two breasts are like two fawns, twins of a gazelle, that feed among the lilies.

'Your two breasts are like two fawns': this refers to Moses and Aaron.

Just as a woman's breasts are her glory and her ornament, so Moses and Aaron are the glory and the ornament of Israel.

Just as a woman's breasts are her charm, so Moses and Aaron are the charm of Israel.

Just as a woman's breasts are her honour and her praise, so Moses and Aaron are the honour and praise of Israel.

Just as a woman's breasts are full of milk, so Moses and Aaron are full of the Torah.

Just as whatever a woman eats the infant eats and sucks, so all the Torah that our lord, Moses, learned he taught to Aaron: 'And Moses told Aaron all the words of the Lord' (Exodus 4:28).

And rabbis say, 'He actually revealed the Ineffable Name of God to him.'

Just as one breast is not larger than the other, so Moses and Aaron were the same: 'This Moses and this Aaron' (Exodus 6:27), 'These are the Aaron and Moses' (Exodus 6:26), so that in knowledge of the Torah Moses was not greater than Aaron, and Aaron was not greater than Moses. Happy are these two brothers, who were created only for the glory of Israel.

That is what Samuel said, '[It is] the Lord . . . who appointed Moses and Aaron and brought your fathers up [out of the land of Egypt]' (1 Samuel 12:6).

Thus 'Your two breasts are like two fawns': this refers to Moses and Aaron.[5]

Not only are Moses and Aaron represented through feminine metaphors, so too are Abraham, Isaac and Jacob, as well as the tribal progenitors, Jacob's sons.

In the following passage feminine Israel is ornamented by all of the jewellery contained in the treasure of the Torah: all of the acts of faith are paraded as marks of the beauty of Israel in the explicit setting of Israel's feminine relationship to the masculine God:

'Behold, you are beautiful, my love; behold, you are beautiful; [your eyes are doves]':

'Behold you are beautiful' in religious deeds,

'Behold you are beautiful' in acts of grace,

'Behold you are beautiful' in carrying out religious obligations of commission,

'Behold you are beautiful' in carrying out religious obligations of omission,

'Behold you are beautiful' in carrying out the religious duties of the home, in separating priestly rations and tithes,

'Behold you are beautiful' in carrying out the religious duties of the field, gleanings, forgotten sheaves, the corner of the field, poor person's tithe, and declaring the field ownerless,

'Behold you are beautiful' in observing the taboo against mixed species,

'Behold you are beautiful' in providing a linen cloak with woollen show-fringes,

'Behold you are beautiful' in [keeping the rules governing] planting,

'Behold you are beautiful' in keeping the taboo on uncircumcised produce,

'Behold you are beautiful' in keeping the laws on produce in the fourth year after the planting of an orchard,

'Behold you are beautiful' in circumcision,

'Behold you are beautiful' in trimming the wound,

'Behold you are beautiful' in reciting the Prayer,

'Behold you are beautiful' in reciting the Shema,

'Behold you are beautiful' in putting a *mezuzah* on the doorposts of your house,

'Behold you are beautiful' in wearing phylacteries,

'Behold you are beautiful' in building the hut for the Festival of Huts,

'Behold you are beautiful' in taking the palm branch and etrog [citrus fruit] on the Festival of Huts,

'Behold you are beautiful' in repentance,

'Behold you are beautiful' in good deeds,

'Behold you are beautiful' in this world,

'Behold you are beautiful' in the world to come.[6]

The feminine and masculine virtues complement one another, and neither is complete without the other. The process comes to fulfilment in this representation as feminine of all the acts of sanctification that God has commanded and that submissive Israel carries out.

How does the sexual imagery convey deep theological meaning? The message of *Song of Songs Rabbah* is that if Israel is feminine now, she will resume her masculinity in the world to come. That is a much more subtle and profound statement, a judgement on the androgyny of Israel that makes the union of traits, feminine and masculine, something other than a static portrait of a world at rest. In fact, the metaphor of the feminine Israel and the masculine God is subsumed within the more profound message of redemption and carries a critical element in that message: Israel must be patient, submissive and deeply trusting in God now, so that in the world to come Israel may resume its fulfilled masculinity. It follows that Israel is represented as androgyne, feminine, then masculine:

Rabbi Berekhiah in the name of Rabbi Samuel ben Rabbi Nahman said, 'The Israelites are compared to a woman.

'Just as an unmarried women receives a tenth part of the property of her father and takes her leave [for her husband's house when she gets married], so the Israelites inherited the land of the seven peoples [Canaan], who form a tenth part of the seventy nations of the world.

'And because the Israelites inherited in the status of a woman, they sang a song [in the feminine form of that word], as in the following: "Then Moses and the people of Israel sang this song [given in the feminine form] to the Lord" (Exodus 15:1).

'But in the age to come they are destined to inherit like a man, who inherits all of the property of his father.

'That is in line with this verse of Scripture: "From the east side to the west side: Judah, one portion (Ezekiel 48:7) . . . Dan one, Asher one . . ." and so throughout.

'Then they will say a song in the masculine form of that word, as in the following: "Sing to the Lord a new song" (Psalms 96:1).

'The word "song" is given not in its feminine form but in its masculine form.'

Rabbi Berekiah and Rabbi Joshua ben Levi: 'Why are the Israelites compared to a woman?

'Just as a woman takes up a burden and puts it down [that is, becomes pregnant and gives birth], takes a burden and puts it down, then takes up a burden and puts it down and then takes up no further burden,

'so the Israelites are subjugated and then redeemed, subjugated and then redeemed, but in the end are redeemed and will never again be subjugated.

'In this world, since their anguish is like the anguish of a woman in childbirth, they say the song before him using the feminine form of the word for song,

'but in the age to come, because their anguish will no longer be the anguish of a woman in childbirth, they will say their song using the masculine form of the word for song:

' "In that day this song [in the masculine form of the word] will be sung" (Isaiah 26:1).'[7]

So the real message lies in the femininity of Israel in this world in contrast to its masculinity in the world to come. Not only so, but there is another qualification of considerable urgency. It is that feminine Israel must then be masculine in its aggressive relationship to the gentile nations, and here, once more, we find what we may call temporal, or serial, androgyny: feminine now, masculine in the age to come. Obviously the system is the work of men and states a masculine viewpoint, which makes the systemic androgyny all the more remarkable. Israel is one thing to God, another to the gentile nations; it will remain feminine and submissive to God, but will become masculine and aggressive to the gentile nations of the world.

The following passage makes the point of serial androgyny with respect to Israel's relationship with God, who responds to Israel's character:

'[What is your beloved more than another beloved, O fairest among women? What is your beloved more than another beloved, that you thus adjure us?] My beloved is all radiant and ruddy, distinguished among ten thousand.'

The Israelites answer them, 'My beloved is all radiant and ruddy.'

'Radiant': to me in the land of Egypt,

'and ruddy': to the Egyptians.

'Radiant': in the land of Egypt, 'For I will go through the land of Egypt' (Exodus 12:13).

'And ruddy': 'And the Lord overthrew the Egyptians' (Exodus 14:27).

'Radiant': at the Sea: 'The people of Israel walked on dry ground through the sea' (Exodus 14:29).

'And ruddy': to the Egyptians at the Sea: 'And the Lord overthrew the Egyptians in the midst of the sea' (Exodus 14:27).

'Radiant': in the world to come.

'And ruddy': in this world.

'Rabbi Levi ben Rabbi Hayyata made three statements concerning the matter:

' "Radiant": on the sabbath.

' "And ruddy": on the other days of the week.

' "Radiant": at New Year.

' "And ruddy": on the other days of the year.

' "Radiant": in this world.

' "And ruddy": in the world to come . . .'

Said Rabbi Abba ben Rabbi Kahana, 'A mortal king is known by his ceremonial garments, but here he is fire and his ministers are fire: "He came from the ten thousands of holy ones" (Deuteronomy 33:2).

'He is marked in the midst of "the ten thousands of holy ones".'[8]

hupartory

When Israel is 'radiant' it is feminine, accepting God's dominion. When Israel is 'ruddy' it is masculine, acting in its own behalf. Thus 'radiant in the world to come' but 'ruddy in this world'; 'radiant on the Sabbath' but 'ruddy on the other days of the week'. Israel when feminine is whole with God, who is represented in a companion source as 'lord of the dance'.

The emotions, classified as feminine, encouraged by Judaism in its formative age, such as humility, forbearance, accommodation, a spirit of conciliation, exactly correspond to the political and social requirements of the Jews' condition in that time. And the reason that the same repertoire of emotions persisted with no material change through the unfolding of the writings of the sages of that formative age was the constancy of the Jews' political and social condition. Emotions lay down judgements. They derive from rational cognition. What Judaism teaches the private person to feel links her or his heart to what Judaism states about the condition of Israel in history and of God in the cosmos. All form one reality, in supernatural world and nature, in time and in eternity wholly consubstantial (so to speak). In the innermost chambers of deepest feelings, the Israelite therefore lives out the public history and destiny of the people, Israel. The genius of Judaism, the reason for its resilience and endurance, lies in its power to teach Jews in private to feel what in public they also must think about the condition of both self and nation. The world within and the world without are so bonded that one is never alone. The individual's life always is lived with the community. And, we now realize, the virtuous man, as much as the virtuous woman, will exhibit women's virtues of attitude and emotion.

The oral Torah's consistent treatment of emotions means that early, middle and late, a single doctrine and programme dictated what the rabbis had to say on how Israel should tame its heart – by behaving like a virtuous woman. And it is not difficult to see why. In this world, Israel was a vanquished nation, possessed of a broken spirit. The sages' Judaism for a defeated people prepared the nation for a long future. The broken-hearted nation that had lost its city and its temple had moreover produced a group from its midst to take over its Scripture and much else. In its intellectuals, as represented by the rabbinic sages, that defeated people found refuge in a mode of thought that trained people to see things otherwise than as the eyes perceived them. And that way of seeing things accounts also for the specific matter of the feminization of Israel: Israel now was to endure as a woman, so that, in the age to come, it would resume its masculine position among the nations: dominant and determinative. Among the diverse ways by which the weak and subordinated accommodate to their circumstance, the one of iron-willed pretence in life is most likely to yield this way of thinking: that things never are, because they cannot be, what they seem. The uniform tradition on emotions persisted intact because the social realities of Israel's life proved permanent, until, in our own time, they changed. The upshot was that rabbinic Judaism's Israel was instructed on how to tame its heart and govern its wild emotions, to accept with resignation, to endure with patience, above all, to value the attitudes and emotions that made acceptance and reconciliation matters of honour and dignity, and therefore also made endurance plausible.

The Halakhah: Women in the Social System of Rabbinic Judaism

So much for the theological reading of gender in the aggadic documents. How is woman portrayed in the halakhah? In the canonical documents of rabbinic Judaism – Scripture as mediated by the halakhah of the Mishnah, Tosefta and Talmuds – women are perceived as abnormal in a world in which men define what is normal.

In the law of Judaism, women matter when, and only when, they relate to men, and men are assumed to form the structure and guarantee the stability of the entire society. Much of the law that touches on women is devoted to the formation and dissolution of the marital bond. The focus, then, is upon the two crucial stages in the transfer of women and of property (women being considered as the property of men) from one domain to another: a woman leaving her father's house for her husband's on marriage; and her leaving her husband's house at the marriage's dissolution through divorce or through the husband's death or the wife's infidelity. There is yet a third point of interest, though it is much less important than these first two stages: the duration of the marriage. But the handful of rules on that subject hardly matches the enormous and dense corpus of laws on betrothal, marriage contracts, divorce, levirate marriage (when a childless widow is obliged to marry her brother-in-law) and adultery (of wives).

In the design of the Israelite household put forward by Judaism, the woman is essential and central. But she is not critical. She sets the stage for the processes of the sacred. She can be made sacred to man, or cease to stand within a man's sacred circle. But only God and man have the power of sanctification. God exercises that power by his nature. Man does so when he expresses his will and intention through formal documents – a marriage-contract or a writ of divorce, for example – the one effecting the sanctification of a relationship, the other ending it, and thus bringing about or removing holiness from a transaction. Women are a principal part of the realm of the sacred, but man on earth, like God in heaven, possesses the power to sanctify.

The law of Judaism does not imagine that men live apart from women or that women exist outside their relationship with, and therefore under the control of, men. Women have rights, protected by man and God alike. The law addresses and means to create an ordered and well-regulated world. It states the order and regulation for such a world, including with whom a woman may have sexual relations, and with what consequences. It is assumed that, from long before the advent of puberty, a girl may be married, and that from puberty onward she will be married. But what is selected for intense and continuing concern is whom she may legitimately marry, and with what economic and social effect. There is no sexual deed without public consequence; and only rarely will a sexual deed not yield economic results, involving the transfer of property from one hand to another. What is anomalous is a woman's sexuality, which is treated in a way wholly different from a man's: men are assumed to be chaste by nature; women as unchaste. The purpose of the Mishnah's section on women is to bring under control and force into stasis all the wild and unruly potentialities of sexuality, with their dreadful threat of uncontrolled shifts in personal status and material possession alike.

The law invokes God's interest in the most critical moment for individual and society alike: when a woman passes from her father's to her husband's house, with the accompanying transfer of property and future progeny. Its conception is that what is rightly done on earth is confirmed in heaven. A married woman who has sexual relations with any man but her husband has not merely committed a crime on earth. She has sinned against heaven. It follows that when a married woman receives a writ of divorce and so is free to enter into a relationship with any man of her choosing, the perception of that woman is changed in heaven just as much it is on earth. What before the divorce would have been a crime and a sin, after it is holy, not subject to punishment at all. The woman may contract a new marriage on earth which God will oversee and sanctify. What is stated in these simple propositions is that those crucial and critical turning points at which the ownership of a woman changes hands produce concern and response in heaven above as much as on earth below. Heaven is invoked specifically at those times, and in those circumstances, in which the law confronts a situation of anomaly or disorder and proposes to effect suitable regulation and sought-after order.

Marriage finds its definition, therefore its rules and obligations, in the tasks assigned by the social order to it – child-bearing and child-raising, on the one hand, and the maintenance of the political economy of the holy people, Israel, on the other. The purpose of marriage is to produce the next generation and to support it. Marriage finds its meaning in the larger social context that the Torah sets forth for Israel.

Husbands and wives owe one another loyalty to their common task and reliability in carrying out their reciprocal obligations, which are sexual, social and economic. Out of mutual trust and shared achievements – children raised, the household maintained – may emerge emotions of affection and love. For example, the sages counsel husbands to afford sexual satisfaction to their wives, saying that if the wife reaches orgasm first, male children, which men are assumed to want, will result. But romantic attitudes do not enjoy a high priority. The governing language is theological, with the keyword being 'holiness'. The family is formed when a man betroths himself to a woman and consummates the betrothal, and the word for 'betroth' is 'sanctify'. The relationship of that woman to that man is one of sanctification; she is uniquely his, having consented to be consecrated to him. God has a big stake in what is set apart as sanctified, whether an offering in the Temple on his altar, or a wife in the household in bed.

In the polygamous society of Judaism,[9] a husband owed his wives not a counterpart relationship of sexual sanctification but reliable support, material and conjugal. A wife could have sexual relations only with her husband, but since he had several wives, he did not enter into a counterpart sanctified commitment of fidelity to her. When it comes to adultery, the sages condemn a husband's as much as a wife's. This view is expressed in the context of their discussion of the ordeal imposed upon a wife accused of adultery. The pertinent verse of Scripture is, 'And the man shall be free from iniquity, and the woman shall bear her iniquity' (Numbers 5:31): 'The sense of the foregoing verse of Scripture is that when the man is free of transgression, the water puts his wife to the test [described in Numbers 5:16–28], and if the man is not free of transgression, the water does not put his wife to the test.'[10] That is to say, the ordeal imposed on the wife is null, if to begin with the husband is not free of transgression.

The practical statements of the law of the Torah set forth in the Mishnah define what the wife owes the husband and the husband the wife. The law focuses, for the wife, on the labour that she owes, and for the husband, on the restraint he must exercise, and the respect for his wife's autonomy he must display. Stated simply: the wife or wives represent participants in the household, and a wife owes her husband the fruit of her labour. The husband reciprocates by honouring his wife's desires and attitudes and refraining from trying to control and isolate her. The wife's domestic duties encompass these:

These are the kinds of labour which a woman performs for her husband:

she (1) grinds flour, (2) bakes bread, (3) does laundry, (4) prepares meals, (5) gives suck to her child, (6) makes the bed, (7) works in wool.

[If] she brought with her a single slave girl, she does not (1) grind, (2) bake bread, or (3) do laundry.

[If she brought] two, she does not (4) prepare meals and does not (5) feed her child.

[If she brought] three, she does not (6) make the bed for him and does not (7) work in wool.

If she brought four, she sits on a throne.

Rabbi Eliezer says, 'Even if she brought him a hundred slave girls, he forces her to work in wool,

'for idleness leads to unchastity.'

Rabban Simeon ben Gamaliel says, 'Also: he who prohibits his wife by a vow from performing any labour puts her away and pays off her marriage contract. For idleness leads to boredom.'[11]

A wife is her husband's partner, having a particular area of responsibility. She is respected in her work and many depend on her management. The good wife described in Proverbs 31:10–31 is the model here:

A good wife who can find? She is far more precious than jewels.
The heart of her husband trusts in her, and he will have no lack of gain.
She does him good, and not harm, all the days of her life.
She seeks wool and flax, and works with willing hands.
She is like the ships of the merchant, she brings her food from afar.
She rises while it is yet night and provides food for her household . . .

A wife is expected to conduct herself in a modest and pious manner, and if she does not do so, her husband may divorce her without paying the alimony that is required in the marriage-agreement, a huge incentive for the wife to keep the law:

And those women go forth without the payment of the marriage contract at all:
    She who transgresses against the law of Moses and Jewish law.
    And what is the law of Moses [which she has transgressed]? [If] (1) she feeds him food which has not been tithed, or (2) has sexual relations with him while she is menstruating, or [if] (3) she does not designate a piece of dough for the priest when she bakes bread, or [if] (4) she vows and does not carry out her vow.
    And what is the Jewish law? If (1) she goes out with her hair flowing loose, or (2) she spins in the marketplace, or (3) she talks with just anybody,
    Abba Saul says, 'Also: if she curses his parents in his presence.'
    Rabbi Tarfon says, 'Also: if she is a loudmouth.'
    What is a loudmouth? When she talks in her own house, her neighbours can hear her voice.[12]

A husband, for his part, owes his wife not only the required domestic support for which Scripture provides – food, clothing and conjugal relations – but also an allowance that she may spend as she sees fit:

He gives her in addition a silver ma'ah [a sixth of a denarius] for her needs [per week].
    And she eats with him on the sabbath night [when sexual relations are owing].

And if he does not give her a silver ma'ah for her needs, the fruit of her labour belongs to her. [She may sell what she makes, for example spun wool, and use the money at will.]

And how much work does she do for him?

The weight of five selas of warp must she spin for him in Judea (which is ten selas' weight in Galilee), or the weight of ten selas of weft in Judah (which are twenty selas in Galilee).

And if she was nursing a child, they take off [the required weight of wool which she must spin as] the fruit of her labour, and they provide more food for her.

Under what circumstances?

In the case of the most poverty-stricken man in Israel.

But in the case of a weightier person, all follows the extent of his capacity [to support his wife].[13]

What we see in the requirements of husband to wife and wife to husband, then, is a heavy emphasis upon shared personal and material obligations. The wife brings to the marriage her dowry, which stands for her share in her father's estate; this reverts to her (hence to her father) in the event of divorce or her husband's demise. So the marriage represents the formation of a partnership based on quite practical considerations. Matters of emotion enter in, but mainly as the husband's responsibility. What we see in all is very little sentimentality but a great deal of respect and dignity.

What does the husband owe the wife? As to sexual relations, however many wives a husband has, each woman's rights are to be carefully respected; marital rape is forbidden, and a woman who invites sexual relations is highly praised and will produce remarkable children:

Said Rabbi Ammi bar Abba in the name of Rabbi Assi, 'It is forbidden for someone to rape his wife or force his wife to carry out the religious duty (of sexual relations): "And he that hastens with his feet sins" (Proverbs 19:2).'

And said Rabbi Joshua ben Levi, 'Whoever rapes his wife will have unworthy children.'

Said Rabbi Samuel bar Nahmani in the name of Rabbi Jonathan, 'Any man whose wife calls him to sexual relations will have children of the like of which the generation of our lord, Moses, didn't have, as it is said, "Choose wise, understanding and experienced men, according to your tribes and I will make them rulers over you'' (Deuteronomy 1:13); and, ''So I took the chiefs of your tribes, wise and experienced men'' (Deuteronomy 1:15), without reference to ''understanding''. And with reference to Leah, it is written, ''Leah went out to meet him [Jacob], and said, ''You must come in to me, for I have surely hired you'' (Genesis 30:16), and it is written, ''Issachar [Leah's son] is a strong ass'' (Genesis 49:14), and elsewhere, ''And [the children] of Issachar, men who had understanding of the times'' (1 Chronicles 12:33).' This was Leah's reward, proving that it is meritorious for a woman to demand sexual relations.[14]

That this perspective is the husband's presents no surprise, the entire system being framed by men. But treating a wife with delicacy and respect brings rewards, and a wife's sexual desires are to be responded to. Correct behaviour with women requires modesty and deference:

He who counts out coins into a woman's hand from his own in order to have a chance to stare at her, even if such a one has in hand the Torah and good deeds like Moses, our master, will not be quit of the judgement of Gehenna [punishment after death]. For it is said, 'Hand to hand, he shall not escape from evil' (Proverbs 11:21). He shall not escape from the judgement of Gehenna.[15]

A husband may not abuse his wife, may not try to keep her away from the normal social relations that she should enjoy as an independent person, and must accord to her all of the rights and dignities of a free woman:

He who prohibits his wife by vow from deriving benefit from him

for a period of thirty days, appoints an agent to provide for her.

for a longer period, he puts her away and pays off her marriage contract.

Rabbi Judah says, 'In the case of an Israelite, for [a vow lasting] one month he may continue in the marriage, but for two [or more], he must put her away and pay off her marriage contract.

'But in the case of a priest, for two months he may continue in the marriage, and after three he must put her away and pay off her marriage contract.'[16]

Since the husband receives property on his marriage that, in the event of divorce, he must restore to his wife's father's household, divorce is not undertaken lightly. It involves not only a year of alimony, but also loss of considerable capital or real estate. Hence the husband has a strong incentive not to make a vow that denies his wife the right to gain benefit from him – to eat at his table, share his bed, and the like.

The same considerations strongly discourage a husband from brow-beating or otherwise trying to manipulate or control his wife. If he imposes on her a vow not to eat even one sort of fruit or vegetable, he must divorce her, giving her her freedom and losing the capital she has brought into his household:

He who prohibits his wife by vow from tasting any single kind of produce whatsoever

must put her away and pay off her marriage contract.

Rabbi Judah says, 'In the case of an Israelite, [if the vow is] for one day he may persist in the marriage, but [if it is] for two he must put her away and pay off her marriage contract.

'And in the case of a priest, [if it is] for two days he may persist in the marriage, but [if it is] for three he must put her away and pay off her marriage contract.'[17]

The law shows remarkably little patience for a controlling husband, who would transform his wife into his slave, lacking all freedom of will. The same protection encompasses a wife's right to adorn herself as a beautiful woman; such petty annoyances become very costly:

He who prohibits his wife by a vow from adorning herself with any single sort of jewellery must put her away and pay off her marriage contract.

Rabbi Yosé says, 'In the case of poor girls, [if] he has not assigned a time limit [he must divorce them].

'But in the case of rich girls, [he may persist in the marriage if he set a time limit] of thirty days.'[18]

A husband must permit his wife to maintain a circle of friends and relationships beyond the limits of the household. He may not interfere in her relationships with her father and family; nor stop her from seeing her relatives:

He who prohibits his wife by a vow from going home to her father's house,

when he [her father] is with her in [the same] town,

[if it is] for a month, he may persist in the marriage.

[If it is] for two, he must put her away and pay off her marriage contract.

And when he is in another town, [if the vow is in effect] for one festival season he may persist in the marriage. [But if the vow remains in force] for three, he must put her away and pay off her marriage contract.[19]

A wife thus has the absolute right to visit her father's household pretty much when her duties permit. Nor may a husband interfere with his wife's normal social intercourse. Here too, if he tries to keep her caged at home and cut off her ties to other people, particularly the society of women, he loses heavily:

He who prohibits his wife by a vow from going to a house of mourning or to a house of celebration must put her away and pay off her marriage contract,
    because he locks the door before her.
    But if he claimed that he took such a vow because of some other thing, he is permitted to impose such a vow.

Finally, intimate details of the marriage must be kept private; a woman has a right to her dignity:

If he took a vow, saying to her, 'Lo, you are as an offering [forbidden] to use unless you say to so-and-so what you said to me [when having sexual relations]', or 'what I said to you', or 'unless you draw water and pour it out on to the ash heap [a euphemism for practising a form of birth control]',
    he must put her away and pay off her marriage contract.[20]

In these and other ways, a husband is given weighty incentives to treat his wife with enormous respect. And, as we have seen, if a woman behaves improperly, not keeping the Torah of Moses – committing adultery, for example – she too loses the assets she has brought to the marriage and the household. The provisions of her marriage-settlement are null: the husband keeps the dowry, and she loses everything.

In a number of specific contexts, moreover, a man and woman are differentiated in the functions that they perform or to which they are obligated:

For every commandment concerning the son to which the father is subject, men are liable, and women are exempt.
    And for every commandment concerning the father to which the son is subject, men and women are equally liable.
    For every positive commandment dependent upon the time [of year], men are liable, and women are exempt.
    And for every positive commandment not dependent upon the time, men and women are equally liable.

For every negative commandment, whether dependent upon the time or not dependent upon the time, men and women are equally liable,

except for not marring the corners of the beard, not rounding the corners of the head (Leviticus 19:27), and not becoming unclean because of the dead (Leviticus 21:1).[21]

A woman is exempt from religious duties that take her away from responsibilities only she can carry out. She has fixed obligations, for example to feed her baby. No religious duty pertains that interferes with these obligations. In the life of the synagogue, woman played a subordinated role. They were not called upon to declaim the Torah, nor could they serve as the voice of the congregation in the presentation of public prayers and so lead services. Women were given an elementary education, but it was rare indeed for a woman to be taught the Talmud, and there are no instances in which women issued legal rulings. As to the study of the Torah, the highest form of service to God, women were not educated as men were, though it was common for them to receive instruction deemed appropriate to their gender. Does the fact of their subordination mean women were alienated by the system? In the writings of Glückel of Hameln (1646–1724) we find that was not so. Glückel's message expresses precisely the same religious world-view as that of contemporary rabbinic sages, all of them male. We find in her memoir a robust piety and we see clearly why Judaism assigned to women the critical tasks of nurture and character-formation:

In my great grief and for my heart's ease I begin this book in the year of Creation 5451 – God soon rejoice us and send us His redeemer soon. Amen.

With the help of God, I began writing this, my dear children, upon the death of your good father in the hope of distracting my soul from the burdens laid upon it, and the bitter thought that we have lost our faithful shepherd. In this way I have managed to live through many wakeful nights, and springing from my bed have shortened the sleepless hours.

I do not intend, my dear children, to compose and write for you a book of morals. Such I could not write, and our wise men have already written many. Moreover, we have our holy Torah in which we may find and learn all that we need for our journey through this world to the world to come. Of our beloved Torah we may seize hold . . . We sinful men are in the world as if swimming in the sea and in danger of being drowned. But our great, merciful and kind God, in His great mercy, has thrown ropes into the sea that we may take hold of them and be saved. These are our holy Torah where is written what are the rewards and punishments for good and evil deeds . . .

I pray you this, my children: be patient when the Lord, may He be praised, sends you a punishment; accept it with patience and do not cease to pray to Him; perhaps He will have mercy upon you . . . Therefore, my dear children, whatever you lose, have patience, for nothing is our own, everything is only a loan . . . We men have been created for nothing else but to serve God and to keep His commandments and to obey the Torah, 'for that is thy life, and the length of the days'.

The kernel of the Torah is: 'Thou shalt love thy neighbour as thyself.' But in our days we seldom find it so, and few are they who love their fellow-men with all their heart. On the contrary, if a man can contrive to ruin his neighbour nothing pleases him more . . .

The best thing for you, my children, is to serve God from your heart without falsehood or deception, not giving out to people that you are one thing while, God forbid, in your heart you are another. Say your prayers with awe and devotion. During the time for prayers do not stand about and talk of other things . . .

Moreover, set aside a fixed time for the study of the Torah, as best you know how. Then diligently go about your business, for providing your wife and children with a decent livelihood is likewise a mitzvah – the command of God and the duty of man.[22]

If we look in vain for evidence that Glückel was discontented with her status as a woman, it is because, within the system, her work was as important as her husband's. She was one who shaped and transmitted Judaism, as much as her husband, but she did it in a different context; she had a different job to do. And she carried out her work unselfconsciously and in a thoroughly accepting spirit. Only in the late nineteenth century would women come to assert themselves as equal participants in Israel's polity, and even then they accomplished their goals with great difficulty.

Women in the Contemporary Synagogue:
Women Now Tell Judaism's Story, Too

The classical writings of Judaism do not prepare us for the revolution in women's role in Judaism that has taken place in the past quarter-century. This shift raises the larger question, what has happened in modern and contemporary times to the story that Judaism tells? The answer is, extraordinary changes, captured by the fact that today in synagogue life and in the councils of rabbinical leadership women participate in telling, and shaping, the story of Judaism. They are ordained as rabbis and make their way as scholars of Judaism, even authorities of the law.

In public roles and activities women have attained equality with men in synagogue life. The change is captured by the fact that, from the 1970s, women have been ordained as rabbis in Reform and Reconstructionist Judaism, and in the 1980s in Conservative Judaism. Important sectors of contemporary Orthodoxy are finding, within the halakhah, roles for women to carry out, even as religious authorities in synagogue life. They have opened yeshivot for women, and women have come to the fore as teachers of the sacred texts. In Reform, Reconstructionist and Conservative Judaism women have taken a position of complete equality with men, conducting religious services, declaiming the Torah, and otherwise participating like men in all regards. In some instances they don the religious garb of worship — skull caps, prayer shawls and phylacteries. Women make a significant proportion of the student body of the Reform, Conservative and Reconstructionist seminaries in the USA and overseas, and with the passage of time, women rabbis will make up a significant part of the membership of rabbinical organizations. The changes have proved so profound and far-reaching that their full implications are not yet clear. But the entire shape and structure of Judaism are now subject to a profound metamorphosis as the sexes attain parity.

In speaking of Reform, Orthodox, Conservative, and other Judaisms, I have got ahead of my story. It suffices here to note that the change in the position of women signals much else that has changed and requires explanation. With the remarkable changes in the status of women in mind, it is time to see how today's worlds of Judaism retell, and renew, the ancient, forever-renewing tale.

11

Contemporary Communities
of Judaism

The Advent of Modern Times:
Rabbinic Judaism Meets Competition

For long centuries, down to the present day, a single story has served to make the statement of the paramount, normative Judaism. It is the story that Scripture set forth, as mediated by the rabbinic sages in theology and law, belief and practice. And alongside some told, in addition, the version of the same story conveyed by the kabbalah. Judaism's story endures, if not intact, then forever unimpaired. But it has also evolved, and, furthermore, Israelites in the very recent past have told other stories of who and what it means to be Israel. All of these, the enduring, the evolving, the new and different, embody the condition of Judaism in contemporary times.

For the larger number of the Jews who practise Judaism, Judaism's story lives, as it has always lived, in the classic form just now portrayed, in everyday life and learning, in halakhah and aggadah. Without stipulations or apologies or excuses, the story still is told as a factual account of God's plan for Creation and the response of humanity to that plan. It is then the story of God's yearning for Israel's love, and Israel's frail but ever-hopeful response. It is normative, because vast communities of Judaism, realized in synagogues and yeshivot, at home and in the street, tell about themselves the relevant chapters of the received and classical tale.

Visit communities of Judaism today, both in the State of Israel and in the Diaspora, and at life-cycle events and in the liturgical year of the synagogue, in yeshivot and study groups, you will hear chapters of that same master narrative. Go to a home where Judaism is practised at Passover, and the songs will sing of liberation; at the sabbath, and wine will be blessed in commemoration of the perfection of Creation.

So the master narrative continues to define Judaism and, more to the point, for many Israelites it has no competition. For them, the story that is told encompasses the whole of the life of Israel, both public and personal. Stated simply: it is Judaism, the story of a singular, unique people on earth, dwelling apart, sanctifying the here and now in the serene hope of salvation at the end of the world, a short, sweet story indeed.

But now there are other ways of telling that same story. In the nineteenth century the received tradition of telling the story met competition and in some, limited circles, mainly in Western Europe and the USA and English-speaking Diaspora, it evolved. So the master narrative endured intact but among some was also modulated to accommodate new communities of Judaism and their storytelling.

What has changed? These revisions in the tale provided for an ambiguity in the lives of the new communities. They both preserved the received narrative and also left open space for other chapters besides those pertinent to Israel. They made provision for other roles for the Israelite players besides the roles assigned to them by the Torah. The evolving narrative in these particular nineteenth-century communities of Judaism that continue today, called Reform, Orthodox and Conservative Judaisms respectively, now contemplated Israelites who were not only, not solely, not always Israel. The story accommodated Israelites who had other loyalties, lived out other lives, besides the loyalty to Israel and the life of holy Israel. To give a single concrete example: they explained why Israel, in addition to studying the Torah, could and should acquire a secular education as well, even at the cost of time better spent in Torah-learning. These communities of Judaism insisted on the compatibility of a double story: Israel always, but something else some time as well.

So the basic outline of Judaism's story remained familiar, but also evolved in new emphases and proportions. The received stories continued to impart sense and meaning to the corporate life of Israel. But nuance and adjustment to how they were told made provision for a different Israel from the one of the received tradition. The main change in the story was simple. Now, Israelites also constituted citizens of Germany or France or Britain or the USA, for example. And 'Israel' consequently meant an entity other than that unique, all-consuming holy community, practising a religion that also constituted a culture and a politics, an ethnicity and a vocation, a mode of thought and a comprehensive philosophy of life. The old, and continuing, version of Israel's story, as we have seen, made no provision for Israelites ever to be anything other than Israel; left no space for the secular.

For these new storytellers, 'Judaism' became a 'religion' in the sense in which religion covered only a limited sector of culture and politics: faith and its rites, in place of the theology and law of God for the whole of human existence. And 'Israel' became a community of faith, with faith defined in doctrinal and ritual terms, and with a vast realm of the secular and the neutral left altogether untouched by religion. What emerged in the nineteenth-century West and flourished in the twentieth century were, first, Reform Judaism, then, in response to Reform, an integrationist ('modern' or 'Western') Orthodox Judaism, and finally, a mediating in-between called in Europe Positive Historical Judaism, in the USA Conservative Judaism and in today's State of Israel Mesorti ('traditional') Judaism. All three nineteenth-century developments presented the master narrative in such a way as to provide space for Israelites to participate in other stories besides the Israelite one, and that provision represented a considerable innovation, whether called Reform or Orthodox or Conservative.

Let us place into perspective this shift, for some, in the telling of Judaism's story. The Jews of the West, preoccupied with change in their political position, formed only a small minority of the Jews of the world, the Western frontier of the Jewish people. But their confrontation with political change proved paradigmatic. They were the ones to invent the Judaisms of the nineteenth century. Each of these Judaic systems exhibited three characteristic traits. First, it asked how one could be both Jewish and something else, that is, also a citizen, a member of a nation. Second, it defined 'Judaism' (that is, its system) as a religion, so leaving ample space for that something else, namely, nationality, whether German, British, French or American. Third, it appealed to history to prove the continuity between its system and the received rabbinic Judaism. The resort to historical fact, the claim that the system at hand formed the linear development of the past, the natural increment of the entire 'history' of Israel, the Jewish people, from the beginning to the new day, masked a profound conviction that the meaning of the facts was self-evident and required no argument or even discussion. It was a deeply felt religious belief – only the focus was now secular and this-worldly. The urgent question at hand, the political one, produced a self-evidently correct answer out of the history of politics constituted by historical narrative.

How was it that some Jews in some places, or at some levels of society, formed the aspiration to participate not only as Israelites in eternal Israel but as citizens of the nations where they lived, even to fight and die for cities not their own, nations that afford them no warm welcome? This represented a genuinely new politics for Israel. For, as we have seen, from the time of Constantine to the nineteenth century, Jewry in Christendom sustained itself as a recognized, and ordinarily tolerated minority: it was always Israel, and it was only Israel. The Jews formed not only a religion, but, like many others, something akin to a guild, specializing in certain occupations – for example, in Eastern Europe, entrepreneurial trade, crafts and commerce. Until the twentieth century, the Jews formed one of the peoples permanently settled in Europe, first in the west, later in the east. But it was only in modern times that the Jews as a whole found, or even aspired to, a position equivalent to that of the majority population in European societies.

Prior to that time the Jews found themselves subjected to legal restrictions as to where they might live and how they might earn a living. They enjoyed political and social rights of a most limited character. In Eastern Europe, where most Jews lived, they governed matters of personal status and other aspects of the life of their own communities through their own administration and law. They spoke their own language, Yiddish; wore distinctive clothing; ate only their own food; controlled their own sector of the larger economy and ventured outside it only seldom; and, in all, formed a distinct and distinctive group, a nation among nations in a poly-ethnic mosaic. Commonly, the villages in which they lived had Jews and Christians living side by side, but in many of those villages Jews formed the majority of the population. These facts made for long-term stability and autonomy. In Western Europe, the Jews formed only a tiny proportion of the population, but, until modern times, they lived segregated from the rest of the country, behind the barriers of language, custom and economic calling. So the Jews for a long time formed a caste, a distinct and clearly defined group but within the hierarchy ordered by the particular society that surrounded them.

Political Emancipation

Politics explains the change in Israel's narrative explanation of itself. The movement for emancipation, which encompassed serfs, women, slaves and Catholics (in Protestant countries – for instance, Britain and Ireland), encompassed the Jews as well. Benzion Dinur defines this process of emancipation as follows:

Jewish Emancipation denotes the abolition of disabilities and inequities applied specially to Jews, the recognition of Jews as equal to other citizens, and the formal granting of the rights and duties of citizenship. Essentially the legal act of Emancipation should have been simply the expression of the diminution of social hostility and psychological aversion toward Jews in the host nation . . . but the antipathy was not obliterated and constantly hampered the realization of equality even after it had been proclaimed by the state and included in the law.[1]

The political changes began in the revolutions of the late eighteenth century, and in a half-century affected the long-term stability that had characterized the Jews' social and political life from Constantine onward. These political changes raised questions not previously found urgent, and, it follows, also precipitated reflection on problems formerly neglected. The answers to the questions flowed logically and necessarily from the character of the questions themselves. And, for those who asked the new questions, the questions answered by the received system, and the answers that they gave, no longer applied.

To place the formation of new communities of Judaism into its political context, I shall look at France, Britain, Germany and the USA. Dinur traces three periods in the history of the Jews' emancipation: 1740–89, ending with the French Revolution; 1789–1878, to the Congress of Berlin; and 1878–1933, to the rise of the Nazis to power in Germany. The first period marked the point at which the emancipation of the Jews first came under discussion, the second marked the period in which

Western and Central European states accorded to the Jews the rights of citizens, and the third brought to the fore a period of new racism that in the end annihilated the Jews of Continental Europe.

In the eighteenth century advocates of Jewish emancipation maintained that religious intolerance accounted for the low status assigned to the Jews. Liberating the Jews would mark another stage in overcoming religious intolerance. During this first period the original ideas of Reform Judaism came to expression, although the important changes in religious doctrine and practice were realized only in the early part of the nineteenth century. The French Revolution and Napoleon's conquests eventually brought Jews political rights in France, Belgium, the Netherlands, Italy, Germany and Austria-Hungary as the nineteenth century progressed. Dinur explains:

It was stressed that keeping the Jews in a politically limited and socially inferior status was incompatible with the principle of civic equality . . . 'it is the objective of every political organization to protect the natural rights of man', hence, 'all citizens have the right to all the liberties and advantages of citizens, without exception'.[2]

The adoption of the American Constitution in 1787 confirmed the US position on the matter: free white Jewish males would enjoy the rights of other free white male citizens.

Reform Judaism, which began in Germany, made it possible for Jews to hold together the two things they deemed inseparable: their desire to remain Jewish, and their wish also to be one with their 'fellow citizens'. By the middle of the nineteenth century, Reform had reached full expression and had won the support of a sizable part of German Jewry.

The end of the nineteenth century saw the rise of anti-Semitism as a social and political movement. Jews began to realize that, in Dinur's words, 'the state's legal recognition of Jewish civic and political equality does not automatically bring social recognition of this equality'. Jews continued to form a separate group which was seen by many as racially 'inferior'. The impact of this new racism would be felt in the twentieth century. The Judaisms of the twentieth century raised the questions of political repression and economic dislocation, as these faced the Jews of Eastern Europe and America. I shall now look at the main nineteenth- and twentieth-century Judaisms.

Reform Judaism

Reform Judaism insisted that change in the religion, Judaism, in response to new challenges represented a valid continuation of that religion's long-term capacity to evolve. Reform Judaism denied that any version of the Torah enjoyed eternal validity. It affirmed that Jews should adopt the politics and culture of the countries where they lived, preserving differences of only a religious character, narrowly construed. How, exactly, did Reform Judaism define itself?

For Reform Judaism in the nineteenth century the full and authoritative statement of the system and its world-view came to expression not in Europe but in the United States, in an assembly in Pittsburgh in 1885 of Reform rabbis. At that meeting of the Central Conference of American Rabbis, the Reform Judaism of the age, by now about a century old, took up the issues that divided Judaism and made an authoritative statement on them, one that most people could accept. The statement, known as the 'Pittsburgh Platform', would be revised in synods held through the twentieth century, but while doctrines changed, modes of thought and theological inquiry remained constant.

Critical to rabbinic Judaism was its view of Israel as God's people, a supernatural polity, living out its social existence under God's Torah. In Reform Judaism too we find an emphasis on who is Israel, with that definition exposing for all to see the foundations of the way of life and world-view that these rabbis had formed for the Israel they conceived:

We recognize in the Mosaic legislation a system of training the Jewish people for its mission during its national life in Palestine, and today we accept as binding only its moral laws and maintain only such ceremonies as elevate and sanctify our lives, but reject all such as are not adapted to the views and habits of modern civilization . . . We hold that all such Mosaic and rabbinical laws as regular diet, priestly purity, and dress originated in ages and under the influence of ideas entirely foreign to our present mental and spiritual state . . . Their observance in our days is apt rather to obstruct than to further modern spiritual elevation . . . We recognize in the modern era of universal culture of heart and intellect the approaching of the realization of Israel's great messianic hope for the establishment of the kingdom of truth, justice, and peace among all men. We consider ourselves no longer a nation but a religious community and therefore expect neither a return to Palestine nor a sacrificial worship under the sons of Aaron nor the restoration of any of the laws concerning the Jewish state . . .[3]

The Pittsburgh Platform takes up each component of the system in turn. Who is Israel? What is its way of life? How does it account for its existence as a distinct, and distinctive, group? The answer is unambiguous. Israel once was a nation ('during its national life') but today is not a nation. It once had a set of laws that regulated diet, clothing, and the like. These no longer apply, because Israel now is not what it was then. Israel forms an integral part of Western civilization. The reason to persist as a distinctive group is that the group has work to do, namely to realize the messianic hope for the establishment of a kingdom of truth, justice and peace. For that purpose Israel no longer constitutes a nation. It now forms a religious community. What that means is that individual Jews do live as citizens in other nations. Difference is acceptable at the level of religion, but not at the level of personal nationality, a position that accords fully with the definition of citizenship in Western democracies. In the language of the emancipationist side of the French Revolution, 'To the Jews as citizens, everything; to the Jews as a nation, nothing.'

Reform Judaism's Israel does not propose to eat or dress in distinctive ways. Its Israelites do seek a place within 'modern spiritual elevation . . . [the] universal culture of heart and intellect'. They impute to that culture the realization of 'the messianic hope', a considerable stake. The single self-evident proposition taken fully into account by this Judaism is that political change has changed the entirety of 'Judaism', but Reform Judaism has the power to accommodate to that change. So change in general forms the method for dealing with the problem at hand, which is change in the political and social standing the Jews now enjoy.

How did this evolving version of Israel's story begin? It was, appropriately, in the setting of synagogue worship. Reform Judaism dates its beginnings to changes, called reforms, in trivial aspects of public worship in the synagogue,[4] such as giving sermons in the vernacular language, rather than Hebrew, which few understood. The motive for these changes derived from the simple fact that many Jews rejected the received system. People were defecting from the synagogue. Since, it was taken for granted, giving up the faith meant surrendering all ties to the group, these first changes were designed to make the synagogue more attractive so that others would not leave, and defectors would return. The reforms therefore took cognizance of something that had already taken place. And that was the loss, for the received system, of its standing as self-evident truth. The many who were staying within Jewry looked in a new way on what, for so long, had scarcely demanded examination at all. But, of course, the real issues involved not the synagogue but society at large. It would take two generations before Reform Judaism would find the strength to address that much larger issue, and a generation beyond for the power of the ideas ultimately formulated in the Pittsburgh Platform to be felt.

The Reformers maintained that change was validated by historical precedent: others had undertaken to revise the tradition, and each generation had the task of updating it. For its part, rabbinic Judaism too has accommodated new modes of thought and their doctrinal, and narrative, consequences. Rabbinic Judaism endured, never intact but always unimpaired, because of its power to absorb and make its own the diverse events of culture and society. So long as the structure of politics remained the same, with Israel an autonomous entity, subordinated but recognized as a cogent and legitimate social group in charge of some of its own affairs, the system answered the paramount question. The trivial ones could work their way through and become part of the consensus, to be perceived in the end as 'tradition' too. A catalogue of changes that had taken place over fifteen hundred years would encompass many more dramatic and decisive sorts of change than those matters of minor revision of liturgy, such as sermons in the vernacular language rather than Hebrew, that attracted attention at the dawn of the Reform movement.

The vital difference was that people were taking a stance external to the received mode, and effecting change as a matter of decision and policy, rather than as a matter of what was purported to be restorative and timelessly appropriate. For those people, Judaism in its received form had already died. The received system no longer defined matters but had now become subject to definition. And that marks the move from self-evidence to self-consciousness.

What formed the justification for reform was the theory of the incremental history of a single, linear Judaism, of which change was characteristic and Reform Judaism the necessary outcome. The earliest

Reformers were laymen rather than rabbis, and they rested their case on an appeal to the authoritative texts. Change was legitimate, and these changes in particular wholly consonant with the law, or the tradition, or the inner dynamics of the faith, or the dictates of history, or whatever out of the past worked that day. They tried to demonstrate that their changes fitted in with the law of Judaism. Reform even at the outset claimed to restore, to continue, to persist in the received pattern. The justification for change always invoked precedent. People who made changes had to show that the principle that guided what they did was not new, even though the specific things they did were. So to lay down a bridge between themselves and their past they laid out beams resting on deep-set piles. The foundation of change was formed of the bedrock of precedent. And they claimed change restores, reverts to an unchanging ideal. So the Reformer claims not to change at all, but only to regain the correct state of affairs, one that others, in the interval, themselves have changed. That forms the fundamental attitude of mind of the people who make changes and call the changes reforms. The appeal to history, a common mode of justification in the politics and theology of the nineteenth century, therefore defined the principal justification for the new Judaism: it was new because it renewed the old and enduring, the golden Judaism of a mythic age of perfection. Arguments on precedent drew the reformers to the work of critical scholarship as they settled all questions by appeal to the facts of history.

Affirming the integrity of the individual over the claim of the group as a whole, and therefore rejecting the claim of the halakhah to dictate practice, Reform Judaism rejected the belief that the Torah was the literal record of what God said to Moses at Sinai. It further denied the authority of the rabbinic writings that are represented as the oral part of the Torah. Rather, it held that Judaism was the result of historical processes which represented divine will. The prophets, with their stress on ethics ('I desire steadfast love and not sacrifice', Hosea 6:6, for example) defined the ideal Judaism, and social action for the improvement of the condition of the world formed the highest calling of the Israelite. Reform Judaism became the paramount Judaism of Germany and the United States in the later nineteenth and twentieth centuries. It made inroads elsewhere as well, in particular in Austria-Hungary, Britain and Canada. The earliest rabbinical school in the United States (Hebrew Union College), the first rabbinical synod and association (the Central Conference of American Rabbis), and the initial union of synagogues (the Union of American Hebrew Congregations) all originated in Reform Judaism.

Reform Judaism defined itself as the natural outcome of the ages, a system that stressed ethics over ritual; Israel as bearing responsibilities to all humanity and bearing a special mission to the gentiles; and, in all, a universalist aspiration. Its religious services were immediately accessible, in the local vernacular, to all comers. The principal figure of Reform Judaism in the USA, Isaac Mayer Wise, believed that in a short period of time all humanity would adopt Reform Judaism. In the twentieth century, particularly in response to the Holocaust, Reform Judaism revised its sunny optimism about humanity and its capacities, and it adopted some of the practices of the rabbinic tradition that in the nineteenth century it had given up. But it remained the bastion of individualism over communal adherence to the law, of the Israelite over the community of Israel, the people subject to the Torah that halakhic Orthodoxy stressed.

Orthodox Judaism

Many people reasonably identify all 'traditional' or 'observant' Judaism with Orthodoxy, and they furthermore take for granted that all Judaisms that keep the Torah as received at Sinai are pretty much the same. But a wide variety of Judaisms all affirm the Torah, oral and written, and abide by its laws, as interpreted by their masters, who differ from one another on many important points. We may call all such Judaic systems 'the Torah camp', meaning the Judaic systems that concur on basic doctrinal matters concerning the origin and authority of the Torah, oral and written: that they record verbatim God's word to Moses at Sinai. The components of the Torah-camp are readily differentiated into those which affirm Israel's self-segregation from the gentiles, and those which in some ways validate Israel's integration, though not assimilation, among them.

Called 'Modern' or 'Western', integrationist Orthodox Judaism both affirms the divine revelation and eternal authority of the Torah, oral and written, and favours the integration of Jews ('holy Israel') into the national life of the countries of their birth. Self-segregationist (also Orthodox) Judaisms (and they are many and diverse) affirm the Torah but favour the segregation of Jews from other people in the countries where they live, including the State of Israel. Indicators such as clothing, language, and above all the legitimacy of secular education, differentiate integrationist from segregationist Judaisms.

How shall we identify integrationist Orthodoxy? When Jews who kept the law of the Torah, for example as it dictated food choices and sabbath observance, sent their children to secular schools in addition to, or instead of, solely Jewish ones, or when, in Jewish schools, they included in the curriculum subjects outside the Torah, they crossed the boundary that distinguished self-segregation from integration. For while the notion that science or German or Latin or philosophy deserved serious study would not have been alien to some of the rabbinic sages, in the nineteenth century it seemed wrong to those for whom the received system remained self-evidently right. Those Jews did not send their children to gentile schools, and in Jewish schools did not include anything in the curriculum other than Torah-study. The self-segregationists in Austria-Hungary, Russia and Germany strongly resisted the efforts of their national governments to include secular subjects in the Jewish schools' curriculum, even those of a vocational character.

Integrationist Orthodox Judaism come into being in Germany in the middle of the nineteenth century, about two generations after the advent of Reform. It represented Jews who rejected Reform and made a self-conscious decision to remain within the way of life and world-view that they had known and cherished all their lives. They framed the issues in terms of change and history. The Reformers held that Judaism could change, and that Judaism was a product of history. Their Orthodox opponents denied that Judaism could change and insisted that Judaism derived from God's will at Sinai and was eternal and supernatural, not historical and man-made. In these two convictions, of course, the Orthodox recapitulated the convictions of the received system. But they found some components of that system more persuasive than others, and in this picking and choosing, and in the articulation of the view that Judaism formed a religion to be seen as distinct and autonomous of politics or society – 'the rest of life' – they entered that same world of self-consciousness that the reformers also explored.

Integrationist Orthodox Judaism dealt with the same urgent questions as did Reform Judaism, questions raised by political emancipation, but it

gave different answers to them. Orthodoxy maintains the world-view of
the received dual Torah, constantly citing its sayings and adhering with
only trivial variations to the bulk of its rules for everyday life. At the
same time Orthodoxy holds that Jews adhering to the dual Torah may
wear the same clothing as non-Jews and do not have to wear distinctively
Jewish (even, Judaic) clothing; may live within a common economy and
not practise distinctively Jewish professions (however these professions
may be defined in a given setting), and in diverse ways may take up a life
not readily distinguished in important characteristics from the life lived
by people in general. So for Orthodoxy a portion of Israel's life may
prove secular, in that the Torah does not dictate and so sanctify all details
of life under all circumstances.

The term 'Orthodoxy' in Judaism takes on meaning only in the contrast
to Reform, so in a simple sense Orthodoxy owes its life to Reform
Judaism. The term first surfaced in 1795.[5] Obviously, so long as the
Torah camp's position struck the generality as self-evident of Jewry,
'Orthodoxy' as a distinct and organized Judaism did not exist. It did not
have to, what else was there? Similarly, the conception of 'tradition' was
articulated only in response to 'change'. If, in concrete terms, Reform
Judaism made minor changes in liturgy and its conduct, Orthodox Judaism
rejected even those that, under other circumstances, might have found
acceptance. Saying prayers in the vernacular, for example, provoked
strong opposition. But everyone knew that some of the prayers, said in
Aramaic, in fact were in the vernacular of an earlier age. The Orthodox
thought that these changes, not reforms at all, represented only the first
step of a process leading Jews out of the Judaic world altogether.

In Germany, where the Reform movement attracted the majority of
members of many Jewish communities, the Orthodox faced a challenge
indeed. There the community's institutions in the hands of the Reform
movement did not obey the law of the Torah as the Orthodox understood
it. So, in the end, Orthodoxy took the step that marked it as a self-
conscious Judaism: it separated from the established community
altogether. The Orthodox set up their own organization and seceded
from the community at large. The next step prohibited Orthodox Jews
from participating in any non-Orthodox organizations. Isaac Breuer, a
leading theologian of Orthodoxy, would ultimately take the position that
'refusal to espouse the cause of separation was interpreted as being

equivalent to the rejection of the absolute sovereignty of God.'⁶ Rabbinic Judaism had addressed all Jews and Orthodoxy recognized that it could not do so. Integrationist Orthodoxy acquiesced, however, in recognizing the split in the unity of the Jewish community, a situation that lay beyond the imagination of the framers of rabbinic Judaism, who had always taken it for granted that holy Israel was indivisible and ruled by the Torah.

True, the Orthodox had no choice. Their seceding from the community and forming their own institutions ratified the simple fact that they could not work with the reformers. But the upshot remained the same. That supernatural entity, Israel, of normative rabbinic Judaism now gave up its place, and a natural, sociological Israel, a this-worldly political fact, succeeded. Pained though Orthodoxy was by this fact, it nonetheless accommodated the new social reality, and affirmed it by reshaping the sense of Israel in the supernatural dimension. Orthodox Judaism no less than the Judaism of the Reformers stood for something new – a birth not a renewal; a political response to a new politics. True enough, for Orthodoxy the politics was that of the Jewish community, divided as it was among diverse visions of the political standing of the Jewish people. For the Reform movement, by contrast, the new politics derived from the establishment of the category of neutral citizenship in an encompassing nation-state. But the political shifts flowed from the same large-scale changes in Israel's consciousness and character, and, it follows, Orthodoxy as much as Reform represented a set of self-evident answers to political questions that none could evade.

Where did integrationist Orthodoxy part company from the self-segregationist Judaic systems of the Torah camp? The single most significant trait of integrationist Orthodoxy is its power to see the Torah as 'Judaism', a 'religion', and therefore concerned with the life of faith, as distinct from 'secular' life. Those distinctions were lost on the received system of rabbinic Judaism, of course, which legislated for matters we should today regard as entirely secular or neutral – for example, the institutions of state (for example, king, priest, army). The recognition that Jews were like others, that the Torah fell into a category into which other and comparable matters fell, was long in coming.

For Christians and for Reform Judaism it had become a commonplace in Germany and other Western countries to see 'religion' as distinct from other components of the social and political system. While the Christian

Orthodox Church in Russia identified with the tsarist state, or the Catholic Church in Poland with the national aspirations of the Polish people, for example, in Germany two Churches, Catholic and Protestant, competed. The terrible wars of the Reformation in the sixteenth and seventeenth centuries, which ruined Germany, had led to the uneasy compromise that the prince might choose the religion of his principality, and from that self-aware choice people understood that a particular world-view, rites and rituals were regarded as a religion, and that one religion might be compared with some other.

The conception of the Torah as a unique truth, incomparable and unlike all other religions, gave way. By the end of the nineteenth century, complex societies had decided that they would tolerate difference in matters of religious belief and private practice, but not in matters of citizenship. The notion of the nation-state, in which all the citizens conformed to a single law and carried out uniform obligations, could then accommodate variation in citizens' private beliefs about supernatural matters. In that way religion was both privatized and trivialized.

That conception that religion could be separated out from all the other concerns of people, registered as a fundamental shift in the understanding and interpretation of the Torah, which was now seen as a body of belief and practice, an -ism along with other -isms. A mark of the creative power of the Jews who formed the integrationist Orthodox Judaic system derives from their capacity to shift the fundamental category in which they framed their system. The basic shift in category is what made Orthodoxy a Judaism on its own, not simply a restatement of rabbinic Judaism.

Integrationist Orthodox Judaism took the view that one could observe the rules of the traditional Judaic system and at the same time keep the laws of the state. More important, it took full account of the duties of citizenship, so far as being a good citizen imposed the expectation of conformity in certain aspects of everyday life. So a category, 'religion', could contain the Torah, and another category, 'the secular', could allow Jews a place in the accepted civic life of the country. The importance of the category-shift therefore lies in its power to accommodate the political change so important, also, to Reform Judaism. The Jews' differences from others would fit into categories in which difference was (in Jews' minds at any rate) acceptable, and would not violate those lines to which all citizens had to adhere.

Integrationist Orthodox Judaism found it possible by recognizing the category of the secular to accept the language, clothing and learning of those countries. And these matters serve openly to exemplify a larger acceptance of gentile ways – not all of them but enough to lessen the differences between the Holy People and the gentiles. Both integrationist Orthodox and Reform Judaism understood that some things were sacred, others not, and that understanding marked these Judaisms off from rabbinic Judaism.

Once the category-shift had taken place from 'Torah' to 'Judaism', the difference was to be measured in degree, not kind. For Orthodox Jews maintained distinctive beliefs of a political character in the future coming of the Messiah and the reconstitution of the Jewish nation in its own land that Reform Jews rejected. But, placing these convictions in the distant future, Orthodox Jews nonetheless prepared for a protracted interim of life within their adopted homelands, seeing themselves like the Reform movement as different in religion, not in nationality as represented by citizenship. What follows is that Orthodoxy, as much as Reform, signals remarkable changes in the Jews' political situation and, more important, aspiration. They did want to be different, but not so different as rabbinic Judaism would have made them. By adopting for themselves the category of religion, and by recognizing a distinction between religion and the secular, the founders of Orthodoxy validated the exercise of choice and selectivity.

So much for the integrationist Orthodox Judaism that responded in Western countries to the changes of the nineteenth century. Self-segregationist Orthodox Judaism was not much in evidence in Central and Western Europe and the United States, but it was paramount in Eastern Europe. There the received definition of the Torah and the traditional practice thereof predominated. There was little or no representation of Reform Judaism east of the German frontier except in Hungary; and integrationist Orthodoxy was scarcely known either. Traditional self-segregationist Orthodoxy persisted there and in the twentieth century found a new setting for itself in the State of Israel and in certain neighbourhoods and cities of Western Europe and the United States, particularly Antwerp, London, Gateshead, and New York City and its suburbs. Today self-segregationist Orthodoxy in its various expressions, some of them deriving from Hasidism, successfully competes with integrationist Orthodoxy. At issue in the diverse modes of expressing the same uniform Torah of Sinai is what God meant in the Torah for his Israel to be, and who authentically realizes God's will. To the self-segregationist Orthodox camp, it is self-evident that the traditional modes of dress, vocation and education (distinctive clothing, particularly Jewish callings, study of the Torah narrowly defined) are the only authentic ones. To the integregationist Orthodox camp, as we have seen, that is by no means self-evident: they believe that God had in mind an Israel engaged by the science and culture that celebrates Creation and the Creator.

Conservative Judaism

A Judaic religious system with roots in the German Judaic response to the development of Reform, then Orthodox Judaism, and also the immigrant response to the conditions of American life in the twentieth century, Conservative Judaism seeks a centrist position on the issues of tradition and change. The Historical School, a group of nineteenth-century German scholars, and Conservative Judaism, a twentieth-century Judaism in America, both took the middle position, each in its own context. They form a single community of Judaism, because they share a single viewpoint. The Historical School began among German Jewish theologians who advocated change but found Reform extreme. They parted company with Reform on some specific issues of practice and doctrine – observance of the dietary laws and belief in the coming of the Messiah, for example. But they also found Orthodoxy immobile. Conservative Judaism in America in the twentieth century carried forward this same centrist position and turned a viewpoint of intellectuals into a Judaism: a way of life and world-view addressed to an Israel. The Historical School shaped the world-view, and Conservative Judaism later on brought that view into full realization as a way of life characteristic of a large group of Jews – nearly half of all American Jews by the middle of the twentieth century.

The Historical School in Germany and Conservative Judaism in America affirmed a far broader part of rabbinic Judaism than Reform, while rejecting a much larger part of the rabbinical world-view than did Orthodoxy. The Historical School concurred with the Reform movement in their basic position but with the Orthodox in their concrete way of life. The Reformers held that change was permissible and claimed that historical scholarship would show what change was acceptable and what was not. But the proponents of the Historical School differed in matters of detail. Their emphasis on historical research in settling theological debates explains their name. Arguing that its positions represented matters of historical fact rather than theological conviction, the Historical School maintained that 'positive historical scholarship' would prove capable, on the basis of historical facts, of purifying and clarifying the faith, joined to far stricter observance of the law than the Reformers required.[7] Rabbis of this same centrist persuasion organized the Jewish Theological Seminary of America in 1886–7, and from that rabbinical college the Conservative Movement developed. The order of the formation of the several Judaisms of the nineteenth century therefore is Reform, then Orthodoxy, and finally, Conservatism – the two extremes, then the middle. Reform defined the tasks of the next two Judaisms to come into being. Orthodoxy framed the clearer of the two positions in reaction to Reform, but, in intellectual terms, the Historical School in Germany met the issues of Reform in a more direct way.

The Historical School added up to a handful of scholars writing books, and a book is not a Judaism. In America, by contrast, Conservative Judaism did reach full realization in a way of life characteristic of large numbers of Jews. In many cities it soon constituted the majority of those that practised Judaism, promulgating a world-view that, for those Jews, explained who they were and what they must do; a clearly articulated account of who is Israel. In the language of the great theologian of Conservative Judaism in the first half of the twentieth century, Mordecai Kaplan, the Jews now formed a people, not a religion or a religious community, and it was their task to preserve the folklore and traditions of that people not because a supernatural God had commanded them to do so, but because they constituted the customs of the people. In his *Conservative Judaism*, Marshall Sklare has argued that this Judaism served to express the viewpoint of the children of the late nineteenth-century immigrants to America from Eastern Europe. These people emphasized the folk aspect and the way of life, while rejecting the world-view and the supernaturalism, of rabbinic Judaism. They treated the commandments of God to carry out certain rites as customs and ceremonies, secular ethnic traditions. For example, they reinterpreted the obligation to sanctify the sabbath as a means of preserving the Jewish people, a matter of the life-style of Jews, not of a divine imperative for holy Israel. So too, they translated the dietary restrictions into an ethnic cuisine, so 'kosher-style' cooking for Jewish palates replaced kosher food. Now Jews were assumed not to eat pork because they did not like pork, not because God forbade it. Sklare further identified Conservative Judaism with the area of second settlement, that is to say, the neighbourhoods to which the Jewish immigrants or their children moved once they had settled down in this country. But the centre's fundamental definition of the urgent issues and how they were to be worked out in both nineteenth-century Germany and twentieth-century America proved remarkably uniform, right up to the present.

The stress of the Historical School in Europe and Conservative Judaism in America lay on two matters: scholarship, with historical research assigned the task of discovering those facts of which the faith would be composed; and observance of the rules of rabbinic Judaism. A professedly free approach to the study of the Torah, specifically through what was called 'critical scholarship' therefore would yield an accurate account of the essentials of the faith. But scholars and lay people alike would keep and practise nearly the whole of the tradition, just as the Orthodox did. The ambivalence of Conservative Judaism, speaking in part for intellectuals deeply loyal to the rabbinical way of life, but profoundly dubious of the world-view they had inherited from it came to full expression in the odd slogan: 'Eat kosher and think *traif*' (*traif* means not kosher). That statement meant people should keep the rules of the holy way of life but ignore the convictions that made sense of them. Orthopraxy is the word that refers to correct action, as against Orthodoxy, right doctrine. Some would then classify Conservative Judaism in America as an orthoprax Judaism defined through works, not doctrine.

Conservative Judaism saw the Jews as a people, not merely a religious community, and celebrated the ethnic as much as the more narrowly religious side of Jewish life. German integrationist Orthodoxy, for all its openness to secular learning, could not concur. When the organized Jewish communities in Germany fell into the hands of Reform Jews, the Orthodox sector left the organized community and set up its own institutions. Reform Judaism rejected the position that the Jews constitute a people, not merely a religious community. Conservative Judaism emphasized the importance of the unity of the community as a whole and took a stand in favour of Zionism as soon as that movement got under way.

What separated Conservative Judaism from Reform was the matter of observance. It affirmed change: more than Orthodoxy but not so much as Reform. When considering the continued validity of a traditional religious practice, the Reform movement asked why, the Conservatives, why not. The Orthodox, of course, asked no questions to begin with. The fundamental principle of Conservatism, that the world-view of the Judaism under construction would rest upon (mere) historical facts, came from Reform Judaism. Orthodoxy could never have concurred. Integrationist Orthodoxy, represented by Hirsch, believed in the Torah despite the evidence of the world. The Conservatives wanted to prove the truth of the Torah as historical fact. That is why they called themselves 'the positive historical school', and deemed their Judaic religious system to constitute nothing other than a collection of historical facts. When history moved to a more critical view of the Torah's narratives, as we saw in Chapter 3, Conservative Judaism faced a theological dilemma not readily resolved by historical scholarship.

History thus served, as in Reform Judaism, as an instrument of reform. The emphasis on research as the route to historical fact, and on historical fact as the foundation for both change and also the definition of what was truly authentic in the tradition further tells us that the Historical School was made up of intellectuals. In America a pattern developed that contradicted the original emphasis of the Positive Historical School upon deeds instead of beliefs. The synagogues of Conservative Judaism were made up of generally non-observant, or not strictly observant, Jews, who wanted their rabbis to keep the law in a strict way. So the original Conservative stress on keeping the law while thinking in new ways was lost, and Conservative synagogues would be distinguished from Reform ones only in superficial traits. But since the rabbis of the Conservative synagogues kept to a higher standard of learning and observance than their Reform counterparts, many of the intellectual problems that occupied public debate concerned rabbis more than lay people, since the rabbis were responsible, so the community maintained, for not only teaching the faith but, on their own, embodying it. It was widely remarked that this Judaism was made up of Orthodox rabbis serving Conservative synagogues made up of Reform Jews. But in the more traditional liturgy and the emphasis on observance of the dietary taboos, sabbath and festivals which did, and still does, characterize homes of Conservative more than of Reform Jews, Conservative Judaism in its way of life as much as in its world-view did establish an essentially mediating position between Orthodoxy and Reform Judaism. And the conception that Conservative Judaism is a Judaism for Conservative rabbis in no way accords with the truth. This is the Judaism that for a long time enjoyed the loyalty of fully half of the Jews in the United States and today still holds the central and influential position there. The viewpoint of the centre influences the more traditional circles of Reform and the more modernist sectors of Orthodoxy.

The point at which a school of thought became a Judaism is not difficult to locate. The Historical School in Germany and a handful of moderate rabbis in the United States defined themselves as a movement in Judaism (in my terms, a Judaism) in response to a particular event: the adoption, by the Reform rabbis, of the Pittsburgh Platform of 1885. At that point a number of European rabbis now settled in America decided to break away from the Reform movement and establish what they hoped would be simply 'traditional' Judaism in America. In 1886 they founded the Jewish Theological Seminary of America, a new rabbinical college for 'the knowledge and practice of historical Judaism',[8] and that is the point at which Conservative Judaism as a religious movement began.

The urgent issue of the age was to address political change. If we want to understand Conservative Judaism, we have to follow its mode of sorting out the legitimate changes from the unacceptable ones, for that method marked the middle off from the extremes on either side. The fundamental premise of the Conservatives' emphasis on history rested on the conviction that history demonstrated the truth or falsity of theological propositions. We would look in vain in all the earlier Judaic Literature for a precedent for this belief, which was self-evident to the nineteenth- and twentieth-century system-builders. The appeal to historical facts was meant to lay upon firm, factual foundations whatever change was to take place. The Conservatives sought reassurance from the history of Judaism that some change, if not a great deal of change, would not endanger the enduring faith they wished to preserve. But there was a second factor.

The laws and lessons of history would then settle questions of contemporary public policy. Both in Germany in the middle of the century and in America at the end the emphasis was on the 'knowledge and practice of historical Judaism as ordained in the law of Moses expounded by the prophets and sages in Israel in Biblical and Talmudic writings', as the articles of incorporation of the Jewish Theological Seminary of America Association stated in 1887. Calling themselves 'traditionalists' rather than 'Orthodox', the Conservative adherents accepted for most Judaic subjects the principles of modern critical scholarship.

Nowadays Conservative Judaism has problems of self-definition that do not face either Reform or integrationist Orthodoxy. Daniel Elazar and Rela Geffen have stated, 'No more than 40,000 to 50,000 members . . . live up to the standards of Conservative Judaism as defined by its leadership . . . out of an estimated million and a half Jews affiliated with Conservative synagogues . . . the Movement is only the equivalent of a fair-sized Hassidic sect'.[9] When Conservative Judaism took shape within the Positive Historical School of the nineteenth century and was carried to the Jewish Theological Seminary of America at the turn of the twentieth century, it advanced a theology of hypocrisy and cynicism: eat kosher and think *traif*. And it caught on: the middle of the road is never crowded. An elite minority chose to eat kosher and think kosher, but a wildly successful mass movement (between a third and half of American Jews who practise any Judaism identify themselves as Conservative) has opted to eat *traif* and think *traif*. Unstable and constantly in quest of self-definition, Conservative Judaism, as distinct from its well-run institutions at the synagogue and community level, faces an uncertain future because it believes nothing in particular for very long. Reform Judaism from the beginning adopted coherent principles of behaviour and belief in a highly cogent system, and Orthodox Judaism, integrationist and self-segregationist alike, always affirmed the enduring tradition. Stuck somewhere in the middle, Conservative Judaism has paid a heavy price for its transient popularity and success, with constant erosion of its more traditional members to Orthodoxy and of the more liberal to Reform.

From Torah to Judaism

The principal communities of Judaism of the nineteenth-century West (Germany, Britain, France and the United States) share principles in common and diverge on matters of detail. All are reformist, on the model of Reform. The power of Reform Judaism to create and define its opposition in Orthodoxy in Germany and Conservative Judaism in the United States tells us how accurately the Reform movement had outlined the urgent questions of the age. Reform, after all, had treated as compelling the issue of citizenship and raised the core question – how could Jews aspire to return to the Holy Land and form a nation and at the same time take up citizenship in the lands of their birth and loyalty? Jews lived a way of life different from that of their neighbours, with whom they wished to associate. Judaism had to explain that difference. The answers of all three Judaisms accepted the premises framed, to begin with, by Reform. Integrationist Orthodoxy maintained one could accept citizenship and accommodate political change, but also adhere loyally to the Torah. Conservative Judaism affirmed Zionism – that the Jews formed one people, and should build a Jewish state in Palestine – but concurred with Reform Judaism that Jews could live like their gentile neighbours except in certain specific details – for example, food regulations and the holy day calendar – where they differed for religious reasons. Conservative Judaism specified as essential fewer aspects of the received way of life than did Orthodoxy, but more than Reform. In many ways, therefore, Reform Judaism defined the agenda for all of the Judaisms of the nineteenth century, and its success lay in imposing its fundamental perspective on its competition.

For nineteenth-century Reform, integrationist Orthodox and Conservative theologians alike, the category 'Judaism' in place of 'Torah' stood for 'what the Jews believe', or 'the Jewish religion'. All three Judaisms viewed 'Judaism' as a system and as a whole: thus 'Judaism' constituted a philosophical category. It was an -ism, instructing thinkers to look for the system and the order and structure of the ideas within it. Hence theologians investigated the doctrine of this, the doctrine of that; and used the category 'Judaism' when they proposed to speak of the whole of Judaic religious existence. But the received tradition expressed itself not solely, or principally, in doctrine but in the halakhic structure, which expressed doctrine through a pattern of actions, and which deemed that the holy way of life realized 'the Torah' and so constituted what the gentile world called 'Judaism'.

To the Jews who remained within rabbinic Judaism in its classical formulation, the discovery of the possibility of an integrationist Orthodoxy represented an innovation, a shift from the perceivably self-evident truths of the Torah. For the word for Judaism in Judaism was and is 'Torah', and when the self-segregationist Orthodox wanted to refer to the whole of the tradition, all together and all at once, they used the word 'Torah'. They not only used a different word, but in fact referred to different things. The two categories, 'Judaism' and 'Torah', which are supposed to refer to the same data in the same social world, in fact encompass different data. 'Judaism' speaks of matters of doctrine, while 'Torah' refers to the narrative of the holy people making their way through time towards eternity. 'Torah' realizes matters of doctrine by portraying a holy way of life that the holy people lead. The difference between religion, with its creeds and doctrines, and culture, with its all-pervasive account of the social order, corresponds to the difference between Judaism and Torah. The -ism category does not invoke an encompassing symbol, image, experience or story, but the systematization of thought. Judaism is an 'it' – an object, a classification, an action. Torah, for its part, is everything in one thing – symbol, image, experience and narrative. When I quoted Father Greeley in the Prologue, 'Religion is experience, image and story before it is anything else and after it is everything else', it was because his singular definition of religion best serves for this book. That is because his emphasis on religion as story captures the fullness of the Torah in a way in which the word 'Judaism' does not. That is why I cannot imagine a more separate and unlike set of categories than 'Judaism' and 'Torah', even though both encompass the same way of life and world-view and address the same social group. So Torah as a category serves as a symbol, everywhere present in detail, holding all the details together, while Judaism as a category makes a statement of the main points, the intellectual surface of it all.

The conception of Judaism as an organized body of doctrine, as in the phrase, 'Judaism teaches . . .' or 'Judaism says . . .' rather than 'the Torah tells . . .', derives from an age in which people had determined that a religion was something that teaches or says, an intellectual exercise of belief and prayer. That is to say, Judaism is a religion, and a religion to begin with was understood as a composition of beliefs. The category of religion as a distinct entity, separate from culture and differentiated from the social order, emerged from Protestant theological thought. For in Protestantism one is saved by faith. But the very components of that sentence – one, an individual, not the people or holy nation; saved, personally, not in history and saved, not sanctified; faith, not law – in fact prove incomprehensible in the categories constructed by the Torah. In the modes of thought and speech of rabbinic Judaism, you cannot state, 'One is saved by faith'. You have to make 'Israel' not 'one' the subject. And you have to address not only the individual life but all of historical time, so 'saved' by itself does not suffice. And 'saved' also does not suffice since the idea of sanctification, not just salvation, must be included. Finally, someone fluent in the language of the Torah will use the term 'mitzvot', commandments, alongside 'faith'. The upshot is, if Protestantism defined the model of a religion, then 'Judaism' could accommodate itself to the Protestant model, but the Torah could not fit within the model at all.

The point is simple: in the nineteenth century, the response to emancipation was to recast 'the Torah' into 'Judaism', that is, the tradition into a religion like other religions. This represented a substantial reform of the received tradition of the Torah. That is not to suggest rabbinic Judaism did not lay down doctrines, even dogmas. It was, and is, animated by a theological system, which we reviewed in Chapter 7. Nor is it correct to suppose that integrationist Orthodoxy erred in recasting the received way of life so that faithful practitioners of the Torah could enter into secular society, politics and learning. It is only to stress how much changed in the transformation of the tradition into a religion on the Western, Protestant model. Contrast the language – 'Judaism teaches', but 'the Torah requires'. Notice the difference between 'Judaism teaches that God is one' and 'Hear O Israel, the Lord our God, the Lord is one'. The one represents a statement of faith, the other an act of submission to God's rule, the acceptance of the yoke of the Torah, the acting out in the here and now of the narrative of Creation, revelation and redemption. The category Judaism thus organizes doctrines. The category Torah teaches what 'we', God's holy people, are and what, by reason of our story, 'we' must do.

When in rabbinic Judaism one studied the Torah, what one studied was not an intellectual system of theology or philosophy, but a document of revealed narrative and law. That is not to suggest that the theologians of nineteenth-century Orthodox or Reform Judaism did not affirm the Shema, or that the philosophers who taught that 'Judaism teaches ethical monotheism' did not concur that, because of that, one has to recite the Shema. A book on Judaism explains the doctrines, theology or philosophy of Judaism. A book *of* Judaism, that is, a book of the Torah, expounds God's will as revealed in 'the one whole Torah of Moses, our rabbi', as the sages taught, and embodies God's will. I cannot imagine two more different books, and the reason is that they represent totally different categories of intelligible discourse and of knowledge. The proof of this is that the books that claim a place as part of the Torah are literally unreadable. They are to be used as part of a genuinely oral exercise, to be cited sentence by sentence and expounded in the setting of other sentences from other books, the whole made cogent by the speaker. That process of homogenization is how the Torah works as an organizing, encompassing, unifying category.

True, the two distinct categories come to bear upon the same body of data, the same holy books. But the consequent compositions, selections of facts, ordering of facts, analyses of facts, statements of conclusion and interpretation, and above all, modes of public discourse (meaning, who says what to whom) bear no relationship whatsoever to one another. Indeed, the compositions more likely than not do not even adduce the same facts, or even refer to them.

How did the category readily perceived as imposed, extrinsic and deductive, namely 'Judaism' (in place of 'Torah') attain the status of self-evidence? Categories serve because they are self-evident to a large group of people. 'Judaism' serves because it enjoys self-evidence as part of a larger set of categories that are equally self-evident. In all of these categories, religion constitutes a statement of belief distinct from other aspects and dimensions of human existence, so religions form a body of well-composed -isms. The source of the categorical power of 'Judaism' derives from the Protestant philosophical heritage that has defined scholarship, including category formation, from the time of Kant onward. 'Judaism' constitutes a category asymmetrical to the evidence adduced in its study. The category does not work because the principle of formation is philosophical and does not emerge from an unmediated encounter with the Torah. In simple terms: when people began to speak in philosophical terms about 'Judaism', a religion, they no longer portrayed religion as experience, image and story. That represented a considerable change in the presentation of Israel's master narrative.

But Reform, integrationist Orthodox and Conservative Judaism continued the received system far more than they diverged from it. While the differences in the grounds of separation from the received system prove formidable, still more striking and fresh are the several arguments adduced once more to establish a firm connection to rabbinic Judaism, or, more accurately, to 'the tradition'. For the Judaisms of continuation characteristically differ in the several ways in which each, on its own, proposed to establish its continuity with a past perceived as discontinuous. Each of the three Judaisms respectively enjoyed ample justification for the insistence that it carried forward the entire history of Judaism and took the necessary and ineluctable step beyond where matters had rested prior to its own formation. The Reform movement in this regard found itself subjected to vigorous criticism, but in saying that 'things have changed in the past, and we can change them too', it established its primary position. It too pointed to precedent, and, in doing so, implicitly conceded the power of the received system to stand in judgement. The integrationist Orthodox and Conservative theologians went even further in affirming that same power and placing themselves under the judgement of rabbinic Judaism. All three claimed to represent the continuation of that Judaism. In the coming century, systems took shape that did not make that claim at all.

Zionism

The twentieth century marked a new occasion for telling the story of Judaism. Because of exterminationist anti-Semitism, Jews were singled out as an ethnic group, not as a religious community, and marked for death: a third of the Jews in the world in 1939 were murdered in the German onslaught that ended in 1945. Indeed, for a time, Judaism as experience, image and story fell silent before the crisis precipitated by the politics of exterminationist anti-Semitism that would define the Jews' situation and present to the Judaic narrative a question beyond all imagining: how is holy Israel to face a world that produces only despair and promises only death?

What made the twentieth century utterly different from all preceding ages in the history of Judaism? It was the full force of the twentieth-century innovation of totalitarianism, whether Soviet-Communist or German-Nazi, which made its imprint also upon the Jews', and also the Judaic, agenda. The nineteenth century had made necessary the question, can the Jews be Israel and something else? The twentieth century asked whether the Jews could *be*; what right did they have to live at all? And the replies, systems that took up as their urgent question the political survival of the Jewish people, came not from the master narrative of Judaism but from the ethnic consciousness of the Jews. Fundamentally ethnic, and not religious, in their character, these systems for the social order of the Jews, each with its definition of Israel, way of life and world-view, are represented by Zionism, a political, not a religious, system to begin with. But this secular political system of ethnic culture and community also recapitulates the same pattern of exile and return that the original system laid out.

Zionism, the Jews' movement of national-political self-emancipation, arose in response to a political crisis: the failure, by the end of the nineteenth century, of the gentile nations' promises of political improvement in the Jews' status and condition. Germany, France, Britain and the USA all witnessed the growth, from 1880 forward, of mass movements of political anti-Semitism, complemented by cultural anti-Semitism within the elite classes of society. Just when masses of Jews faced a violent, politically sponsored anti-Semitism in Eastern Europe, particularly Russia, the Western democracies began to close the doors that had seemed to open with the French Enlightenment and the political emancipation of the late eighteenth and earlier nineteenth centuries. Zionism called to the Jews to emancipate themselves by facing the fact that gentiles in the main hated Jews. The Zionist system of Judaism declared as its world-view this simple proposition: that the Jews form a people, one people, and should transform themselves into a political entity and build a Jewish state where Jews could free themselves of anti-Semitism and build their own destiny.

Zionism came into existence at the end of the nineteenth century, with the founding of the Zionist Organization in 1897, and reached its fulfilment, and the dissolution of its original form, with the founding of the State of Israel on 15 May 1948. It was as successful a secular, political enterprise as any in modern times; as fully realized as the American Revolution that began in 1776.

Zionism began with the definition of its theory of Israel: a people, one people, in a secular sense. Then came the world-view, which composed out of the diverse histories of Jews a single, singular history of the Jewish people (nation), leading from the Land of Israel through exile back to the Land of Israel. This component of the Zionist world-view constituted an exact recapitulation of the scriptural narrative, even though it derived not from a religious but from a nationalist perspective. The way of life of a Zionist activist required participation in meetings, organizing within the local community, attendance at national and international conferences; a focus of their life's energy on the movement. Later, as settlement in the Land itself became possible, Zionism defined the most noble way of living life as migration to the Land and (for the Socialist wing of Zionism) building a collective community or kibbutz. So Zionism presented a powerful, complete and fully articulated system for a Jewish social order in its day, prior to its complete success in the creation of the State of Israel in 1948.

Zionism enunciated a powerful doctrine of the community of Israel as 'a people, one people'. Given the Jews' diversity, people could more easily concede the supernatural reading of Judaic existence than this national construction. Scattered across the Christian West as well as the Muslim world, Jews did not speak a single language, follow a single way of life, or adhere in common to a single code of belief and behaviour. What exactly made them one people and validated their claim and right to a state of their own, constituted the central theme of the Zionist world-view. No facts of perceived society validated that view. In no way, except for a common fate, did the Jews form one people. True, in Judaic systems they commonly did. But rabbinic Judaism and its continuators imputed to Israel, the Jewish people, a supernatural status – a mission, a calling, a purpose. Zionism did not: a people, one people, that is all.

Zionist theory had the task of explaining how the Jews formed one people. This led to the invention of 'Jewish history' that is, a past now read in a secular framework as a single and unitary story. In this way

Zionist theory solved the problem by showing how the Jews all came from one place, travelled together, and were going back to that same place. So as a matter of secular fact they were shown to constitute one people. Zionist theory therefore derived strength from the study of history, much as had Reform Judaism, and in time generated a great renaissance of Judaic studies as the scholarly community of the nascent Jewish state took up the task. The sort of history that emerged took the form of factual and descriptive narrative. But its selection of facts, its recognition of problems requiring explanation, its choice of what mattered and what did not, were all determined by the larger programme of nationalist ideology. So the form was secular and descriptive, but the substance ideological in the extreme.

Yet the principal components of Zionism's world-view fit entirely comfortably within the paradigm of the Torah concerning exile and return. For the Torah held, for its own reasons based on genealogy, that the Jews form one people, and should (when worthy) have the Land back and build a State on it. It is not surprising at all that Zionism found in the writings about the return to the Land ample precedent for its programme, linking today's politics to something very like God's will for Israel, the Jewish people, in ancient times. Zionism would reconstitute the age of the return to Zion from exile in Babylonia after the destruction of the first Temple, so carrying out the prophetic promises. The doctrine of Israel in rabbinic Judaism maintained that the one thing Israel should not do is arrogant deeds. That meant waiting for God to save Israel, assigning to Israel the task of patience, loyalty, humility and obedience, all in preparation for God's intervention. The earliest pronouncements of a Zionist movement, received in the Jewish heartland of Eastern Europe like the tocsin of the coming Messiah, for that same reason impressed many sages of the dual Torah as blasphemy. They believed that God will do it, or it will not be done. Considerable time would elapse before the contemporary rabbinic sages could make their peace with Zionism, and a few of them never did.

But for many Zionism formed into a single whole the experiences of remarkably diverse people living in widely separated places, showing that all those experiences formed a single fact, of a single sort – exclusion, victimization and anti-Semitism – which Zionism could and did confront. Among the Judaic systems of the twentieth century, Zionism attained the status of a mass movement, competing only with Orthodox, Reform and Conservative Judaism, and even within significant sectors of all these movements infusing their religious communities with new energy and meaning.

Telling the Story After the Holocaust

'The Holocaust' refers to the murder by the Germans before and during the Second World War of nearly six million men, women and children, solely because they were born to Jewish families. For many, the story of the Holocaust and that of the creation of the State of Israel form a seamless narrative. The Jews of Europe were unable to escape from the German exterminationists because there was no Jewish state to afford them refuge and hope. The creation of that state in 1948 represented a solace and a guarantee that a Holocaust would never again take place.

In line with that story, Jews, both religious and secular, make pilgrimages from the USA and Western Europe in two stages. First they travel to the death camp sites in Poland, such as the principal one in Auschwitz, where huge masses of Jews, as well as numbers of Poles and other conquered peoples, were murdered in gas chambers, their bodies burned in crematoria. In Auschwitz the pilgrims conduct rites of remembrance and recite the Kaddish prayer. Then they continue their journey to Jerusalem. They visit the western wall of the ancient Israelite Temple there, as well as the Holocaust memorial in Jerusalem, called Yad Vashem, and other sites of renewal and rebuilding. In this way the story of Holocaust and redemption plays itself out in a dramatic, personal experience. In the State of Israel and among overseas Jewish communities as well, a day of remembrance of the Holocaust is observed prior to the celebration of the date in the lunar calendar that marks the declaration of the State of Israel's independence.

In these rites of remembrance, contemporary Judaism encompasses the events of our own time within the ancient narrative of exile and redemption. The story of exile and return begins in the Torah, as we have seen. It begins with the destruction of the Temple and the exile of the people from the Land of Israel in 586 BCE and their return a generation or so later, in c. 530. Each telling of Israel's story followed that same model, whether in the way in which classical Judaism told it or in the Zionist framing of matters. The one spoke of exile 'because of our sins' which was to come to an end with the advent of the Messiah and the return of Israel to the Land of Israel under his aegis. The other spoke of political exile and the creation of a secular state. The pattern is the same, the details different. The enormous events of 1933–1945 on the one hand and 1948 on the other, fitted the pattern and found a place in the Judaic story for the otherwise senseless happenings of mass murder and political upheaval.

The impact of the Holocaust on the faith of believing Jews took two forms. First, for large numbers of survivors and their families, the events of 1933 to 1945 led to a renewal of their religious devotion to the Torah and its way of life that defined the holy community they now embodied. Various expressions of Orthodox Judaism were reinvigorated in the generations after 1945. In the State of Israel and in Britain, Europe, Canada and the USA, the survivors and their descendants renewed the covenant that bound Israel to God, accommodating the catastrophe within the long-told tale of the Torah. Orthodox belief and practice have flourished from 1945, schools of traditional learning have multiplied, standards of religious activity risen, and synagogues embodying the ancient law been strengthened. The greatest challenge to the faith of holy Israel found its response in a reaffirmation of the Torah.

Second, the Holocaust raised in acute form the chronic problem of evil that Judaic monotheism faces. If God is all-powerful, then he cannot be good. If he is good, then he cannot be all-powerful. That, in a rough way, expresses the problem of justifying God that the Holocaust presented to the theologians of contemporary Judaism. In more classical terms, it may be framed in this way: a religion of numerous gods finds many solutions to one problem; a religion of only one God presents one solution to many problems. Life is seldom fair. Rules rarely work. To explain the reason why, polytheisms adduce multiple causes of chaos: a god per anomaly. Diverse gods do various things, so, it stands to reason, outcomes conflict. Monotheism explains many things in a single way. One God rules. Life is meant to be fair, and just rules are supposed to describe what is ordinary, all in the name of that one and only God. So in monotheism a simple logic governs to limit possible ways of making sense of things.

But that logic contains its own dialectics. If one true God has done everything, then, since he is all-powerful and omniscient, all things are credited to, and blamed on, him. In theory he might be good or bad, just or unjust, but in the Torah he has presented himself as just and merciful. The oral Torah thus takes it as its task to reveal the justice of the one and only God of all Creation. God is not only God but also good.

From the Second World War onward, all Judaic theologians contended with the theological crisis presented by the Holocaust. As we have noted, it was not a crisis of faith for those who practised Judaism and told its story as their own account of themselves. But for the systematic religious thinkers, the issues of philosophy and theology worked out by the received religious narrative and system were no longer so readily sorted out. Various readings of the events of 1933–1945 have contended. In the characterization of Zachary Braiterman,

[Richard L.] Rubenstein and [Emil] Fackenheim have argued that the Holocaust represented a unique and radical evil in human history that has ruptured traditional theological categories like theodicy [justifying God]. Against Rubenstein and Fackenheim, other scholars maintain that the Holocaust was only one of many catastrophes in Jewish history; as such, it neither requires nor has generated any unique theological response . . . A uniquely modern catastrophe with uniquely modern implications befell the Jewish people in the twentieth century . . .[10]

The problem of the Holocaust framed in theological language has captured the attention of secular Jewish thinkers more than the faithful of the religion. Braiterman notes, 'Little to no post-Holocaust thought appears among ultra-Orthodox Jews, who have wanted nothing from either modernity or modernism. The Holocaust intensified an already-strained relation between Judaism and modern cultural currents.'[11] It follows that an account of religious and secular thought within the ethnic Jewish community would dwell on the Holocaust as a unique problem, probably beyond solution, in faith and culture. But those who practise Judaism, even the Holocaust theologians of Orthodox and Conservative origin, in the main have built their systems on the foundations of the received Torah and its narrative, not on the nihilism yielded by Auschwitz without Jerusalem, exile without return and renewal.

What this means in concrete terms captures the power of the halakhah to raise the stakes of human life. In the face of mass murder, the Torah camp has reaffirmed the halakhah as the means for capturing the presence of God in the everyday world. To live a halakhic life, as the Jews who practise Orthodox Judaism do, whether integrationist or self-segregationist – and these form the majority of those who practise Judaism in the world – means not only to study the ancient books and their extensions in medieval and modern times (Maimonides's *Mishneh-Torah*, for example, with its recapitulation in his framework of the Mishnah itself); it means to engage in decisions about how to carry on many of the transactions of ordinary life. For new situations constantly arise: halakhic decisions come up in every hour of the day – how to do business, how to speak with people, what to eat or not eat, when to have sexual relations or not, and so on through the entire fabric of life. The classical sources do not provide practical guidance on such matters. The halakhah is renewed continually in this engagement with unprecedented circumstances. And by its nature, life is unprecedented – that is the lesson drawn by living Judaism from the Holocaust. And it explains why the diverse communities of Judaism that call themselves 'Orthodox' form a powerful response to the Holocaust and constitute the most vital component of the world of contemporary Judaism.

The Israel of Sinai, the State of Israel, the Jewish People, and Judaism in the Twenty-first Century

The creation of the Jewish state in 1948 has written a new chapter in the tale told by Judaism, and most Judaic systems, including all Reform, Conservative and integrationist Orthodox Judaisms in the Diaspora as well as most of their Israeli counterparts, encompass the advent of the State of Israel within the story that they tell. This renaissance of the Judaic narrative, linking the Holocaust to the State of Israel as the foretaste of redemption at the end of the world, has enormous appeal to most, though not all, of the camps of Judaism today, including the greater part of the Torah camp.

An important qualification is required. Not all Orthodox Judaisms are Zionist, and some of them are anti-Zionist and reject the Zionist premises on which the State of Israel is founded.[12] Radical anti-Zionism recognized the religious imperative brought to Zionism and rejected it. As we have seen, anti-Zionism was best known in the West as the response of Reform Judaism in Germany and the United States. But that negative reading of the religious meaning implicit in Zionism in fact dominated among the Jews of Eastern Europe, both Hasidic and traditional Orthodox. Messianic, religious Zionism took up the same position – that Zionism is an event in Judaism – but treated Zionism as the medium of realizing the messianic aspiration and, later on, imputed to the State of Israel the status of 'the beginning of our redemption', and similar language. That is the Gush Emunim Orthodox Judaism that animates the Jews who have taken up residence in Samaria and Judea, also known as the West Bank. The third response treats Zionism as neutral, neither messianic nor having religious consequence at all, and is associated with the Agudath Israel movement in the United States and the State of Israel. So any representation of Orthodoxy as uniform in its support of Zionism and the State of Israel misses the complexity and diversity of Orthodox opinion on this as on other fundamental questions posed by the encounter of the Torah with the world of the nineteenth and twentieth centuries.

Naming the Jewish state 'Israel' has complicated matters for, as we have seen, by 'Israel' Judaism means the holy people who assembled at Sinai and accepted the Torah. From the Hebrew Scriptures forward through the oral Torah to the liturgy of the synagogue, the protagonist of God is called 'Israel'.[13] In the religion of Judaism, 'Israel' means the community of the faithful, comprised of those who take for granted that Israel's story, which they find in the Hebrew Scriptures of ancient Israel, refers to them in particular. The story of Judaism is the story of a family that is transformed into the holy, eternal people by their covenant with God at Mount Sinai. That family-people constitutes the supernatural social group, 'Israel' which forms the focus of the story of Judaism. Scripture leaves no ambiguity there.

The communities of the faithful, those who practise Judaism, form 'Israel' because in their conviction they continue, and identify with, the story of the Israel of which the Torah speaks. But in today's world there are two other 'Israels': the State of Israel, and the people of Israel, the Jewish people. The one is a secular, political nation-state, the other an ethnic group, formed by a common identity of fate, not defined by a common faith. It is self-evident that the State of Israel, a place and a nation-state, a political identity, does not present itself as 'eternal Israel', a spiritual entity formed by believers. Possessing an Israeli passport does not mark the holder as a person who practises the Torah's imperatives, though as a matter of fact many Israelis do practise Judaism. Similarly, a person can be ethnically Jewish, and thus part of 'Israel' the Jewish people, but not practise Judaism, therefore not a member of the holy community of Israel brought into being at Sinai by God's giving, and Israel's accepting, the Torah. The interplay of religion and ethnicity creates a variety of complications and yields anomalies.

Judaism is not a culture religion or an ethnic religion or a state religion, closed to all not related by sentimentality or family genealogy or nationality. Just as one may practise Islam without being an Arab, living in the Middle East or speaking Arabic, even though it is the language of the Koran, so one may practise Judaism in Sydney, Moscow, Berlin, Washington or Tel Aviv, without being born Jewish, adopting citizenship of the State of Israel or speaking Hebrew (except in worship and religious study). So Judaism is not a matter of culture but conviction. 'Israel' in Judaism corresponds with 'the Church' ('the mystical body of Christ') in Christianity. A gentile can become an Israelite through a religious rite of conversion, just as a person becomes a Christian in the same kind of process. So Judaism is not a matter of ethnicity. And just as not all Bosnians are Muslim and not all Italians or Brazilians are Catholic, so not all Israelis are Israelites, and not all Jews practise Judaism.

But would that matters were so simple! There is a reason for people to interpret the social traits of Judaism in such a way as to conclude Judaism is an ethnic, national or cultural religion. For the theological definition of 'Israel' that is set forth in the law of Judaism contains another complication. Its 'Israel' encompasses everyone born of a Jewish mother,[14] so in the theology of Judaism 'Israel' is constituted by the ethnic group of common ancestry: the Jews. That legal and theological fact is conveyed by the rule, 'even though an Israelite may sin, he remains an Israelite'. If a Jew adopts a religion other than Judaism, he or she remains not only an ethnic Jew in self-designation but an Israelite from the perspective of the law of Judaism. And that is not a matter of mere theory. Those who practise Judaism (we might call them 'Judaists') without exception through all time have correctly regarded themselves, and have been regarded by others, as Jews by ethnic identification. When someone converts to the religion, that person is automatically deemed part of the Jewish ethnic group. The story central to the Judaic account of humanity presents two points: first, God is one and unique; and second, we are created in God's image, after God's likeness (Genesis 1:26). Together, these facts of the faith preclude any ethnicity based on race or biology.

Not all Jews practise Judaism in any way. Some of them are secular and affirm no religion. Others practise Christianity or Buddhism or other religions of the day. Even if a Jew converts to another religion his or her status within 'Israel' the holy people is indelible, and if and when the same person reverts to Judaism, no rite of conversion is required. Still, these points of clarification should not obscure the simple fact that most Jews who practise any religion practise a form of Judaism.

There is no way to simplify these ambiguities and anomalies. But for the purpose of studying Judaism the religion, there is no such ambiguity or unclarity. In Judaism to be Israel individually and corporately is to know God as God has made himself known in the Torah of Sinai, and to be responsible for acting in accordance with that revealed knowledge of God. In Judaism to form part of the holy community, Israel, is to accept the Torah as God's account of what this community is, who its members are, and what they are to do. In Judaism everyone born of a Jewish mother or converted to Judaism belongs, willy-nilly, to the holy community, Israel. And nearly every one of them will rise from the grave, be judged and be received into the life of the world to come. That is the story not of an ethnic group, let alone a nation-state, but of the community of the Torah, offered by God at Sinai to all humanity.

The Perpetual Power of Judaism's Story

Whither and when? No one but God knows the future, and God gives us the free will to shape our own future. The Talmud teaches that the Messiah will come when Israel wants him to, meaning, when all Israel properly observes a single sabbath. That has not yet happened.

So we do not know how to tell the next chapter in Judaism's story. But the past yields one sure lesson: the story will be told, and there will be people who will make that story their own. The master narrative of the human condition accounts for its own success; the faithful would add, because it is God who to begin with tells the story. But, even in a secular framework, if the history of Judaism yields one certainty, it is this: the story is still there to be told, and it can and will sustain many and diverse retellings.

True, the Jews are not a numerous group, and among them those who practise Judaism are fewer still. So people worry, with reason, about the future of the faith. The power of Judaism's story is captured by a doleful Hasidic tale of foreboding and decline, as told by S. J. Agnon:

When the Baal Shem [the eighteenth-century founder of Hasidism] had a difficult task before him, he would go to a certain place in the woods, light a fire and meditate in prayer, and what he had set out to perform was done.

When a generation later the 'Maggid' [preachier] of Meseritz was faced with the same task, he would go to the same place in the woods and say, 'We can no longer light the fire, but we can still speak the prayers,' and what he wanted done became reality.

Again, a generation later, Rabbi Moshe Leib of Sassov had to perform this task. And he too went into the woods and said, 'We can no longer light a fire, nor do we know the secret meditations belonging to the prayer, but we do know the place in the woods to which it all belongs, and that must be sufficient'; and sufficient it was.

But when another generation had passed and Rabbi Israel of Rishin was called upon to perform the task, he sat down on his golden chair in his castle and said, 'We cannot light the fire, we cannot speak the prayers, we do not know the place, but we can tell the story of how it was done.'

And the story that he told had the same effect as the actions of the other three.[15]

But this does not capture the tale of Judaism. For the enduring religion, Judaism, merely remembering the telling of the story does not write the last chapter. That has not been, and today is not, the fate of the tale. Rather, the very same eternal Israel of which the story speaks, the Israel formed at Sinai and realized in the Jewish people throughout all time, still endures, still tells the story, still knows the place, always lights the fire, every day says the prayers, and what Israel sets out to perform comes about, when God wills. This year and next and for years beyond, the synagogues will be crowded on the Day of Atonement, families will assemble on the eve of Passover, on sabbath days and weekdays the sacred scrolls will be removed from their holy place and unfurled and declaimed for holy Israel, which will sing with joy: 'This is the Torah that Moses set before the Children of Israel at the Lord's instruction.'

Notes

Prologue

1 Andrew M. Greeley, 'Why do Catholics stay in the Church? Because of the Stories', *New York Times*, reprinted in Greeley, *White Smoke* (New York, 1996), pp. 448–58. Father Greeley proceeds: 'Catholics like their heritage because it has great stories . . . the heritage for most people most of the time was almost entirely story, ritual, ceremony, and eventually art . . . Catholicism has great stories because at the center of its heritage is "sacramentalism", the conviction that God discloses himself in the objects and events and persons of ordinary life.'

1 What Is 'Israel'?

1 These definitions have no bearing on the contemporary secular debate concerning who is a Jew. In the state of Israel, that question requires an answer, for the citizenship law of the state of Israel extends Israeli citizenship automatically to any Jew who applies. It follows that knowing who a Jew is has practical consequences. For deciding who should live and who should die, the National Socialists in Germany defined a Jew as anyone who had one Jewish grandparent. So each context produces its own definition.

2 The lunar year is 354 days and the solar year is 365 days. The eleven-day difference is accounted for by adding a lunar month every few years, so that the solar seasons and the lunar celebrations are kept synchronized. The month of Adar, corresponding to March, is doubled.

3 Known in the Bible as 'tabernacles', but 'huts' captures the humble and transient character of the structures much more accurately. 'Tabernacles' invokes constructions altogether too grand for the context.

4 Shavuot is not the sole point at which the Israelite accepts God's kingdom. In

their prayers, morning and night, when Israelites recite the declaration of their faith in one God ('Hear O Israel, the Lord our God, the Lord is one'), they accept the dominion of God's kingdom. And in the synagogue service when the scroll containing the Torah is removed from the ark and displayed to the congregation of Israel, the congregation proclaims, 'This is the Torah that Moses set before the children of Israel at the instruction of God.'

5 The Messiah who is prophesied in Judaism to appear at the end of the world to raise the dead and announce the last judgement is not the same as Jesus Christ.

6 I use this term and Before Common Era (abbreviated CE and BCE) throughout in preference to the specifically Christian AD and BC.

7 A small case containing verses from scripture, attached to the doorpost.

8 *Ruth Rabbah* XX:i.3−4.

9 *Avodah Zarah* I:i.1.2/2A−B, in the Talmud of Babylonia.

10 *Ruth Rabbah* III:i.2−3.

11 Leviticus 23:33, 42−43.

12 Deuteronomy 1:26, 34−5.

13 Contemporary Reform and Reconstructionist Judaisms add, 'or of a Jewish father', thus matrilineal or patrilineal descent serves equally to establish the status of a Jew. Orthodox and Conservative Judaism adheres to the received law.

2 Who Is 'Israel'?

1 The same Hebrew word, *Yisrael*, refers in the liturgy and in the canonical writings both to the entire community of Judaism, Israel, and to the individual male members of that community, also referred to in the singular as *Yisrael*. Female members are commonly called *bat Yisrael*, a daughter of an Israelite.

2 *Sanhedrin* 14:5, in the Mishnah.

3 Joshua 7:19.

4 *Sanhedrin* 6:4, in the Mishnah.

5 Leviticus 16:29−30, 34.

6 All the quotations in this section are from *Mahzor for Rosh Hashanah and Yom Kippur: A Prayer Book for the Days of Awe*, ed. Jules Harlow (Rabbinical Assembly, New York, 1972).

7 Genesis 22:1−13.

8 *Pesiqta deRab Kahana* XXIII:III.

9 The root for all three words is 'SB' ' − *shin bet ayin*.

10 'in the name of' is used throughout the rabbinical texts to mean 'quoting'.

11 *Pesiqta deRab Kahana* XXIII:IX.

12 *Pesiqta deRab Kahana* XXIII:X.

13 This view of Israel and not-Israel was complicated by the advent of Christianity and Islam, both of which affirm monotheism and carry forward the heritage of holy Israel. Medieval and modern theologians of Judaism take account of that fact and recast matters, recognizing that all of humanity cannot be divided so simply between idolaters on one side and those that worship God on the other.

14 *Pesiqta deRab Kahana* XXIII:I.

15 Ibid.

16 *Nedarim* 3:1 I.14 ff/22A–B, in the Talmud of Babylonia.

17 *Genesis Rabbah* XIX:IX.1–2.

18 *Sifra* CXCV:I.2–3.

19 *Taanit* 1:1 II:5, in the Talmud of the Land of Israel.

20 *The Talmud of the Land of Israel* (University of Chicago Press, 1987), pp. 5–6.

21 Ibid.; nowadays the eradication of debt is circumvented by a legal fiction, the prosbol, which transfers the debt's ownership to the court, so that it is not remitted.

22 Leviticus 25:8–10.

23 The portable sanctuary that the Israelites carried with them in the wilderness, and which was the model for the Temple.

3 The Historical View
of the Formation of Judaism

1 Contemporary communities of Judaism debate the factual and historical authenticity of the Scriptural narratives. The Torah-camp (the various Orthodox Judaic systems, some culturally integrationist, some self-segregationist) affirms the literal historical facticity of Scripture. Reform, Conservative, Reconstructionist and other Judaisms do not. I have tried to frame matters in such a way that most of the faithful can concur, emphasizing the positive side.

2 *The Fathers According to Rabbi Nathan* IV:V.2.

4 Chapters of the Tale of Judaism
in the Life Cycle of the Israelite

1 Lifsa Schachter, 'Reflections on the Brit Mila Ceremony' in *Conservative Judaism* 38 (1986), pp. 38–41.

2 1 Kings 19:10–14; I have modernized the language of the Revised Standard Version here.

3 *Pirke deRabbi Eliezer*, Gerald Friedlander (London, 1916), pp. 212–14.

4 Genesis 17:1–5, 9–10.

5 'Reflections on the Brit Mila ceremony'.

6 *Genesis Rabbah* XXXIX:XIV.

7 *Rabbi's Manual*, ed. Jules Harlow (Rabbinical Assembly, New York, 1965), p. 67.

8 *Yebamot* 4:12 I.47/47A–B, in the Talmud of Babylonia.

9 Ezekiel 36:25–8; my translation.

10 *Rabbi's Manual*, p. 78.

11 Rashi's commentary is included in standard Judaic editions of the Pentateuch.

12 *Rabbi's Manual*.

13 All translations of the marriage rite derive from the *Rabbi's Manual*.

14 Jeremiah 33:10–11.

15 *Rabbi's Manual*.

16 *Weekday Prayer Book*, ed. Gerson Hadas with Jules Harlow Rabbinical Assembly, New York, 1966), pp. 54–5.

5 God in the Here and Now

1 Psalm 137:1, 5–6.

2 Psalm 126:1–2, 4–5.

3 *Weekday Prayer Book*, ed. Gerson Haas with Jules Harlow (Rabbinical Assembly, New York, 1966).

4 The fringes are today attached to the prayer shawl worn at morning services by Conservative and some Reform Jews, and perpetually worn on a separate undergarment for that purpose by male Orthodox Jews; they remind the Jew of all the commandments of the Lord.

5 *Weekday Prayer Book*, *passim*.

6 Ibid.

7 Both quotations are from *Pirke Avot* 3:6.

8 Ibid.

9 *Genesis Rabbah* XLII:IV.

10 Ibid., LXIII:X.

11 Ibid., LXXV:IV.

12 *Baba Mesia* 4:11 I.15/59A–B, in the Talmud of Babylonia. The quotation from Exodus differs from the biblical version.

6 The Story of the Good Life:
Judaism's Ethical Imperatives

1 *Sifra* CC:III.7.
2 *Shabbat* 30B–31A/2:5 I. 12, in the Talmud of Babylonia.
3 *Avot* 2:8–9, in the Mishnah.
4 *Taanit* 1:4 I, in the Talmud of the Land of Israel.
5 Ibid.
6 Ibid.
7 Ibid.
8 *Kiddushin* 1:10 I.10/40A, in the Talmud of Babylonia.
9 *Genesis Rabbah* XXXI:VI.1.
10 *Hagigah* 1:7 I:3, in the Talmud of the Land of Israel.
11 *Sanhedrin* 106b/11.1–2 XII.5, in the Talmud of Babylonia.
12 *Horayot* 3:1–2 I.11/10B, in the Talmud of Babylonia.
13 *Sifré to Deuteronomy* CCCXVIII:I.1ff.
14 *Pesiqta deRab Kahana* V:III.3ff.
15 *Leviticus Rabbah* XVIII:III.2ff.
16 *Rosh ha-Shanah* 4:4 I.6A–E/31 A–B.
17 *Sifré to Numbers* CLXI:III.2.
18 *Pesiqta deRab Kahana* I:I.3, 6.

7 The Theology of Judaism:
Revealing the Rationality of Being

1 *Sotah* 1:7, in the Mishnah.
2 *Makkot* 3:16, in the Mishnah.
3 *Arakhin* 3:5 II.3/15A–B, in the Talmud of Babylonia.
4 *Sifré to Numbers* CXI:I.1–2.
5 *Pirke Avot* 3:15.
6 *Genesis Rabbah* LXXVII:I.1.
7 *Sanhedrin* 10:1, in the Mishnah.
8 *Lamentations Rabbati* CXL:I.1–2.
9 For a succinct introduction to kabbalah see Ithamar Gruenwald, 'Major Issues in the Study and Understanding of Jewish Mysticism', in J. Neusner, ed., *Judaism in Late Antiquity*, vol. 2, *Historical Syntheses* (E. J. Brill, Leiden, 1995), pp. 1–52. See also Gershom G. Scholem, *Major Trends in Jewish Mysticism*, (Schocken Books,

New York, 1941), and *On the Kabbalah and its Symbolism* (New American Library, New York, 1974); Fischel Lachower and Isaiah Tishby, eds, *The Wisdom of the Zohar*, vols. 1–2 (The Littman Library of Jewish Civilization, London and Washington, 1989). I consulted Professors Ithamar Gruenwald, Tel Aviv University, and Elliot R. Wolfson, New York University, in writing this section, and I owe them thanks for generously sharing their learning and insight with me.

10 *Zohar: The Book of Enlightenment*, Daniel Chanan Matt (Paulist Press, New York and Toronto, 1983), p. xv. I found this the best introduction to the *Zohar* in the English language.

11 *Zohar, The Book of Splendor: Basic Readings from the Kabbalah*, ed. Gershom G. Scholem (Schocken Books, New York, 1963), pp. 29–30.

12 *Zohar: The Book of Enlightenment*, p. 24.

13 Abraham J. Heschel, 'The Mystical Elements of Judaism', in *The Jews: Their History, Culture, and Religion*, ed. Louis Finkelstein (Harper & Row, New York, 1971); quotations are from the *Zohar*.

14 Ibid., p. 284.

8   The Law of Judaism

1 Leviticus 19:2–4.

2 *Sifra* CC:III.

3 *Makkot* 23b–24a, in the Talmud of Babylonia.

4 *Baba Qamma* 83b/8:1 I.1A–B, in the Talmud of Babylonia.

5 Deuteronomy 22:4–12.

6 *Eruvin* 54b/5:1 I.43, in the Talmud of Babylonia.

7 *Pirke Avot* 1:1.

8 *Hagigah* 1:8, in the Mishnah.

9 Leviticus 16:1–5, 29–34.

10 *Yoma* 8:1, in the Mishnah.

11 *Kippurim* 4:1, in the Tosefta.

12 Ibid., 4:5.

13 *Yoma* 8:6, in the Mishnah.

14 *Kippurim* 4:6–8, in the Tosefta.

15 *Yoma* 8:7, in the Mishnah.

16 *Kippurim* 4:9, in the Tosefta.

17 Ibid., 4:10–11.

18 Ibid., 4:13.

19 Ibid., 4:15.

9 The Success of Judaism's Story

1 Julius Guttmann, *Philosophies of Judaism: The History of Jewish Philosophy from Biblical Times to Franz Rosenzweig*, trans. David Silverman (Holt, Rinehart & Winston, New York, 1964), p. 158.

2 Quoted by Isaak Heinemann in 'Judah Halevi, Kuzari', in *Three Jewish Philosophers*, ed. Isaak Heinemann, Alexander Altmann and Hans Lewy (Jewish Publication Society, Philadelphia, 1960), p. 33.

3 Ibid., p. 72.

4 Ibid., p. 75.

5 Professor Alan Nadler of Drew University and Dr Benjamin Brown of Hebrew University were kind enough to read this section and correct it for me. I appreciate their help.

6 Quoted by Louis Jacobs in 'Basic Ideas of Hasidism', *Encyclopaedia Judaica*, vol. 7 (Keter, Jerusalem, 1971), col. 1,404.

7 Ibid., col. 1,405.

8 Gershom Scholem, 'Shabbetai Zevi' in *Encyclopaedia Judaica*, vol. 14, col. 1,222.

9 Ibid., col. 1,223.

10 Ibid.

10 Women in the Aggadah and the Halakhah

1 *Song of Songs Rabbah*, Song 7:10.

2 Ibid., 6:2.

3 Ibid., 8:6.

4 Ibid., 4:12.

5 Ibid., 4:5.

6 Ibid., 1:15.

7 Ibid., 5:3.

8 Ibid., 5:10.

9 Jews practised polygamy until the tenth century CE in Christian countries, and until 1948 in Muslim countries.

10 *Sotah* 5:1 I:1D/28A, in the Talmud of Babylonia.

11 *Ketubot* 5:5, in the Mishnah.

12 Ibid., 7:6.

13 Ibid., 5:9.

14 *Eruvin* 10:10:8 II.9/100B, in the Talmud of Babylonia.

15 *Berakhot* 9:1 XVII.6, 8/61B, in the Talmud of Babylonia.

16 *Ketubot* 7:1, in the Mishnah.

17 Ibid., 7:2.

18 Ibid., 7:3.

19 Ibid., 7:4.

20 Ibid., 7:5.

21 *Kiddushin* 1:7, in the Mishnah.

22 Franz Kobler, *A Treasury of Jewish Letters*, vol. 2 (Jewish Publication Society of America, Philadelphia, 1954), pp. 565–7.

11   Contemporary Communities
of Judaism

1 Benzion Dinur, 'Emancipation' in *Encyclopaedia Judaica* vol. 6 (Keter, Jerusalem, 1971), cols. 696–718.

2 Ibid., col. 699.

3 The Pittsburgh Platform, quoted in Jakob J. Petuchowski, 'Reform Judaism', *Encyclopaedia Judaica*, vol. 14, col. 26.

4 Jakob J. Petuchowski, 'Reform Judaism' in *Encyclopaedia Judaica* vol. 14, cols. 23–8.

5 Nathaniel Katzburg and Walter S. Wurzburger, 'Orthodoxy' in *Encyclopaedia Judaica* vol. 12, cols. 1,486–93.

6 Ibid., col. 1,488.

7 Arthur Hertzberg, 'Conservative Judaism,' *Encyclopaedia Judaica* vol. 5, cols. 901–6.

8 Ibid., col. 902.

9 Daniel J. Elazar and Rela Mintz Geffen, *The Conservative Movement in Judaism: Dilemmas and Opportunities* (State University of New York Press, Albany, 2000) p. 93.

10 Zachary Braiterman, *God After Auschwitz: Tradition and Change in Post-Holocaust Jewish Thought* (Princeton, 1998: Princeton University Press), p. 5.

11 Ibid., p. 6.

12 See Aviezer Ravitzky, *Messianism, Zionism and Jewish Religious Radicalism*, translated by Michael Swirsky and Jonathan Chipman (The University of Chicago Press, 1996).

13 When, in 1948, the Jewish state was founded in what Judaism knows as 'the

Land of Israel', the founders introduced a new meaning for the word 'Israel', no longer a people, wherever located – a religious community or an ethnic group – but a nation-state in a particular place. When Scripture speaks of 'Israel' it means not a location but a vocation, and when in the prayerbook of Judaism people pray for 'Israel', they have in mind the people that follow the Torah, wherever they live.

14 In contemporary Reform, Reconstructionist and other Judaisms that deem the law of Judaism to possess a voice but not a veto, the child of a Jewish father and a non-Jewish mother is also regarded as 'Israel'. Orthodox and Conservative Judaisms abide by the law of Judaism that affirms matrilineal, but not patrilineal, descent. Both accept converts, as do all the contemporary communities of Judaism.

15 Quoted by Gershom G. Scholem in *Major Trends in Jewish Mysticism* (Schocken Books, New York, 1941), pp. 349–50.

Glossary

586 BCE: date of the destruction of the Temple in Jerusalem by the Babylonians under Nebuchadnezzar.

70 CE: date of the destruction of the Temple in Jerusalem by the Romans under Vespasian and Titus.

Abraham: the first human being in the sequence of twenty generations (ten from Adam to Noah, and ten from Noah to Abraham) who exhibited faith in God and loyalty to his commandments. He and his wife, Sarah, produced Isaac, the father of Jacob, also called Israel. With his wives Leah and Rachel, Jacob produced the twelve tribes that formed 'the children of Israel'. Jacob and his family went down to Egypt in a time of famine in the Promised Land and were enslaved there. Called by God, Moses prevailed upon the Pharaoh of Egypt, to let the people go, and led them to Sinai. There they received the Torah, or Instruction, of God and covenanted with God to keep the laws of the Torah and to build a kingdom of priests and a holy people. All who accept the Torah become children of Abraham and Sarah and part of the people of Israel. This account of a family that became a covenanted holy people forms the foundation story of Judaism.

aggadah ('telling', 'narration'): rabbinic teaching which is not about actual laws (halakhah). Aggadah includes lore, theology, fable, scriptural exegesis and ethics. The exposition of theological and ethical topics.

Akiva or Aqiba: sage who lived in the early second century CE, principal teacher of the sages who created the Mishnah.

Aleinu ('It is our duty'): this is the first word of the concluding prayer of the liturgy – 'It is our duty to praise the Lord of all, to accord greatness to the Creator of Creation . . .'

Arakhin: tractate in the Talmud of Babylonia dealing with the valuation of vows described in Leviticus 27.

Avodah Zarah: tractate in the Talmud of Babylonia dealing with idolatry.

Baba Mesia: tractate in the Talmud of Babylonia expounding civil law.

Babylonia: ancient Middle Eastern kingdom, later a province in the Iranian empire, corresponding to the area around Baghdad in central Iraq today. Location of those exiled from Judaea in 586 BCE and of a community of Judaism from then until the creation of the State of Israel and the exodus of the Iraqi Jewish community in 1948–9.

BCE: before the common era; used in place of BC.

Berakhot: tractate in the Talmud of Babylonia dealing with blessings and the recitation of daily prayers.

CE: common era; used instead of AD.

Conservative Judaism: religious movement, reacting against the early Reform movement, which attempts to adapt Jewish law to modern life on the basis of principles of change inherent in traditional laws.

Constantine: Roman emperor who in 312 CE issued an edict permitting the free practice of Christianity, and who before he died converted to Christianity; his successors established Christianity as the religion of the Roman Empire.

cult: I use this word in the text to mean simply a system of religious worship, a mode of serving God.

David: king of ancient Israel, *c*. 900 BCE, who unified the Israelites and extended the borders of the Israelite domain. His son, Solomon, built the first Temple in Jerusalem.

Day of Atonement (Yom Kippur): the day that wipes away sins committed in the past year and brings about a reconciliation with God and a sinless beginning to the new year. It is a day of forgiveness and penitence for sin, observed through fasting, prayer, confession of sin and supplication for forgiveness.

Deuteronomy: the fifth of the Five Books of Moses (which form the Pentateuch, the original Torah), Deuteronomy recapitulates the story of Moses' leadership of Israel from Egypt to the borders of the Promised Land and also the laws revealed to him at Sinai.

Diaspora: the dispersion or exile of Jews from the Land of Israel; Jews who live elsewhere than Israel.

dietary laws: taboos pertaining to animal food; pious Jews may eat only fish that have fins and scales, or animals that part the hoof and chew the cud (sheep and cattle, for example, but not camels, pigs, shellfish, worms, snails or flesh torn from a living animal). Animals must be ritually slaughtered by a humane method of slaughter accompanied by a blessing. Any mixture of meat and milk is forbidden; after eating meat, one may not eat dairy products for a period of time (one to six hours, depending on custom).

Edom: A neighbour and enemy of ancient Israel, this kingdom lay across the River Jordan, south of the Dead Sea.

Eighteen Benedictions, *see* The Prayer.

Eliezer [ben Hyracanus]: One of the principal sages involved in the foundation of the Mishnah legal code, who lived at the end of the first century CE. He was a disciple of Yohanan ben Zakkai and, along with Joshua ben Hananiah, he smuggled Yohanan out of Jerusalem, which was besieged by the Romans, and brought him to the Roman Emperor Vespasian, who gave him permission to join other rabbinic sages at Jabneh, south-west of Jerusalem.

Elijah: prophet in ancient Israel in the time of Ahab who is present at every Passover banquet and every rite of circumcision in an Israelite family.

Eruvin: tractate in the Talmud of Babylonia dealing with providing a sabbath boundary to establish a single domain out of multiple private domains in order to keep the sabbath.

Esther: heroine who saved the Israelites in the fifth-century BCE Persian Empire from destruction by the vizier, Haman, an event celebrated at the Festival of Purim.

Exodus: the second of the Five Books of Moses, tells the story of the exodus of the Israelites from Egyptian slavery and their receiving the Torah at Sinai; also describes the tabernacle (portable sanctuary) and the divine service in the wilderness of Sinai.

Fathers According to Rabbi Nathan: rabbinic amplification of *Pirkei Avot*.

Five Books of Moses: Genesis, Exodus, Leviticus, Numbers, Deuteronomy; all attributed to the prophet, Moses; also known as the Pentateuch; *see* Torah.

Genesis: first of the Five books of Moses, tells the story of Creation, Abraham's response to God's call and the founding of the family of Abraham and Sarah as God's family, the continuation of the family through Isaac and Rebecca, Jacob and Rachel and Leah, and their descent to the Land of Egypt in a time of famine in the Promised Land.

Genesis Rabbah: rabbinic commentary to the Book of Genesis, *c.* 450 CE. Reads the events of contemporary Israelite life in the light of the narratives of Genesis.

Hagigah: Talmud of the Land of Israel commentary on the Mishnah tractate on festival offerings.

halakhah ('the way things are done'): the prescriptive, legal tradition. Halakhah defines the norms of conduct, whereas aggadah refers to norms of conviction.

Hillel: first-century Pharisaic master, founder of a House, or school, that bears his name. Principal saying: 'What is hateful to you, don't do to your fellow. That is the entire Torah, all the rest is commentary. Now go, study.' (*Shabbat* 30b, in the Talmud of Babylonia)

Historical School: school of thought in German traditional Judaism that laid heavy emphasis on historical research in determining what may or may not be subject to revision in the law of Judaism.

Horayot: the subject of erroneous instruction by the authorities of Judaism –

for example, the king, high priest and sage – and how the community atones for error done in good faith but under false instruction; there are three tractates on this subject, in the Mishnah, Tosefta and Talmud.

Isaiah: (1) prophet in the time of the first Temple, *c.* 700 BCE, who taught that Israel should trust in God and not surrender to the Assyrian invaders (Isaiah 1–39); (2) prophet in the time of the second Temple, *c.* 500 BCE, who prophesied that Israel's sin was atoned for by the destruction of the Temple in 586, and that God had reconciled with Israel.

Ishmael [ben Elisha]: rabbinic sage of *c.* 100 CE.

Israel: in Judaism: the holy people, who are children of Abraham and Sarah through their grandson Jacob, who know God and who at Sinai accepted God's rule set forth in the Torah that God revealed to Moses; covers all who accept God's dominion in the Torah as the sole and complete revelation of God's will and affirm belief in one God alone.

Israel, Land of: The ancient homeland of the Jews, corresponding to the area covered by Palestine and the State of Israel today. God originally promised Abraham this Land, and his descendants who were exiled into slavery in Egypt later wandered in search of the homeland God had promised them. The Israelites finally reconquered the Land of Israel only to later be conquered in their turn (though those who remained in that area, known to history as Palestine or Judaea, were still thought of by Jews as living in the Land). The Land of Israel is seen by many rabbinic teachers as analogous to the Garden of Eden. (Not to be confused with the northern kingdom of the Jews *c.* 930–721 BCE – their southern kingdom being Judah – or the modern State of Israel.)

Israelite: child of a Jewish mother, or a convert to Judaism.

Jerusalem: the place God chose for the building of the Temple that Israel was to construct for divine service and offering, as spelled out in the Book of Deuteronomy.

Joshua: succeeded Moses as leader of the Israelites, commanding their entry, conquest and inheritance of the Promised Land.

Joshua [ben Hananiah], Rabbi: principal disciple of the first-century rabbinic sage Yohanan ben Zakkai and primary teacher of the next generation of rabbinic sages.

Judah: a son of Jacob and progenitor of a tribe of ancient Israel. The name also refers to the territory in the mountains around Jerusalem occupied by the tribe of Judah.

Judah, Rabbi: a second-century authority on the Mishnah.

Judah the Patriarch (also known as Judah ha-Nasi): head of the Jewish community in the Land of Israel who compiled the Mishnah code of law, *c.* 200 CE.

kabbalah or qabbalah ('tradition'): the mystical Jewish tradition.

kaddish or *qaddish*: a prayer of praise said at the end of the principal sections of the Jewish service, consisting of praise of God with the congregational response, 'May his great name be praised eternally'. It includes the hope for a speedy advent of the Messiah. Also recited by mourners.

ketubah: marriage contract specifying obligations of husband to wife.

Ketubbot: tractate in the Mishnah devoted to marriage contracts.

Kiddushin or *Qiddushin*: on the subject of betrothals and other transfers of ownership; there are two tractates on this subject, in the Talmud of Babylonia and the Mishnah.

Kippurim [Yoma]: tractate in the Tosefta that supplements the Mishnah's presentation of the law on the Day of Atonement (Leviticus 16).

kosher ('fit', 'proper'): applies to anything suitable for use according to Jewish law. Often applied to food; *see* dietary laws.

Lamentations: scriptural book of dirges attributed to Jeremiah.

Leviticus: third Book of Moses, devoted to the laws of sacrifice, the rules of ritual cleanness and uncleanness, and the preservation of the priestly caste and their rations in a state of ritual cleanness.

Leviticus Rabbah: Rabbinic commentary on the Book of Leviticus, *c.* 450 CE.

Makkot: tractate in the Mishnah on corporal punishment.

Messiah: the anointed descendant of King David prophesied in Scripture to come at the end of time to raise the dead and announce the Last Judgement. In Judaism this Messiah is not the same as Jesus Christ.

mezuzah: a tightly rolled parchment containing verses of Scripture (Deuteronomy 6:4–9 and 11:13–21), put in a case and fixed to the right-hand doorpost of every room in a Jewish home.

midrash: exegesis of Scripture; also applied to collection of such exegeses. Examples include the *Haggadah of Passover*, *The Fathers According to Rabbi Nathan* and *Pirke de Rabbi Eliezer*.

Mishnah: code of law compiled by Judah the Patriarch in the Land of Israel *c.* 200 CE. It is a collection of oral laws divided into six parts: agriculture; festivals and the sabbath; family and personal status; torts, damages, and civil law; holy things; and rules of ritual cleanness. Each part is divided into short treatises or tractates, each on a particular topic; the whole Mishnah therefore consists of sixty-two such legal (halakhic) tractates. Later commentaters on the Mishnah would take one particular tractate and subject it to close reading and amplification.

Mosaic: what pertains to Moses or to the writings attributed to him, for example, Mosaic law.

Nedarim: tractate in the Talmud of Babylonia dealing with vows.

New Year: first day of Tishri (which falls in September). Day of God's remembrance of humanity's conduct in the prior year and his determination of what is to happen as a consequence in the coming year.

Nisan: first lunar month after the spring equinox.

nissuin: consummation of a marriage.

Numbers: fourth Book of Moses; tells the story of Israel's wandering in the wilderness between Egypt and the Land of Israel.

Old Testament: *see* Scripture.

Orthodox Judaism: The belief that the Torah of Sinai, oral and written, is the literal, unaltered word of God and defines God's will for humanity, the entirety representing the exhaustive and complete account of God's plan and requirement for the human race. Orthodoxy from beginning to end involves the practice of the Torah, its ritual and its moral elements equally. It is divided into two main camps: integrationists, who believe that one can practise the Torah and also participate in the cultural and social life of the contemporary secular world, and self-segregationists, who teach that holy Israel keeps the Torah in isolation from modern ways of behaving and believing.

Palestine: secular name of the Land of Israel.

Passover (Hebrew, *Pesah*): festival on the fifteenth day of the lunar month of Nisan, the first full moon after the spring equinox (21 March), celebrating the exodus of the Israelites from Egyptian bondage. Traditionally includes a family ritual banquet or Seder.

Pentateuch: the Five Books of Moses — Genesis, Exodus, Leviticus, Numbers, Deuteronomy — which made up the original Torah.

Pentecost: *see* Shavuot.

Pesikta deRav Kahana: systematic interpretations of Scripture dating from *c.* 500 CE that are singled out for declamation in the synagogue on special sabbaths and festivals.

Pharisee (from Hebrew, *perush* — 'separatist' or 'interpreter'): sect in ancient Judaism teaching, beside the conventional written Torah, an oral Torah revealed at Sinai and preserved through a succession of prophets and sages that culminated in the Pharisaic sect which emerged in *c.* 160 BCE. They espoused prophetic ideals and applied them to everyday life through legislation. Their distinctive beliefs, according to the first-century Jewish historian Josephus, were: (1) the immortality of the soul; (2) the existence of angels; (3) that God controls all things; (4) free will; (5) the resurrection of the dead; (6) the authority of their oral Torah.

phylactery: small box containing scriptural texts worn by men at morning prayer.

Pirkei Avot (or *Abot*; 'The Chapters of the Fathers'; also known simply as *Avot*): a collection of wise sayings of the sages of the Mishnah on Torah-study and related subjects, attached to the Mishnah but topically and formally separate from it. Regularly studied in synagogue on the sabbath, it is the best known of all the Talmudic works.

Pirke deRabbi Eliezer: medieval compilation of stories attributed to or told about Eliezer.

Prayer, The (also known as Amidah – 'standing' – and Eighteen Benedictions, since each prayer ends with a blessing): The main section of obligatory prayers of petition, recited morning, afternoon and evening: (1) God of the fathers; (2) praise of God's power; (3) holiness; (4) prayer for knowledge; (5) prayer for repentance; (6) prayer for forgiveness; (7) prayer for redemption; (8) prayer for healing the sick; (9) blessing of agricultural produce; (10) prayer for ingathering of dispersed Israel; (11) prayer for righteous judgement; (12) prayer for punishment of the wicked and heretics; (13) prayer for reward of the pious; (14) prayer for rebuilding Jerusalem; (15) prayer for restoration of the House of David; (16) prayer for acceptance of prayers; (17) prayer of thanks; (18) prayer for restoration of Temple service; (19) prayer for peace.

rabbi ('my lord'): a master of the Torah; title for a teacher of the oral Torah.

rabbinic: pertaining to the rabbis and teachers of the oral Torah, as written down in the classical sources of the Mishnah, Tosefta, two Talmuds and the midrash compilations.

Rashi: a name for Rabbi Solomon ben Isaac (1040–1105), composed of Rabbi SHlomo Yitzhak; hence *Rashi*. He was the writer of the most widely consulted of all commentaries on the Torah and Talmud.

Rav or Rab: a third-century CE master of the Torah.

Rebbe: title given to a Hasidic master; an intermediary between man and God, a wonder-worker.

redemption: the salvation of humanity from the condition of sinfulness; the salvation of holy Israel from the condition of exile; and the restoration of humanity to Eden and of Israel to the Land of Israel.

Reform Judaism: religious movement advocating changing tradition to conform to the conditions of modern life. Holds halakhah to be a human creation, subject to the judgement of man; sees Judaism as the historical religious experience of Jewish people.

revelation: the giving of the Torah by God to Moses at Sinai.

Rosh ha-Shanah, *see* New Year.

Ruth: scriptural heroine, portrayed by the Book of Ruth as the first convert to Judaism and the ancestress of King David, and thus of the prophesied Messiah.

sabbath: the seventh day, commemorating God's completion of the creation of the world at sundown on the sixth day and also the exodus of Israel from Egypt.

Observed by cessation from acts of servile labour and by repose, feasting, Torah-study and prayer.

Sanhedrin: tractate in the Mishnah dealing with the government of holy Israel, the conduct of trials, the penalties for various sins and crimes, and with the means of inflicting the death penalty to secure atonement for sins or crimes committed in one's lifetime, making certain that at the Last Judgement and the Resurrection nearly all Israelites will be judged worthy of eternal life.

Scripture: the holy books of ancient Israel, known as the Torah. Corresponds to the Christian Old Testament.

Seder ('order'): order of service, in particular, the Passover ceremony that takes place at home, at which the *Haggadah of Passover* is recited, retelling the story of the exodus from Egypt.

Shavuot ('weeks'): festival that takes place fifty days after Passover, celebrating the revelation of the Torah at Sinai and the acceptance of God's rule through the Torah by Israel; also known as Pentecost.

Shema: the proclamation of the unity of God: Deuteronomy 6:4–9, 11:13–21, Numbers 15:37–41.

shofar: ram's horn, sounded during high holy day period, from a month before New Year until the end of the Day of Atonement.

Sifra: rabbinic commentary on the Book of Leviticus, *c.* 300 CE, emphasizing the scriptural foundations of the laws of the oral Torah.

Sifrei to Deuteronomy: rabbinic commentary on the Book of Deuteronomy, *c.* 300 CE.

Sifrei to Numbers: Rabbinic commentary on the Book of Numbers, *c.* 300 CE.

Solomon: son of King David and king of ancient Israel; built the first Temple.

Song of Songs, also known as the Song of Solomon: a love poem that expresses the relationship between God and Israel.

Song of Songs Rabbah: rabbinic interpretation (*c.* 500 CE) of the Song of Songs, spelling out the religious attitudes and actions to be performed by Israel in order to realize the images of love in the scriptural poem.

Sotah: tractate in the Talmud of Babylonia dealing with a wife accused of adultery.

sukkah: hut, tabernacle.

Sukkot, Sukkoth or Succoth ('huts'): autumn harvest festival, ending a season of holy days. Begins on the first full moon after the autumn equinox (21 September).

synagogue: Greek translation of the Hebrew *bet keneset* (house of assembly). Place of Jewish prayer, study and assembly.

Taanit: tractate in the Talmud of the Land of Israel expounding the Mishnah's laws on fast days; how they are determined and observed, and the liturgy on such days.

tabernacle: portable sanctuary constructed by the Israelites in the wilderness, and the precursor to the Temple in Jerusalem. *See also sukkah*; Feast of Tabernacles, *see* Sukkot.

Talmud: the Mishnah plus a systematic exposition of its codes of law and conduct. These commentaries on the Mishnah and its supplement (the Tosefta) were produced in rabbinical academies from *c.* 200 to 600 CE. Two Talmuds were produced – the Talmud of the Land of Israel (including commentaries on the tractates in the first four parts of the Mishnah, completed *c.* 400 CE) and the Talmud of Babylonia (including commentaries on the tractates in parts two to five of the Mishnah, completed *c.* 600 CE). From 500 CE onward the Babylonian Talmud is the primary source for Judaic law and theology.

tanna/tannaite: an authority on the Mishnah or halakhah in the first two centuries CE; also one who studies and teaches.

Temple, the: place of sacrifice to God in Jerusalem ordained in the Books of Exodus, Leviticus and Numbers. (Also used by American Reform Jews to refer to a synagogue.)

Tishri: the lunar month in which the first full moon after the autumnal equinox occurs. The first day of Tishri is the New Year, the tenth is the Day of Atonement, the fifteenth is the first day of Sukkot.

Torah ('revelation'): God's revelation to Israel, including the extension, amplification and interpretation by the rabbinic authorities of all generations in the chain of tradition back to the original revelation at Sinai. At first, 'Torah' meant the Five Books of Moses; then the Scriptures as a whole; and finally the whole corpus of revelation, both written and oral, taught by rabbinic Judaism (also known as the dual Torah). The 'written Torah' refers to the Five Books of Moses. The oral tradition was ultimately written down by the rabbis of the early centuries of the Common Era in the form of the Mishnah, Talmuds and the midrash compilations. The Torah can also refer to the study of, and discussion of, this tradition.

Tosefta: supplements to the Mishnah, *c.* 250 CE.

tractate: a systematic exposition of a topic of the law (halakhah) of the Torah by the rabbinic sages: set forth in the Mishnah, amplified in the Tosefta, and expounded and applied as practical law in the two Talmuds.

Weeks, *see* Shavuot.

Yebamot: tractate expounding the laws of levirate marriage, which obliges a childless widow to marry her dead husband's brother (Deuteronomy 25:5–10).

yeshiva: talmudic academy or circle of disciples of a master of the Torah, engaged in the study of the Torah as expounded in the classics of rabbinic Judaism.

Yom Kippur, see Day of Atonement.

Yoma: tractate on the Mishnah topic of the Day of Atonement (Leviticus 16).

zekut: the result of an act of uncoerced generosity; divine favour that cannot be coerced in response to a human deed that is supererogatory.

Zion: the highest mountain in the Land of Israel, the location of the Temple in the city of Jerusalem. Also used to mean Jerusalem and the Land of Israel.

Zionism: movement to secure a Jewish state in Palestine, founded in 1897 by Theodor Herzl.

Bibliography

Alan J. Avery-Peck, *The Talmud of the Land of Israel* (University of Chicago Press, 1987).

Zachary Braiterman, *God After Auschwitz: Tradition and Change in Post-Holocaust Jewish Thought* (Princeton University Press, 1998).

Benzion Dinur, 'Emancipation' in *Encyclopaedia Judaica* vol. 6 (Keter, Jerusalem, 1971), cols. 696–718.

The Fathers According to Rabbi Nathan: An Analytical Translation and Explanation, Jacob Neusner (University Press of America, Lanham, 2001).

Genesis Rabbah: The Judaic Commentary on Genesis, A New American Translation, Jacob Neusner (3 volumes; University Press of America, Lanham, 2001).

Andrew M. Greeley, 'Why do Catholics stay in the Church? Because of the Stories', article originally published in the *New York Times*, reprinted in Greeley, *White Smoke* (New York, 1996), pp. 448–58.

Ithamar Gruenwald, 'Major Issues in the Study and Understanding of Jewish Mysticism' in *Judaism in Late Antiquity, II: Historical Syntheses*, ed. Jacob Neusner (E. J. Brill, Leiden, 1995), pp. 1–52.

Julius Guttmann, *Philosophies of Judaism: The History of Jewish Philosophy from Biblical Times to Franz Rosenzweig*, trans. David Silverman (Holt, Rinehart & Winston, New York, 1964).

Haggadah of Passover [script for the Passover banquet], Maurice Samuel (Hebrew Publishing Co., New York, 1942).

Isaak Heinemann, 'Judah Halevi, Kuzari' in *Three Jewish Philosophers*, ed. Isaak Heinemann, Alexander Altmann and Hans Lewy (Jewish Publication Society, Philadelphia, 1960).

Arthur Hertzberg, 'Conservative Judaism' in *Encyclopaedia Judaica* vol. 5 (Keter, Jerusalem, 1971), cols. 901–6.

Abraham J. Heschel, 'The Mystical Elements of Judaism' in *The Jews: Their History, Culture, and Religion*, ed. Louis Finkelstein (Harper & Row, New York, 1971).

Louis Jacobs, 'Basic Ideas of Hasidism' in *Encyclopaedia Judaica* vol. 7 (Keter, Jerusalem, 1971), col. 1,404.

Nathaniel Katzburg and Walter S. Wurzburger, 'Orthodoxy' in *Encyclopaedia Judaica* vol. 12 (Keter, Jerusalem, 1971) cols. 1,486–93.

Lamentations Rabbati in *The Components of the Rabbinic Documents: From the Whole to the Parts, IV*, Jacob Neusner (USF Academic Commentary Series; Scholars Press, Atlanta, 1997).

Leviticus Rabbah in *The Components of the Rabbinic Documents: From the Whole to the Parts, X*, Jacob Neusner (USF Academic Commentary Series; Scholars Press, Atlanta, 1998).

Mahzor for Rosh Hashanah and Yom Kippur: A Prayer Book for the Days of Awe, ed. Jules Harlow (Rabbinical Assembly, New York, 1972).

The Mishnah: A New Translation, Jacob Neusner (Yale University Press, New Haven and London, 1987).

Pesiqta deRab Kahana in *The Components of the Rabbinic Documents: From the Whole to the Parts, X*, Jacob Neusner (USF Academic Commentary Series; Scholars Press, Atlanta, 1998).

Jakob J. Petuchowski, 'Reform Judaism' in *Encyclopaedia Judaica* vol. 14 (Keter, Jerusalem, 1971) cols. 23–8.

Pirke Avot in *Torah from Our Sages: Pirke Avot, A New American Translation and Explanation*, Jacob Neusner (Rossel, Chappaqua, 1983; paperback edition 1987).

Pirke deRabbi Eliezer, Gerald Friedlander (London, 1916).

Rabbi's Manual, ed. Jules Harlow (Rabbinical Assembly, New York, 1965).

Ruth Rabbah: An Analytical Translation, Jacob Neusner (University Press of America, Lanham, 2001).

Lifsa Schachter, 'Reflections on the Brit Mila Ceremony' in *Conservative Judaism* 38 (1986), pp. 38–41.

Gershom G. Scholem, *Major Trends in Jewish Mysticism* (Schocken Books, New York, 1941).

Gershom Scholem, *On the Kabbalah and its Symbolism* (New American Library, New York, 1974).

Scripture: translations of passages of Scripture derive from *The Oxford Annotated Bible with the Apocrypha, Revised Standard Version*, edited by Herbert G. May and Bruce M. Metzger (Oxford University Press, New York, 1965).

Sifra in *The Components of the Rabbinic Documents: From the Whole to the Parts, I*, Jacob Neusner (USF Academic Commentary Series; Scholars Press, Atlanta, 1997).

Sifré to Deuteronomy in *The Components of the Rabbinic Documents: From the Whole to the Parts VII*, Jacob Neusner (USF Academic Commentary Series; Scholars Press, Atlanta, 1997).

Sifré to Numbers in *The Components of the Rabbinic Documents: From the Whole to the Parts, XI*, Jacob Neusner (USF Academic Commentary Series; Scholars Press, Atlanta, 1998).

Marshall Sklare, *Conservative Judaism* (Free Press, 1965).

Song of Songs Rabbah: An Analytical Translation, Jacob Neusner (3 volumes; University Press of America, Lanham, 2001).

The Talmud of Babylonia: An Academic Commentary, Jacob Neusner (USF Academic Commentary Series; Scholars Press, Atlanta, 1994–6, 1999).

The Talmud of the Land of Israel: A Preliminary Translation and Explanation, Jacob Neusner (University of Chicago Press, 1982–93).

The Tosefta in English: I. Zeraim, Moed, and Nashim; II. Neziqin, Qodoshim, and Toharot, Jacob Neusner (Hendrickson Publications, Peabody, 2001).

Weekday Prayer Book, ed. Gerson Hadas with Jules Harlow (Rabbinical Assembly, New York, 1966).

The Wisdom of the Zohar, ed. Fischel Lachower and Isaiah Tishby (The Littman Library of Jewish Civilization, London and Washington, 1989).

Zohar: The Book of Enlightenment, Daniel Chanan Matt (Paulist Press, New York and Toronto, 1983).

Zohar, The Book of Splendor: Basic Readings from the Kabbalah, ed. Gershom G. Scholem (Schocken Books, New York, 1963).

Subject Index

Index of Scripture and Rabbinic Literature

READ MORE IN PENGUIN

In every corner of the world, on every subject under the sun, Penguin represents quality and variety – the very best in publishing today.

For complete information about books available from Penguin – including Puffins, Penguin Classics and Arkana – and how to order them, write to us at the appropriate address below. Please note that for copyright reasons the selection of books varies from country to country.

In the United Kingdom: Please write to *Dept. EP, Penguin Books Ltd, Bath Road, Harmondsworth, West Drayton, Middlesex UB7 0DA*

In the United States: Please write to *Consumer Services, Penguin Putnam Inc., 405 Murray Hill Parkway, East Rutherford, New Jersey 07073-2136.* VISA and MasterCard holders call 1-800-631-8571 to order Penguin titles

In Canada: Please write to *Penguin Books Canada Ltd, 10 Alcorn Avenue, Suite 300, Toronto, Ontario M4V 3B2*

In Australia: Please write to *Penguin Books Australia Ltd, 487 Maroondah Highway, Ringwood, Victoria 3134*

In New Zealand: Please write to *Penguin Books (NZ) Ltd, Private Bag 102902, North Shore Mail Centre, Auckland 10*

In India: Please write to *Penguin Books India Pvt Ltd, 11 Community Centre, Panchsheel Park, New Delhi 110017*

In the Netherlands: Please write to *Penguin Books Netherlands bv, Postbus 3507, NL-1001 AH Amsterdam*

In Germany: Please write to *Penguin Books Deutschland GmbH, Metzlerstrasse 26, 60594 Frankfurt am Main*

In Spain: Please write to *Penguin Books S. A., Bravo Murillo 19, 1°B, 28015 Madrid*

In Italy: Please write to *Penguin Italia s.r.l., Via Vittorio Emanuele 45/a, 20094 Corsico, Milano*

In France: Please write to *Penguin France, 12, Rue Prosper Ferradou, 31700 Blagnac*

In Japan: Please write to *Penguin Books Japan Ltd, Iidabashi KM-Bldg, 2-23-9 Koraku, Bunkyo-Ku, Tokyo 112-0004*

In South Africa: Please write to *Penguin Books South Africa (Pty) Ltd, P.O. Box 751093, Gardenview, 2047 Johannesburg*